GROW

BY

LETTING GO

A NEW WAY TO RAISE CHILDREN
WITH EVERYDAY DRAMA
AND SELF-CREATION

Jiawei Liu, Ph.D.

1 Plus Books
San Francisco, 2025

1 Plus Books
https://1plusbooks.com

Title: Grow by Letting Go: A New Way to Raise Children with Everyday
Drama and Self-Creation
Author: Jiawei Liu

ISBN: 978-1-966814-27-6

出版人/Publisher: 刘雁/Yan Liu
定价: US$29.99
Published by 壹嘉出版 ®/ 1 Plus Books®
https://1plusbooks.com
San Francisco, 2025

Introduction

We begin with the assumption that autopoiesis belongs to living systems. It was never meant for anything else. And yet, when we enter a theater space with children, something begins to shift. We are no longer only speaking of cells or organisms; we are speaking of symbolic actions, of roles, and of meaning in motion. Drama becomes a system that lives.

Autopoiesis refers to the capacity of a system to reproduce both its parts and its whole. In biological life, this process is organic. In cities, it often becomes mechanical. Roads are built, utilities maintained, and social rhythms repeated. But even there, we have seen systems that sustain themselves through symbolic means. The Toronto Gorilla policy model demonstrated how structural logic could extend into abstract domains such as language, law, and communication, without relying on physical replication. Because of this, we choose to extend the logic of autopoiesis into education.

But not just any education. What emerges here is an education rooted in dramatic experience. In the theater, a child enters a role not to pretend, but to encounter. The role is not fiction. It is a space of becoming. Through enactment, the child reorganizes self-understanding. Through embodiment, they generate meaning. In this space, autopoiesis begins to operate again. The role becomes a component, the gesture a property, and the emotion a relational thread. The educational system is no longer imposed from the outside. It arises from within.

This is the foundation of Autopoietic Psychodramatic Education for Children, a developmental framework and philosophical system grounded in autopoiesis (Maturana & Varela, 1980), transpersonal psychology (Wilber, 2000), e mbodied drama (Jennings, 1998), and the pedagogical insights of Maria Montessori (1967). The entire model orbits three essential questions.

It is a vision of the child as a living, composite system that is self-generating, self-organizing, and self-regulating. Rather than viewing the child as a single unit observed from the outside, this theory invites us to see from within. To understand the child phenomenologically is to attend to their expressive structure. Voice, movement, hesitation, rhythm, and attachment are not isolated behaviors but components of an evolving system. Their qualities function as properties. Their interactions form the basis of relational organization. The educator becomes not an instructor but a participant in the unfolding of the system. As we shift between perspectives, between whole and part, we begin to grasp what counts as a property such as a gesture or desire, and what counts as a relation, such as how those qualities connect, conflict, and transform. Education, in this model, is not about shaping outcomes. It is about honoring the self-organizing logic of becoming.

The aim is not knowledge acquisition or performance. The purpose is to awaken the child's internal rhythm and provide a symbolic container where identity, emotion, and meaning may emerge and reorganize. Growth is not tracked through benchmarks. It is observed in subtle reorganizations of self and relation (Capra & Luisi, 2014; Siegel, 2012). Dramatic space becomes a medium in which the child's inner landscape becomes visible, tangible, and transformable. The goal is not mastery but emergence. Not control but presence.

Autopoietic principles can be found even in non-biological systems. The Toronto Gorilla policy model revealed how organizations can evolve through symbolic interaction and affective feedback. Education, viewed through this lens, becomes a living system composed of communication, emotion, and relationship. The theater is not a rehearsal hall. It becomes a space in which the self is enacted, witnessed, and reorganized.

Four pedagogical pathways express this framework in applied settings:

1. Dramatic generative spaces allow children to enter symbolic roles that mirror and transform internal experience.

2. Emotional perception mechanisms help children recognize, express, and integrate affective states through embodied and symbolic play.

3. Family co-performance brings parents into shared dramatic interaction, reframing hierarchy as mutual understanding.

4. Developmental rhythm sensitivity encourages educators to re-

spond to the child's natural timing instead of enforcing standardized progression.

In each of these practices, the educator is no longer the authority who imparts knowledge or manages outcomes. The educator becomes a steady and responsive witness who listens, reflects, and protects the child's unfolding process. This vision echoes Montessori's prepared adult and is extended by transpersonal psychology, which sees the child not only as a psychological subject but as a soul in development (Grof, 2000; Maslow, 1971). Education becomes a space of symbolic integration, intuitive knowing, and self-realization.

To support the complexity of such a living and emergent system, we also require the support of reflective technological tools. Artificial intelligence, when designed as an aid rather than a replacement, can serve as a co-observer of rhythm, memory, and developmental pattern. Within an autopoietic framework, AI is not a controlling force. It is a secondary presence that extends our ability to witness the system as it generates itself.

Autopoietic Psychodramatic Education does not seek to mold the child. It seeks to stand beside them. The child is not trained. The child is generated.

Foreword

Autopoietic Psychodramatic Education for Children

Dr. Liu's book shows me how to think about education from a humanistic perspective. I was brought up by a tiger mom who took a more utilitarian approach.

As a father of two young boys, I struggled with what to do when my 5 yo cried foul after teasing and got bantered by his 10 yo brother. The following paragraph resonates with me "Sometimes they go from laughter to fighting in seconds." (P 199) After reading Dr. Liu's book, I found alternative to my old frustrating way of trying to be the referee. I would first acknowledge my own frustration and be curious "who wants to tell me what happened first?", with the intention of letting them feel seen and heard.

Of course, not everything works instantly, but the growth mindset for both my kids and myself, makes me feel hopeful. I started to learn how to observe more and judge less. These also helped me at work, where project discussions could become emotional, and I used to be conflict averting. I would apply the same growth mindset to these work situations.

In AI, researchers have found that supervised learning using examples are only making models into imitation machines. To make the models more intelligent, we need to use reinforcement learning to optimize for long-term rewards instead of greedy incentives.

Another important benefit of a growth mindset is resilience to failures. Instead of repeating one thing for 10,000 hours and becoming a craftsman, AI enables us to iterate 10,000 times to become a jack of all trades (product, engineering, marketing, sales) that build and launch things very quickly to test the product market fit.

The key idea presented in "Grow by Letting Go: A New Way to Raise Children" by Dr. Jiawei Liu is Autopoietic Psychodramatic Education for Children, or APEC, a developmental framework and philosophical system for early childhood education. It challenges traditional educational paradigms, which often view children as "empty vessels to be filled" or "clay needing shaping" Instead, APEC posits that children are "living composite system that is self-generating, self-organizing, and self-regulating." The core of this approach is to foster intrinsic growth and self-realization through dramatic experience, emotional awareness, integrated relationships, and a deep respect for each child's unique developmental rhythm. Following his ground-breaking system, Dr. Liu presents real-world examples in Chapter 3~5 to showcase the impact of the APEC model on children and their parents, which embodied the cycle of "Knowing, Being, and Doing".

The book inspired me to think about the following directions:

The purpose of education is nurturing holistic human beings rather than imparting knowledge.

The role of humans (educator, children, and parents) in an era when AI is rapidly surpassing humans in memorizing and synthesizing knowledge.

AI, as an aid, can be an co-observer to facilitate the APEC system.

As a father of young children, and a machine learning engineer who work

Jiawei's book has vividly and thoroughly answered these questions. Below are my take-aways from reading the book. I hope they can serve as a synopsis to guide you through this treasure trove of educational gems.

1. Autopoiesis is the Foundational Principle

APEC extends the biological concept of "autopoiesis", the capacity of a system to reproduce both its parts and its whole through internal operations, to education. While this process is material in biology, APEC applies it to abstract human systems (like accounting, legal systems, and language) that reproduce themselves through symbolic means, patterns, and communication.

Children are not seen as products to be molded but as dynamic beings with innate capacities to generate meaning and expression. Their behaviors, emotions, and relationships are integral to their self-generation.

2. Dramatic Experience for Education

In Dr. Liu's book, theater is a space of becoming, and drama is central to APEC, serving as a "Generative Theater" where children engage in roles not for pretense, but for "encounter." Children reorganize self-understanding and generate meaning through enactment and embodiment.

3. Emphasis on Emotional Awareness and Integration

Emotions are considered valid languages, not something to be controlled or suppressed. The Generative Theater guides children toward self-understanding by utilizing mirrored movements, symbolic constructions, and improvisational emotional shifts.

APEC prioritizes mental health, promoting emotional fluency, psychological resilience, and inner coherence, rather than emotional suppression. The aim is to cultivate "emotional intelligence, an awareness of feeling, and the ability to navigate it constructively." (p. 27)

Many examples focus on helping children understand and process their emotions in a safe, non-judgmental environment.

Symbolic Expression: An early example that shaped the author's philosophy was a child who silently placed a cloth bag over his head for ten minutes. He later explained that the bag represented his feeling of being "invisible and voiceless". Another story describes Weier, a boy holding in a great deal of anger, which he called "a lot of red". A counselor helped him draw his anger, which allowed him to process and release these feelings, leading to a visible sense of relief and calm.

Fear and Trauma: Xiaozhou, a boy who froze in fear after making a small mistake, revealed that he was hit at home for such errors. A facilitated conversation where he could express his fear and anger to his mother led to an apology, an emotional release, and the beginning of family healing. Similarly, Little Yu, a three-year-old who was aggressive and restless, was held firmly but gently by a counselor. This embrace allowed him to release pent-up fear and pain from being hit at home, eventually leading to calm and connection.

Several narratives focus on overcoming shyness, anxiety, and distrust through patient and responsive care.

The program's first two students included a quiet six-year-old girl who learned trust through a falling-and-catching exercise and an eight-year-old boy with autism who moved from silence and avoidance to connection and laughter through personalized, imitative activities.

The Power of Embrace: Jasper, a boy with significant emotional instability, was helped through a "deep containment embrace" that re-established his sense of security and allowed him to transform from aggressive to collaborative in just three weeks. Eli, a dysregulated thirteen-month-old, was calmed through "rhythmic supportive embrace," which helped him focus, sleep soundly, and engage with others.

4. Redefining the Educator's Role

The educator shifts from an authority figure imparting knowledge to a "steady and responsive witness" who listens, reflects, and protects the child's unfolding process. This echoes Montessori's "prepared adult."

5. Integrated Learning and Holistic Development

The purpose of APEC is not knowledge acquisition or performance, but to "awaken the child's internal rhythm and provide a symbolic container where identity, emotion, and meaning may emerge and reorganize." (p. iv)

"Integrated education consciously nurtures emergent abilities in a child, fostering inner connections across domains and gradually forming a whole being who is independent, autonomous, and creative." (p. 38) It nurtures emergent abilities by fostering inner connections across spiritual (values, beliefs), psychological (emotions, relationships, self-awareness), and physical (embodied action) dimensions.

Learning is deeply embedded in culture, community, and meaningful activity. Children construct understanding through real-life, embodied experiences like caregiving, cleaning, and role-playing.

6. Boundaries, Rules, and Responsibility

Dr. Liu describes boundaries as the enablers of freedom. He states that clear boundaries are not shackles but "riverbanks that allow life to flow forward," providing certainty, peace, and security for the self to grow. They clarify roles, make responsibility clear, and reduce confusion for children. "Boundaries are not shackles. They are more like riverbanks that allow life to flow forward." (p. 62)

Children are given opportunities to make choices and experience natural consequences, fostering an "inner architecture of accountability." This cultivates genuine agency rather than blind compliance. "Responsibility is the capacity to acknowledge the connection between one's actions and their consequences." (p. 92) "When offered real options with genuine outcomes, children experience agency and begin to internalize accountability." (p. 95)

Conflict as Generative Opportunity: Conflict is viewed not as a disruption but as a generative opportunity for learning social rules and relational nuances, leading to empathy and discernment. "Conflict is not inherently harmful. Rather, it is our mode of response... that shapes whether it becomes a source of harm or a path toward growth." (p. 88)

Dr. Liu provides examples of how clear, consistent boundaries help children develop self-regulation and a sense of responsibility.

Redirecting Behavior: Leo, a three-year-old running indoors while pretending to be "Ultraman," did not respond to his mother's increasingly desperate pleas. An educator knelt to his level, acknowledged his play, and then calmly but firmly stated the boundary: "inside, we walk". Leo immediately understood and complied.

Learning from Consequences: Two stories illustrate how offering structured choices cultivates responsibility. Caleb, a five-year-old, was given a clear choice: eat lunch and have dessert, or skip lunch and have no dessert. After two days of choosing to skip both, he decided on the third day to eat his lunch, having learned from the natural consequence. Mateo, a six-year-old, was given the choice to speak quietly and play outside or speak loudly and stay inside. He chose to continue speaking loudly and, after being gently reminded of his choice, accepted the consequence of staying indoors.

Conflict is framed not as a disruption but as a chance for relational learning and deeper understanding.

When two boys, Liam and Noah, had a physical altercation, a counselor helped reconstruct the scene. It was revealed that Liam, whose father was away, had lain on top of Noah not out of aggression, but from a need for physical closeness and connection. Noah, a sensitive child, reacted to the violation of his personal space. The facilitated conversation led to an apology and immediate reconciliation, turning a misunderstanding into a moment of relational insight.

7. Technology as a Reflective Partner

In the age of AI, Dr. Liu considers AI as a "co-observer of rhythm, memory, and developmental pattern," extending the educator's ability to witness the self-generating system. It does not replace humans but complements us.

"Artificial intelligence, when designed as an aid rather than a replacement, can serve as a co-observer of rhythm, memory, and developmental pattern." (p. v) "Our AI system does not judge. It observes. It exists to support adults in responding accurately to children's needs." (p. 23)

8. Family as a Co-Creative System

Jiawei, a father of a young child, embodies his own principal of being a parent as co-learners and co-healers. The way he interacts with his 2 year old son is more like a friend. APEC emphasizes "systems-level coherence between home and school." He designed parent workshops and shared dramatic interactions to transform parents into "conscious participants" and "co-authors of the child's emerging narrative."

"Only when educational institutions and families align in their cognitive approach can a child feel truly held. This shift repositions parents and educators as co-authors of the child's emerging narrative." (p. 30) "Parents revisit their own childhoods, repair old wounds, and find themselves in the very act of supporting their children." (p. 36) The "Life Tree" Metaphor: The totem of the Generative Theater is a "spiraling tree of life," symbolizing education as an open, nonlinear living process rooted in relationships, with experiences forming the trunk and multiple intelligences unfolding as branches. "The roots of this tree are grounded in the soil of relationship. A child's growth does not begin in isolation, but through structural coupling with family, educators, and the environment." (p. 49)

9. Ample Field Studies

In Chapters 3–5 of the book, Dr. Liu uses numerous examples, anecdotes, and case studies to illustrate his principles. These stories highlight how children's behaviors are seen not as problems to be fixed, but as meaningful expressions of their inner worlds. The examples demonstrate how educators and parents can act as responsive witnesses rather than instructors, creating a space for children to self-organize and grow.

The author frames the parents' act of writing their letters as a "moment of generation" in which parents reflect on their own journey, see their children with new clarity, and recognize how much love was there all along.

The letters share several overarching themes:

The Child as a Teacher: Parents repeatedly express that their children have been their greatest teachers, showing them how to slow down, be patient, and love more deeply. One family described their son as a "clear mirror" reflecting back the parts of themselves that needed to grow.

Parental Growth and Apology: Many letters contain heartfelt acknowledgments of parental shortcomings and apologies for moments of impatience, anger, or misunderstanding. The mother of Qianqian writes a particularly moving account of her struggles as a young, overwhelmed mother and thanks her daughter for her forgiveness, which catalyzed her own healing.

Gratitude and Transformation: The letters are filled with gratitude for the children's presence and for the positive changes observed since joining the Generative Theater or Tianjin Ruide Kindergarten. Lele's father describes being moved to tears by his daughter's profound understanding of gratitude for nature, which he attributes to the school's focus on character education. Chenchen's father details his son's remarkable transformation from a shy and dependent toddler into a confident, independent child who learned to read on his own.

Observing Children's Innate Wisdom: Parents often marvel at their children's empathy and kindness. The mother of three-year-old Elena describes how her daughter will pat her on the back and ask, "Mama, are you feeling a little sad?" showing an emotional wisdom beyond her years. Anran's mother tells of how her once-shy daughter found the courage to sing on stage at a wedding simply "because it mattered to me," demonstrating a newfound inner strength.

Conclusion

In APEC (Autopoietic Psychodramatic Education for Children), Jiawei Liu offered a profound shift in educational philosophy. It advocates for an approach that honors the child's inherent capacity for self-generation, emphasizing emotional awareness, dramatic experience, and a supportive ecosystem that includes parents, educators, and technology. The core message is that "Education is not molding. It is becoming." This framework seeks to cultivate not merely knowledgeable individuals, but whole, self-aware beings rooted in intrinsic motivation, emotional intelligence, and a deep, respectful connection with themselves and the world.

Preface

Where shall I begin, dear reader? Should I unravel the tapestry from the threads of method, or perchance from theories profound? Or should my tale commence within the quiet chambers of data and the vivid scenes of case studies? Nay, perhaps my story truly begins with a simple call.

One day, the telephone broke the stillness of my afternoon. At the other end was a mother, her voice anxious and hurried. She had heard from a friend that the children's developmental drama classes I offer held something special. She couldn't quite explain why she felt compelled, yet confessed, "I feel like your place might help him." Sunlight gently filtered through the window, illuminating my quiet contemplation as I had just sent home a child from his first drama experience. Her words, weaving between haste and hesitation, bore the weight of fatigue yet carried within them a delicate thread of hope.

Such calls were no strangers to my experience. Periodically, parents reached out, their voices mingling helplessness, hope, guilt, and urgency. At home, their children withdrew into silence; at school, labeled as "sensitive" or "difficult." Yet within these young hearts lay unspoken cries, emotions yearning to form words. Drama offered them the first chance to find their voice.

Traditional education tends to regard children as clay, needing shaping through structured knowledge, behavioral training, and standardized evaluations. Yet, through numerous practical experiences in educational and psychological fields, we have come to recognize more clearly that children are not empty vessels to be filled but dynamic beings possessing their rhythms, self-organizations, and innate capacities for generating meaning.

Psychology has long reminded us that children's behaviors are outward manifestations of inner states. Carl Jung articulated that individuation is the integration of oneself within society. Jean Piaget emphasized that children actively construct knowledge through interaction rather than passive reception. In the 1970s, the Autopoiesis theory of Chilean biologists Maturana and Varela profoundly influenced me, suggesting that living beings are self-producing, self-defining entities, not externally controlled products. Furthermore, transpersonal psychology enriched this educational framework with Maslow's "peak experiences," Grof's "expanded states of consciousness," and Jung's "symbols and archetypes," all emphasizing the spiritual and symbolic dimensions essential to children's growth.

I vividly remember when the concept of "Autopoietic Children's Drama Education" first dawned on me. It was during the conclusion of a drama class. A child, engaged in improvisation, silently placed a cloth bag over his head, standing motionless for ten long minutes. An extraordinary stillness enveloped the room. I refrained from interrupting, choosing instead to quietly accompany him. Later, he softly confessed that the bag represented his feeling of invisibility and voicelessness. At that very moment, I realized profoundly that if we could create a space where children felt understood without words and recognized within symbolic expressions, genuine growth could truly begin.

Thus, the "Autopoietic Children's Drama Education" gradually took shape.

This educational philosophy has no simple origin, nor does it offer a quick-fix methodology. Rather, it resembles a slowly growing tree deeply rooted in Autopoiesis theory, transpersonal psychology, and drama education, extending branches toward embodiment, emotions, relationships, consciousness, and integration with artificial intelligence-assisted tools.

Its purpose is not to train children, but rather to awaken their inner rhythms; not to design a standardized path, but to protect and honor each child's unique journey of becoming.

The Generative Theater Space: A Container for Growth

Within this educational approach, the foundational point is not the curriculum but the space itself, the "Generative Theater." This is no ordinary stage. It is a psychological domain capable of containing symbols, projections, silence, conflicts, and reconstructions.

A seven-year-old boy once portrayed an "owl who could never sleep," continually pacing, interrupting, speaking. Initially misinterpreted as attention deficiency, his behavior in our theater space was met not with correction but with patient accompaniment. Ultimately, in the third act, he scripted a "tree hollow meditation," discovering his calmness. Later, he shared, "There are many selves inside my head, and they're too noisy." In this theater, he saw himself clearly for the first time.

Emotional Awareness and Symbolic Integration: Becoming Oneself

Emotions, far from being controlled, deserve acceptance as valid languages. In our Generative Theater, we utilize mirrored movements, symbolic constructions, and improvisational emotional shifts to guide children toward clearer self-understanding from initially vague sensations. As Moreno, th e founder of psychodrama, beautifully expressed, "A person's suffering arises not from an inability to feel but from an inability to articulate those feelings." Drama paves the way toward this articulation.

Family Cross Theater: Reconstructing Relationships

A child's development does not occur in isolation. Their emotions, roles, and sense of meaning intertwine deeply with their familial relationships. Hence, we created the "Family Cross Theater," inviting parents into their child's symbolic world to collaboratively enact and reconstruct their shared narratives, thereby enhancing and deepening parent-child connections.

Systemic Rhythm and Generative Order: Observation Rather Than Instruction

Every child possesses a unique rhythm. Within our approach, we discard evaluations and fixed timelines, replacing them with educators' careful observation, focusing on what children naturally generate rather than rushing toward imposed goals. This honors the authentic rhythm and internal order inherent in each child's developmental process.

Peak Ritual Experiences: Anchors of Psychological Memory

Life inevitably encompasses moments of farewell, rebirth, and self-affirmation. Thus, our curriculum incorporates "Peak Ritual Experiences," symbolic narratives assisting children in navigating significant psychological milestones, creating pathways to heal and transcend emotional wounds.

Children are not to be molded into another's image; rather, they journey toward becoming authentically themselves. Our role remains simple yet profound, guarding the theater's threshold, inviting children in, allowing them to create stories, assume roles, remove masks, and gradually, gently flourish in relationships, integrate through symbols, and evolve through actions.

Thus concludes our tale, dear reader.

Yet is it not true that within the theater of becoming,

each ending marks a new beginning?

Table of Contents

Chapter 1: Stepping Into the Theater, Growing Up Together with Children

Growth Begins When Life Speaks in Its Own Language

Autopoiesis offers a compelling theoretical framework for understanding living systems. It describes how certain entities reproduce both their components and their organizational unity through internal operations. This reproduction is not abstract. It is fundamentally material. That distinction is essential. For a system to be autopoietic, it must regenerate itself mechanistically, in accordance with the physical laws of nature. There can be no separation between structure and process. The system exists only insofar as it produces the very conditions of its continuation (Maturana & Varela, 1980; Montévil, 2015).

Understanding what autopoiesis is also requires clarity about what it is not. The theory cannot be directly mapped onto human social systems. The reason lies in reproduction. Human systems do not reproduce their components and their wholeness materially. Common analogies, such as marriage in which two people form a union and produce a child, ultimately miss the point. The baby, while biologically connected to the couple, is not a regenerated part of the marriage. The baby becomes a separate organism. The marriage does not reproduce itself as a self-contained whole. This reveals the fundamental difference between metaphorical continuity and biological autopoiesis (Bitbol & Luisi, 2004; Koskinen, 2013).

However, Maturana and Varela did not confine autopoiesis to biology. They allowed that it could extend to non-practical living systems, systems that operate without material reproduction but nonetheless display systemic closure. In this broader sense, autopoietic logic can illuminate human systems, particularly those organized around symbols, rules, and communication. These systems reproduce themselves not through cells or molecules, but through patterns, structures, and meaning (Maturana, 1987).

A vivid example of such abstract autopoiesis is the global system of accounting. This system is constructed from a small set of core rules, which may number no more than ten or twenty. The most fundamental among them is that debit and credit must always balance. From this principle emerges a network capable of organizing billions of dollars across global institutions. Regardless of whether a company earns or loses money, its accounting structure must remain internally consistent. Every ledger, report, and financial statement is interrelated. Each transaction, no matter how complex, is an instantiation of these foundational rules. The system functions as a closed, internally regulated whole. Its coherence does not depend on external outcomes. It is sustained through its own logic (Achterberg & Vriens, 2010; Oxford Reference, n.d.).

This raises an important question: if autopoietic logic can apply to abstract systems, how might it inform our understanding of education? Can we design classrooms and learning environments as self-organizing systems whose parts and wholes are internally coherent?

To approach this question, we must turn to Niklas Luhmann (1984), whose contribution to systems theory is essential. Luhmann argued that human systems are not made up of people but of communications. Each act of communication refers to previous communications and anticipates future ones. In this way, communication systems reproduce themselves recursively. This recursive reproduction does not require material form. It depends entirely on language. Through language, systems define their own boundaries, sustain their internal logic, and evolve over time. Luhmann's theoretical work, articulated in detail across thousands of pages, offers a comprehensive map of how symbolic systems sustain coherence without requiring physical regeneration (Luhmann, 1984; Teubner, 1992).

In applying this to education, language becomes central. Language is not just a medium of instruction. It is the operational condition that makes learning possible. Within an educational program, the components such as students, teachers, tasks, and interactions are organized into a systemic whole. At any given moment, this system occupies a particular state, shaped by the relationships and internal conditions it holds. When the environment introduces a stimulus, such as a question, a conflict, or an unexpected insight, the system adjusts in response. This adjustment, however, does not occur randomly. It occurs in accordance with the system's internal organization. This is the process known as structural determination (Maturana & Varela, 1980; Allen & Friston, 2018).

When a system changes in response to an external event, it undergoes a transition. These transitions from one state to another, always shaped by internal logic, form the process of structural coupling. The system and the environment are linked through recurrent interaction. But the environment does not dictate change. It triggers responses. The form of those responses is shaped by the system's existing structure. Through continued interaction, the system reorganizes itself while preserving its identity.

These transitions cannot happen without language. Language enables the system to move from one state to another. It also allows internal perspectives to shift toward external observation and back again. From within, a teacher must see how the classroom functions as a whole. From the outside, an observer may see the structure's unity but not the internal operations. What is visible to an external observer is the unity of the system, perceived as its external form or shell. However, this unity should not be mistaken for the properties of the individual components within it. The unity has emergent properties that exceed the sum of its parts (Kauffman, 2019; Thompson, 2007).

Learning, in this framework, is not the accumulation of discrete facts. It is the outcome of reorganization. As students engage with new inputs, the system enters new configurations. This learning is understood as a structural shift. It is recursive, relational, and linguistic. The entire process is grounded in communication. Through language, meaning is generated. Through language, identity is sustained. And through language, systems adapt.

Autopoiesis, when reframed in this way, reveals that the architecture of learning is systemic. It is dynamic, closed, and continually self-producing. Understanding education as an autopoietic system allows for deeper insight into the unfolding of learning, which is better conceived not as a process of transmission, but as one of transformation.

Generation Moves from Cell to Stage

Autopoiesis is a theory developed to explain biological systems, specifically living systems. One of the most precise examples is the individual cell, which demonstrates six fundamental characteristics. Among these, the existence of a boundary, a membrane or wall, is crucial. This wall provides the first and most essential act: the power to distinguish. First, we distinguish the boundary. Then, we discern the components within that boundary. Finally, we perceive the relationships among those components. No matter how one moves within this structure, one remains within the closed system.

This insight leads Maturana and Varela to a fundamental conclusion: living is doing, and doing is knowing. In the context of a cell, this is expressed as a circular process. The organism produces its parts, the parts maintain the whole, and the whole reproduces itself. This circularity only applies to living things.

Mechanistically, this process depends on both passive and active dynamics. Passive mechanics include diffusion processes, such as water moving from high to low salt concentration. Active mechanics involve electrochemical interactions, positive and negative charges, electron exchanges. Together with the laws of physics, these constitute the mechanistic basis of autopoiesis. And yet, the resulting system is so elegantly self-sustaining that many have wondered whether such a model can apply to human organizations.

In organizational settings, such as schools, marriages, or dance partnerships, there may appear to be an analogous self-sustaining structure. There are leaders and followers, shared purposes, and relational coherence. However, to assume these systems are autopoietic is a categorical error. Why? Because autopoiesis demands the internal generation of both components and structure. Human organizations do not reproduce their parts. A classroom does not regenerate teachers and students. A married couple does not continuously re-create each other. Even reproduction, childbirth, produces something external to the couple, not the couple themselves. Autopoiesis, in its strict sense, remains internally self-contained.

This is why applying autopoiesis to human organizations without adjustment inevitably fails. Critics argue that it is conceptually inaccurate or even misleading. A corporation, classroom, or tango couple does not literally create its own components anew. Thus, applying autopoiesis directly to human institutions becomes philosophically untenable.

But this is not the end of the discussion. Influential thinkers such as Niklas Luhmann and Humberto Maturana opened a crucial window by arguing that autopoiesis can apply not just to material systems but to abstract ones as well. What does this mean? It means that systems based on ideas, rules, and symbolic relations can also be autopoietic if they are self-referential and autonomous.

Take accounting. With just a handful of rules, such as debit and credit, left and right, plus and minus, the system organizes and sustains itself. Every transaction must balance. There is no external logic required. Accounting is not a communication system; it is a system of relations. As such, it exemplifies autopoiesis in the abstract.

The legal system is another, though more complex, example. With hundreds of interwoven rules, the system governs itself by recursive logic. Natural language operates similarly. Each language maintains its own generative rules and expands through internal consistency.

Even artificial languages, such as those used in AI or computer programming, follow this principle. They form internally complete, recursive structures that self-maintain meaning and function.

This reopens the question, can human organizations, when viewed through the lens of abstraction, be seen as autopoietic systems? Here, the answer becomes more nuanced.

Consider tango again, not simply as a dance, but as an embodied abstract system. In tango, a leader and a follower interact through relational cues. They do not create each other, but their roles are defined and redefined through ongoing mutual engagement. The movement is governed by physical laws, but the structure is abstract. This makes tango a hybrid system, with real bodies enacting symbolic logic.

Such insight is deeply phenomenological. One need not explain tango; one enacts it. You see it, feel it, do it. Even when one cannot execute the steps, one can perceive their logic. The body understands what the mind does not yet articulate.

This brings us to education, particularly in drama-based learning environments. In a drama classroom, students assume roles. Each child expresses distinct properties such as voice, gesture, timing, and emotion. These are the components. The interactions between students form the relationships. The class becomes a system of interrelated parts.

The teacher or facilitator, too, enters this system with their own properties. They observe and interact, shifting between inside and outside perspectives. From the outside, one sees the class as a unified system. From the inside, one perceives the properties of each student and the dynamic relations among them.

This dual perspective is essential. To build such a system, one must ask: What are the properties of the components? What are their interrelations? How does the system relate to its environment? These are not rhetorical questions. They are design criteria.

Furthermore, in human systems, causality does not operate in linear, mechanical ways. Instead of cause and effect, we encounter triggers and compensations. The environment does not impose outcomes. It initiates transformations based on the system's internal state.

For example, a child cannot perform a piano concerto just because their parent wishes it. Mastery, or State Two, depends on preparation, or State One. Each step builds upon the previous. Development is a continuous internal transition, not an externally driven leap.

This principle must be embedded in educational design. In drama education, each student develops their own properties. One may project well vocally. Another may excel in gesture or emotional sensitivity. These individual properties matter. But the collective also matters. The ensemble must develop shared relations. The drama class becomes an emergent whole.

The facilitator must hold both views, each part and the whole. They must observe the dynamics among students, between student and teacher, and between the class and its environment.

Ultimately, autopoiesis teaches us that systems must be self-contained and self-generating. In abstract human systems, this means they must be self-referential and autonomous. External influence can only trigger change; it cannot define the system.

This is why phenomenology is critical. It allows us to see and feel the system without dissecting it. When you see, you do. When you do, you understand. And when you understand, you become part of the system's unfolding.

In this light, autopoiesis is not just a biological theory. It is a paradigm for systems of learning, growth, and becoming. It is, at its heart, a drama of living.

Behind Every Educational System Lies a Story

The name "Children's Psychodynamic Theater" was not chosen to sound impressive or fashionable. It emerged from a slow and sincere process of growth. In the very beginning, we started with only two students. They were like two small seeds. We did not expect them to grow into the best at anything. What truly mattered was whether they could grow into themselves.

I remember a mother once joking, "That name sounds way too philosophical. My daughter says she'd rather call it the Happy Little Theater Club." I laughed. The child was not wrong. Of course, this place can be joyful. But joy here does not simply mean smiling or laughing. It comes from being seen, being held, and being understood. That is where the lightness comes from.

We have never prioritized being the best, and we never required quantifiable improvement. Our focus has always been on observing and accompanying. We follow the child's pace, their emotions, and their unfolding relationship with the world. We do not try to shape them into a better version based on any standard. What we hope for is that, through drama, through relationships, and through self-driven growth, they will discover a way of being that is genuinely their own.

We began in a small classroom in the Bay Area. Slowly, more families found their way to us. Many of them had children who felt lost in traditional education systems. Many parents were dealing with deep anxiety. Here, they saw something different. Some children on the autism spectrum began to express themselves. Others, labeled as overly sensitive, started creating their own stories. Teenagers moved from silence to speech, from guardedness to real friendships.

Children's Psychodynamic Theater has never been a packaged teaching product. From the beginning, it has been a space of the heart. In this space, children are not shaped. They emerge. And their emergence is not driven by anyone else's expectations. It comes from their own needs and their own rhythm.

We have not opened many branches. We have made no plans for rapid expansion. Our vision is not to grow larger, but to grow deeper. Even if there is only one child in the room, if that child is able to become more of who they are, then we have already achieved everything we hoped for.

Origins

The initial inspiration for the Children's Psychodynamic Theater emerged through a series of insights I gained while studying transpersonal psychology. As a long-time educator in children's theater, I began teaching drama in the Bay Area in 2012. Back then, my focus was primarily on artistic expression. I had not yet delved into the deeper psychological dimensions of children. It wasn't until 2015, when I was formally introduced to transpersonal psychology, that I felt as if another door had opened. I began to re-examine the meaning of childhood, education, and growth.

Between 1905 and 1906, William James first used the term "transpersonal" in his lectures at Harvard University, introducing psychology to the spiritual dimension of human experience. Carl Jung expanded this with his concepts of the collective unconscious and archetypal symbolism, deepening our understanding of psychological development. Abraham Maslow later identified transpersonal psychology as the "fourth force" of psychology, alongside psychoanalysis, behaviorism, and humanistic psychology. Transpersonal psychology emphasizes wholeness, spirituality, and transcendence. It encourages the expansion of human consciousness beyond the individual to include society, nature, and even the cosmos. This led me to ask whether education could also take such a path. Could it go beyond knowledge, skills, and exams to become a companion in the holistic growth of consciousness?

Around the same time, I also encountered the theory of autopoiesis, which greatly expanded my thinking. The term autopoiesis, coined by Chilean biologists Humberto Maturana and Francisco Varela, describes a living system as one that maintains, replicates , and defines itself through its own organization. According to their theory, life is not the product of external programming but arises through the unfolding of internal rules. Every system continuously regenerates itself while remaining in structural coupling with its environment. In his work on cognitive biology, Maturana wrote th at cognition is life. Consciousness does not result from outside input but from a system's internally generated operations. This theory has since been widely applied in systems theory and artificial intelligence, suggesting that language, society, and even education are all self-organizing systems. We do not simply deliver information to children. We activate their agency and invite their intrinsic responses.

Isn't that exactly how children grow? They are not passive containers waiting to be filled. They are dynamic systems with innate capacities to generate meaning and expression. Their behaviors, emotions, and relationships are the languages of their systems. Our role is not to control them but to observe, to respond, and to resonate.

In 2022, I finally brought together years of psychological theory, theater practice, and systemic thinking to launch the Children's Psychodynamic Theater research project. We had no large facilities or funding team. All we had was a small dance studio in the Bay Area. The first class consisted of just two children. One was a typically developing six-year-old girl. The other was an eight-year-old boy with an autism diagnosis. They became like two mirrors. One reflected societal expectations. The other revealed a more raw and internal reality.

The six-year-old girl was quiet and reserved, with a soft, clear gaze. During the first few sessions, she barely spoke. She simply watched. Eventually, I created a one-on-one trust exercise for her. She closed her eyes and fell backward while I stood behind her, ready to catch her. At first, we stood close together so there was little risk. Gradually, I stepped farther away. Each time, she trusted me and fell. Each time, I caught her.

I am six feet two inches tall and weigh two hundred pounds. At one point I said, "Now it's your turn to catch me." She hesitated. I asked her, "Can you do it?" She nodded seriously and said, "I can." But then I quietly told her we were going to stop. Not because she wasn't brave, but because in this world, even with good intentions, we should not do things that might harm ourselves. Helping others should never come at the cost of self-sacrifice. She never forgot that lesson. From that moment, she became more expressive. She began to see things from different perspectives. She learned to process emotions using something akin to the second-order perspective described in autopoietic theory.

The eight-year-old boy with autism made a different kind of impression. At the end of his first session, I felt a heaviness. He had a handsome face and clear eyes, but his body and emotions remained in a state of guarded defense. He avoided eye contact and physical proximity and said nothing at all. I designed a highly personalized curriculum for him. We began with describing his physical appearance. Then we moved on to imitating my walking. A silent understanding began to develop between us. He eventually started describing his family, mimicking voices, and imitating gestures.

Slowly, he moved from avoidance to response, from silence to imitation, from isolation to open laughter. One day, after class, he hugged my neck tightly and wouldn't let go. In that moment, I knew he had finally established a sense of trust in the space.

I never imposed goals or measurable standards on these children. The only thing that mattered to me was whether they were living in alignment with their inner rhythm. They cried, they laughed, they paused, they ran away and returned. That was their rhythm. That was their self-generation.

This entire approach was deeply influenced by Maria Montessori's educational philosophy. She believed that a child's development unfolds naturally from within and that the adult's responsibility is to prepare the environment, maintain order, and wait. It is this non-interventionist trust that gave me the confidence to integrate transpersonal psychology, autopoiesis, and theatrical experience into one coherent system. Education is not about correction. It is about coexistence.

And so, the Children's Psychodynamic Theater quietly began in a small dance studio in the Bay Area. There was no grand opening, no media, no scoring system. Just a few children and a few educators, growing together through light and fabric, through stories and silences, slowly becoming who they already were.

If the original blueprint of education was sound, why have we questioned it time and again? This question kept me awake through many nights. In today's early childhood education systems, so many so-called standards and principles carry a kind of silent pressure. They demand obedience, compliance, and rule-following, yet rarely listen to the voices within children.

Many parents share this confusion. They ask, "If my child becomes more independent, more honest, and more opinionated, won't that make them harder to manage?" One mother asked me tentatively, "Will children from your program end up too free, too unstructured? What will happen to them later?" I smiled and responded, "Isn't a child who can listen to their inner world, express their feelings, and connect with others exactly the kind of citizen we hope for in the future?"

What many parents are really expressing is a deeply rooted sense of insecurity. It is not that they do not love their children. It is that they fear losing control, fear uncertainty, and fear the unpredictable. Education becomes a repair operation, as if children are born flawed and must be corrected as quickly as possible.

But when I immersed myself in the theater alongside children, joining in their play, silence, conflict, breakdowns, and rebuilding, I discovered something transformative. Children do not need to be educated in the traditional sense. They need to be seen.

In the fall of 2022, we launched our first "Co-Emergence Theater" project in an unassuming house in the Bay Area. Only a few families joined us, and the space looked more like a temporary community center than a school. But the atmosphere was so real, so unfiltered, it could never be replicated in modern classrooms. Children tumbled on floor mats, mimicked each other, pretended freely. The adults watched with tension and wonder. They had never seen their children express emotion this way, and they were unsure how to respond.

One day, a grandmother joined a family session. When she saw her grandson roar and cry during an improvisational activity, her eyes filled with tears. Afterward, he took her hand and said, "Grandma, you should come to drama class too. It would help you." In that moment, I understood something clearly. Theater is not about teaching children to act. It is about helping families truly see each other again.

By 2025, our project had grown into three sites, each still intentionally small. We knew that this kind of system could not be replicated through duplication or standardized curriculum. It is an ecosystem that needs relationships, time, emotion, confusion, and trust. Like soil, it nurtures a child's natural rhythm of development.

During this evolution, I continually sought deeper psychological grounding for our approach. When I encountered transpersonal psychology, I finally found a language for what was happening in our work. Carl Jung's theory of archetypes, Maslow's research on peak experiences, and Stanislav Grof's studies of expanded consciousness, once considered marginal ideas, matched exactly the transformations we saw in children during drama. When a child touches sadness, anger, or fear through role-play, their consciousness expands in ways far beyond what traditional education can offer.

Yet the theory that allowed us to frame all of this systematically was autopoiesis. Originally a concept from biology, it describes how a system maintains its identity and coherence through its own structure and operations. It helped me redefine what growth means. A child is not a vessel to be shaped. A child is a living system capable of organizing, regulating, and generating meaning from within. What they need is not adult control but a relational container that supports their unfolding.

This understanding inspired us to create what we now call Cross-Theater Learning. In this design, children are the starting point and adults are co-learners. Each family theater session invites parents into the child's internal script. Sometimes it takes the form of a fearful dream, sometimes an imaginary hero, and sometimes a quiet shadow crying in the corner. Slowly, adults set aside the role of the instructor and become listeners, companions, and co-healers.

We often ask parents a single question. Do you want your child to change in order to better fit your expectations, or are you willing to accompany them as they become someone uncertain but authentically themselves? Most parents are silent the first time they hear this. And it is that silence that makes room for real growth.

For us, the word education no longer means instruction or correction. It means walking alongside a life as it moves through its own rhythms, its own conflicts, and its own reconciliation. Theater becomes the container where all of this can unfold. And we, the adults, are not directors. We are the lights that never go out.

Growth Is Not Taught. It Is Awakened

We cannot have two back-to-back headers at the same level unless they have some text

In between them. Thus, can you add at least one sentence here? I am putting this text here now

As a placeholder for text that you will insert. We need the text order to have these two headers.

Ten Moments in Theater That Illuminate the Path of Self-Generation

We often say, "A child's pace of growth should be their own." Yet in most education systems, adults are used to setting milestones, academic benchmarks, and development charts. What often gets forgotten is that every child is already a self-generating living system.

In the theater, we do not see a single trajectory of growth. We see countless intertwined paths, spiraling inward and stretching outward. Children develop emotional regulation through expression, build interpersonal boundaries through conflict, and explore cognition and language through improvisation. In relationships, they practice love and courage.

From these years of experience, we have distilled ten moments of growth. These are not curriculum steps or learning outcomes. They are moments we witnessed when children became more fully themselves. Each is a coordinate in their becoming. None of them relied on instruction or reward. They emerged naturally through experience, relationship, and action.

<u>Scene 1</u>:

In p lanting seeds, children glimpse the meaning of life.

In the sky and the soil, they begin to meet themselves.

Children do not learn about life from textbooks. They learn by planting something, rolling in the mud, or staring into the sky. That is often the first time they sense that they exist and begin to feel their place in the world.

<u>Scene 2</u>:

You are my brother. I am your sister.

In our connection, we discover trust and boundaries.

Children shout, "You took my part" or "I want to act with you" again and again in the theater. Each exchange and each moment of tension becomes a chance to practice finding their place, not by retreating or dominating but by negotiating presence.

<u>Scene 3</u>:

I greet myself.

I begin to build a gentle inner dialogue.

They learn to listen inwardly. How do I feel today? What happens in my body when I'm angry? Through mirror games, emotion cards, and small rehearsal scenes, they practice speaking to themselves with honesty and care.

<u>Scene 4</u>:

I can choose.

And I will face the consequences of what I choose.

There are no commands. Only choices. Which character do you want to play? How will this scene unfold? In these questions, children begin to link autonomy with responsibility. They become more accountable, not more obedient.

<u>Scene 5</u>:

I recognize my feelings.

And I learn to process them through words, movement, or stillness.

Children do not need to suppress emotions. They need tools to work with them. Theater is a natural toolbox. Tears become part of performance. Anger gives power to a character. Fear softens under the stage lights.

Scene 6:

I practice cooperation through play.

Through taking turns, I internalize rules.

Rules are not imposed. They emerge from the shared need for rhythm and structure. In creating a shared story or crafting a group adventure, children discover how to coordinate, yield, and stand firm.

Scene 7:

Conflict brings pain.

But it also opens the door to coexistence.

Children discover that not every conflict needs to end in escape. Sometimes they can explain. Sometimes they can pause. Sometimes they can ask for help. They gain courage and skills to navigate complex dynamics.

Scene 8:

In daily life, I begin to express myself.

In community, I begin to belong.

Language becomes more than a tool of desire. It becomes the vessel of identity, emotion, and thought. Through storytelling and performance, children stretch their language and practice listening to others.

Scene 9:

I wonder who I am.

I imagine who I might become.

Their inner compass begins to emerge. They play heroes, parents, explorers. They rehearse alternate selves. In this rehearsal of life, they search for their own direction.

Scene 10:

I embrace my imperfections.

And I learn to restore myself in emotion.

Eventually, children gain the ability to self-regulate. They know they will make mistakes and learn to forgive themselves and start again. That is true freedom.

These ten moments of growth are scenes we have seen unfold time and again in the theater. They move us. They teach us. These are not lessons we deliver to children. They are signs of the living systems each child already is.

Children are not empty vessels waiting to be filled.

They are already whole.

All we wish to do is keep the light in the theater burning, so that every child may step onto their own stage and begin the journey of becoming who they are.

Twelve Emotional Themes—One Journey Across the Year

We do not believe in a single timeline for all children. But we do believe that growth needs rhythm. A child's development is not a race toward progress. It is a spiral of awakening, pausing, transforming, and integrating.

Through embodied theater experiences, everyday rituals, and shared action, we help children meet themselves, connect with others, and become more whole. The calendar is not based on academic units, but on monthly invitations for emotional discovery and human becoming.

January: Growing Wonder. A new year, A fresh world .

As the calendar turns, we slow down to notice the world again. Through morning greetings, nature walks, and evening gratitude circles, children learn not to recite thank you phrases but to notice. They see the sky, their own shoes, a friend's small act of kindness. Wonder becomes the first language of presence.

February: Growing Belonging in the Month of Friendship and Family.

Around Valentine's Day, we explore what it means to feel safe with others. Children make cozy classroom corners, share stories of love, and recognize care in small gestures. Belonging is not about fitting in. It is about being seen and held.

March: Growing Respect for Life Spring Begins. Life Stirs Under the Surface.

As the earth thaws, children plant seeds and watch them grow. They learn to care for sprouts and say goodbye to fallen leaves. Through these moments, they begin to understand growth, change, and the gentle cycle of life.

April: Growing Memory Where did I come from?

In a season of renewal and reflection, children trace personal histories. They create family trees or ancestor mailboxes and invite parents to share stories from long ago. Memory becomes a thread of belonging that grounds identity.

May: Growing Initiative I can do things. I want to try.

During a time of spring energy and Mother's Day, children are invited to contribute to their world. They clean a window, water plants, or make a snack for a friend. These are not chores but choices that say, I can help and it matters.

June: Growing Compassion Summer starts. The heart opens.

As school winds down, we turn to care. Through stories about children or animals in need and role-playing empathy, children learn to comfort and to approach others with kindness. Compassion becomes their quiet strength.

July: Growing Awareness of Difference Independence and inclusion.

During Independence Day celebrations and family travels, we explore what makes each person and culture unique. Children discover new foods, music, and languages. They practice seeing the world through someone else's eyes.

August: Growing Connection Back to school. Rejoining the group.

As the new school year begins, children rediscover how to live together. What are rules? Why do we wait our turn? Through theater games and classroom rituals, they experience belonging not as control but as connection.

September: Growing Respect Honoring teachers and guides.

Labor Day and the return to school invite a deeper conversation about respect. Children design thank-you cards and remember teachers who made them feel seen. Respect is not fear. It is recognition and appreciation.

October: Growing Safety Fall brings change and challenge.

As Halloween nears and safety drills begin, children engage in "what if" theater. They rehearse getting lost, calling for help, and navigating emergencies. These practices build body memory and give them tools for real-life resilience.

November: Growing Responsibility Giving thanks and taking part.

Around Thanksgiving, we explore how actions affect others. Children sort recyclables, care for a shared plant, and help prepare snacks. Responsibility is not a rule. It is a relationship with the world that begins with care.

December: Growing Selfhood Looking back, looking forward.

During the holiday season, we hold a Secret Kindness Circle. Children quietly care for one another through small gestures. At the end of the month, each one shares: This year I learned... Next year I hope to... This is selfhood not as ego but as reflection and renewal.

These twelve months are not a syllabus. They are a way of living in time. In each action, children gain experience. In each experience, they process feeling. In feeling, they begin to know who they are. In knowing, they become.

If childhood is a tree growing, then we offer the right water, the right sunlight, and the right space. Not to shape the tree, but to help it grow true.

The Theater as a Container for Children's Inner Worlds

There are two distinctive features of the Generative Theater. The first is the positioning. The Generative Theater is a developmental education center, not a preschool.

After visiting many preschools, I have often felt a deep sense of unease. Though many institutions claim to have a standard ratio of two teachers and one caregiver, the reality is often just one teacher for a group of twenty to forty children. Even elite private preschools, with class sizes of fifteen, frequently operate within a hierarchical structure where the teacher lectures and the children listen. Children with divergent attention patterns or unique ways of expression are often labeled as disruptive or problematic.

This is not the fault of individual teachers. Their time and energy are limited, and the educational systems they are trained in often emphasize traditional instruction over psychological development and individual emergence. Many children are misunderstood or even punished before they have had the chance to discover who they are.

The Generative Theater is a developmental center, not a preschool. We do not treat children according to uniform benchmarks. Instead, we focus on individual emergence, drawing from psychological counseling, drama education, systems theory, and AI-assisted learning. We create a living ecosystem that supports the integrated growth of a child's body, mind, and spirit. Life is education, and education is generative. Our role is not to manage children but to accompany them in becoming themselves.

The second distinctive feature of the Generative Theater is the environment—it feels like home. Our space is not designed to resemble a school or a theme park. Instead, we model it after a home. As one child told a journalist, "I'm going to my other home to play." For them, the Generative Theater is not a strange institution but a warm and familiar extension. They do not arrive as strangers but return as family.

Each Generative Theater space is divided into small "homes," each with up to fifteen children and two facilitators, whom we call caregivers. We use a mixed-age model, where older children care for younger ones and younger children learn to respect their older peers. This structure supports authentic and respectful peer relationships.

Key Values and Practices

1. Learning From Nature

"Man follows the earth. Earth follows the sky. The sky follows the Tao. The Tao follows nature." Nature is our first and most profound teacher. Our day begins outdoors, learning from sunlight, wind, soil, and water. Children plant flowers and vegetables, observe butterflies, snails, and ants, and feel the rhythm of life in changing weather. This is more than life education. It is a living field of awareness.

In transpersonal psychology, this practice reflects reverence for life. In systems theory, it is the practice of structural coupling.

2. Comparing With Oneself

We do not encourage children to become "the best." We encourage them to become better versions of themselves. There are no external rankings. Instead, we use AI to map behavioral and emotional patterns and combine this with daily observations from caregivers to draw a dynamic picture of each child's growth. Children are invited to reflect on how they have changed from yesterday, not how they measure up to others. This fosters self-awareness and intrinsic motivation. Our AI system does not judge.

It observes. It exists to support adults in responding accurately to children's needs. This is a practical application of the principle that knowing is embodied.

3. Personal Ownership

Each child has their own towel, pajamas, bowl, cup, and space. They learn what is mine and what is yours. This supports a concrete understanding of boundaries. It aligns with the Montessori principle of psychological order and lays the foundation for a sense of body, emotion, and relational structure.

4. Cooperative Relationships

We practice mixed-age community living. Children learn empathy, respect, and collaboration. Older children are not enforcers but gentle role models. Younger children are not just recipients but active contributors. Each small home is a field of co-creation. Children help set rules, negotiate tasks, and co-lead their group. Facilitators are not authority figures but co-participants in a generative process. This reflects structural coupling in systems theory and synchronicity in transpersonal psychology.

5. Independence and Agency

We design support systems not for standardization but for self-regulation. From using a spoon and setting a table to putting on pajamas and cleaning a room, every routine is a chance for self-generation. The AI system tracks progress through these routines, signaling when facilitators can step back and children can step up. This builds true autonomy, not obedience through command but freedom through practice.

6. Understanding Boundaries and Rules

We do not enforce rules through coercion. Instead, we use signage, spatial design, visual charts, and role negotiation to help children experience boundaries and consensus. During free time children can choose from various stations such as cutting, painting, writing, or building. They understand when the kitchen is off-limits and when toys must be returned. Even when they test boundaries, they are learning how order arises through exploration.

7. Delayed Gratification

We do not force children to suppress their desires. Instead, we guide them through practices of moderation. Waiting turns, calming before sleep, and trading roles are experiences that help children build inner rhythm and self-discipline. In systems theory, self-regulation is a core developmental function. Moderation is not suppression. It is the awakening of inner stability. Our AI system monitors these developmental markers such as the beginning of self-paced emotional control.

8.   Cultivating Respect and Responsibility

We believe human beings grow in relationship. Respect is not a rule. It is an early ritual of shared humanity. Each day brings opportunities to greet, share, apologize, forgive, and reflect. Children learn to express conflict and resolve it, replacing "It's okay" with "I accept you" and silence with a hug. We also emphasize care for the environment. Children learn to sort waste, tidy shared spaces, and care for plants.

In real responsibility, they experience compassion for self and world.

All of this is supported by our AI-enhanced generative education system. The technology does not replace humanity. It helps us see and respond to the unfolding of each child's becoming.

- The Generative Theater is a vessel for the soul. It is a theater of becoming.

- We are not instructors. We are companions in co-creation.

- We do not set limits. We create space.

- Here, children are not empty vessels to be filled but living beings becoming who they are.

As we believe:

- Education is not molding. It is becoming.

- Performance is not imitation. It is emergence.

Prioritizing Mental Health: The Second Pillar

Through years of immersive practice in child counseling and developmental therapy, we have come to an enduring conclusion: authentic happiness in children does not stem from performance-based accolades or obedient behavior. Rather, it emerges from a child's capacity to love and accept themselves fully. Yet much of traditional education inadvertently discourages this. Children are often taught not to cry, not to show anger, to behave and make their families proud, and to never disappoint others. Although these messages may sound positive, they cultivate a subtle yet pervasive culture of emotional suppression. Over time, many children learn to silence their inner world, shaping themselves into outwardly agreeable but inwardly conflicted "model children."

At the Generative Theater, mental health is not an auxiliary concern. It stands as one of the three foundational pillars of our developmental framework. Around this axis, we have constructed an ecosystem of educational support that promotes emotional fluency, psychological resilience, and inner coherence. We believe that a child's strength lies not in emotional suppression but in the ability to feel, to express, and to reflect with awareness.

Our approach welcomes emotional expression. We do not stop children from crying or expressing frustration. Instead, we accompany them through these experiences, helping them to name and explore their feelings as a gateway to self-understanding. An AI-supported system continuously monitors emotional and behavioral patterns, not to intervene arbitrarily, but to offer educators and parents timely, compassionate insights. This allows us to perceive subtle shifts in a child's psychological landscape and respond with precision and care.

Our aim is not to produce emotionally "stable" children in the conventional sense. Stability achieved through suppression is brittle. Instead, we cultivate emotional intelligence, an awareness of feeling, and the ability to navigate it constructively. Children learn to articulate emotions in ways that connect their inner life to the outer world. For instance:

- "I am crying because I don't feel understood."

- "I am angry because I want to play alone."

When children can translate emotion into language, the experience of feeling becomes transformative rather than chaotic. Emotional intensity becomes a bridge to insight. In interpersonal conflict, we do not rely on punitive measures or forced compromise. Instead, we guide children through a reflective sequence: restoring the factual context, cultivating self-awareness, and assuming responsibility. This process draws from transpersonal psychology's emphasis on the integrated self and from autopoietic theory's model of structural coupling, wherein the individual and environment co-create meaning through mutual adaptation.

As articulated in "Knowing Being Acting," the process of knowing is inseparable from the states of being and acting. Emotions are not impediments they are vital threads that weave together perception, decision-making, and relational awareness. Our AI system serves not as a surveillance mechanism but as an attuned observer. It helps detect the quiet emergence of deeper aspects of a child's identity, enabling educators to respond with informed empathy.

Honoring Intelligence: The Third Pillar

Though we do not equate educational success with academic credentials, we regard the cultivation of intelligence as an essential and generative endeavor. True learning is not transmitted. It is awakened from within. It occurs when a child's curiosity, pace, and engagement with their environment harmonize to ignite insight.

Each child in the Generative Theater follows a unique and self-authored learning path. There is no one-size-fits-all curriculum. Instead, we design personalized educational experiences grounded in each child's cognitive rhythm, personal interests, and temperament. Here, AI does not assess or grade. It acts as a subtle growth mirror, gathering behavioral data from play, language use, and problem-solving to create a dynamic learning profile. Educators use this profile to track developments in reasoning, linguistic structure, and pattern recognition.

Our language curriculum emphasizes emotional tone, narrative rhythm, and genuine expression. Mathematics is introduced through experiential learning using spatial manipulation and quantity perception rather than rote calculations. Academic concepts emerge organically from real-life engagement. Children internalize sequencing and quantity through setting the table, learn classification while exploring nature, and develop narrative coherence through collaborative storytelling.

As emphasized in "Knowing Being Acting," intelligence enacted through meaningful activity becomes a portal to deeper presence. Knowledge is not merely absorbed. It is constructed through action.

Autopoietic theory reinforces this view. Cognition is not about replicating an external world but about co-creating meaning within one's lived context. In the Generative Theater, as children interact with objects, spaces, and peers, they generate new neural pathways and cognitive structures. These cycles of knowing, being, and acting become self-reinforcing.

AI in this setting is not a substitute for human intuition. It complements it. By documenting subtle transformations in a child's developmental process, AI helps us witness how intelligence becomes identity in motion.

A Return to Society and Life

The Generative Theater does not isolate children from the world. On the contrary, it positions everyday life as the primary arena for growth. We believe that education divorced from daily experience loses its relevance. We take children into neighborhoods, grocery stores, parks, and communal spaces to learn from what is real and immediate.

These excursions build skills far beyond the academic. Children learn to navigate social norms, assess others' needs, observe unspoken rules, and practice mutual responsibility. While they explore these spaces, AI systems quietly record linguistic and behavioral patterns, offering educators rich insight into each child's social fluency and adaptive strategies.

Our approach insists that life is the curriculum. Eggs do not come from boxes but from hens. Milk is not manufactured but sourced from cows. When children reconnect with the origins of what they encounter daily, they begin to see the world not as abstract, but as alive and relational.

This immersion in real life nourishes what transpersonal psychology calls self-transcendence, the ability to move beyond the narrow confines of self into relational consciousness. Through theater, caregiving, and environmental interaction, children deepen their empathy and expand their understanding of what it means to belong. AI amplifies the educator's perceptiveness, enabling more nuanced support as children integrate into social networks and form relational identities.

Integrated Relationships: Partnering With Parents

We do not treat parents as peripheral. In our philosophy, a child's development depends on systems-level coherence between home and school. Alignment in values, language, and intention creates a unified environment for growth.

To facilitate this, we offer weekly parent workshops, monthly data interpretation sessions supported by AI, and daily visual updates on each child's experiences. These practices are not about broadcasting achievements. They aim to foster shared reflection on the child's developmental journey.

We recognize that many parents feel exhausted and uncertain. That is why we center our efforts on transforming parents into conscious participants. By involving them in performances, collaborative tasks, and shared rituals, we create a bridge between school and home. These experiences generate not only understanding but healing. Through co-participation, the parent-child bond is reanimated.

The home is the first theater in which a child's being is staged. Only when educational institutions and families align in their cognitive approach can a child feel truly held. This shift repositions parents and educators as co-authors of the child's emerging narrative.

Conclusion: The Generative Theater is Not a Place. It is a Living Field of Co-created Growth.

We do not cultivate perfection. Nor do we enforce conformity. Our purpose is to hold space for each child to unfold into wholeness, psychologically attuned, intellectually alive, and socially engaged.

Education is not a process of shaping. It is a process of emergence. The Generative Theater is more than a pedagogical system. It is a philosophy of being. A way of belonging. A living culture of mutual becoming.

This is the practice to which we return every day.

Chapter 2: Understanding the Child's Inner World Through Play and Performance

Enter the Child's Inner Theater

Psychologist Erik Erikson p roposed that human development unfolds across eight distinct stages, each serving as a psychological cornerstone in the life cycle of a person.

The first stage, from birth to approximately 18 months, centers on trust versus mistrust. During this period, the relationship between mother and child is of paramount importance. If a child consistently receives warm and reliable care, they begin to form a fundamental trust in others and the world. This trust lays the foundation for emotional security. Conversely, inconsistent or absent caregiving fosters mistrust, sowing fear and alienation.

The second stage, from around 18 months to three and a half years, is marked by autonomy versus shame and doubt. As children begin to explore their environment and test their ability to influence it, they require both encouragement and boundaries. Support nurtures independence and self-efficacy. Excessive control or criticism breeds shame and doubt.

From three and a half to six years of age, children enter a stage of initiative versus guilt. Their curiosity and energy reach a peak, and they seek to understand the world through questions, mimicry, and play. When this initiative is stifled by constant restraint, children internalize guilt, which can dampen future motivation.

The fourth stage, from six years to adolescence, involves industry versus inferiority. As children begin formal education and acquire social skills, their ability to master tasks becomes a key source of self-worth. Encouragement fosters confidence. Without it, feelings of inadequacy may dominate.

The fifth stage, spanning adolescence to young adulthood, centers on identity versus role confusion. This period is a time of existential questioning. A coherent sense of self arises when one's experiences and values can be synthesized into a stable identity. If not, a fragmented sense of self may emerge.

The remaining stages covering intimacy, generativity, and integrity pertain to adult life. Yet their successful navigation is built upon the developmental architecture established in childhood, particularly the pillars of trust, autonomy, initiative, and industry.

The educational model of the Generative Theater draws upon Erikson's framework while also integrating concepts from transpersonal psychology, which emphasizes self-transcendence and holistic integration, and the theory of autopoiesis, which highlights structural coupling between an organism and its environment. Children are not passive recipients of content but active participants in meaning-making processes. Artificial intelligence complements this by functioning as a feedback system. It observes behavioral rhythms, emotional fluctuations, and learning patterns to support educators in crafting individualized responses.

This stage-based developmental map is not merely theoretical. Within the Generative Theater, it becomes an active and adaptive pedagogical structure. Situated cognition theory informs our practice by emphasizing that learning is not a solitary, abstract process but one deeply embedded in culture, community, and meaningful activity. The Theater offers children real-life, embodied experiences such as caring for others, arranging environments, or performing roles through which their developmental challenges are encountered and transformed.

Rather than relying on abstraction, we make knowledge tangible and participatory. The child becomes an agent in constructing understanding. Through shared tasks like cleaning, decorating, and caregiving, they explore social roles, learn responsibility, and engage in collaborative meaning-making.

From the perspective of autopoiesis, the interactions between children, environments, and peers form a constantly evolving, self-organizing system. Cognition, emotion, and value do not emerge through unidirectional transmission. They arise through recursive feedback and dynamic engagement.

Autopoiesis, a term coined by Chilean biologists Humberto Maturana and Francisco Varela, refers to a system that maintains its coherence and identity through structural coupling with its environment. In the context of the Generative Theater, children are not seen as empty vessels to be filled. They are living systems already endowed with the potential for self-organization. The role of education is to provide rich, responsive environments that stimulate this generative capacity. As Varela stated in The Tree of Knowledge, cognition is embodied action. This principle underlies our emphasis on experiential learning and situated practice.

Transpersonal psychology, developed in the 1970s as an extension of behavioral and humanistic psychologies, explores how consciousness can transcend ego-bound awareness and connect with larger fields of meaning. Childhood education benefits from this perspective because it acknowledges the nonlinear nature of development. Growth is not a straight path. It is a spiral of successive self-transcendences.

In the Generative Theater, emotional expression, empathy, and theatrical engagement with otherness serve as vehicles for this transcendence. As described in Knowing Being Acting, performance is not merely imitation. It is a becoming, a return to the core of life. In this sense, the generative process is a relational unfolding of identity.

To illustrate, we share two anonymized stories:

- XiaoGang entered the Generative Theater at two years and ten months. Now five years old, he independently bathes, combs his hair, folds his blanket, and even blows his hair dry. He also cares for his mother when she is unwell. His maturity and attention to others reflect a deeply rooted autonomy. His mother, once anxious and uncertain, now feels grounded and grateful.

- Xiaotong, a four-year-old girl, initially resisted dance lessons due to physical discomfort. Months later, she said to her father, "I was scared then. Now I want to sit with my fear for a while." She had come to an inner agreement with her fear and felt ready to dance again. Her emotional awareness was made possible by consistent support and an environment that allowed for emotional exploration.

These outcomes are not accidental. They arise from a consistent focus on the four developmental pillars of trust, autonomy, initiative, and industry. Moreover, they are cultivated through active participation. Children must do. They must engage in labor. Learning cannot remain in the realm of words or abstract thought.

Labor is not a punishment or duty. It is a concrete entry point into reality. Activities such as folding clothes, washing dishes, preparing food, or cleaning become formative practices. The earlier children are invited to engage the world through their bodies, the more grounded and confident they become. As autopoietic theory suggests, the ongoing vitality of a system depends on its responsiveness to environmental complexity. Labor, then, is a child's most immediate and profound response to the world.

Children's initiation into the Generative Theater begins with psychological accompaniment and the establishment of clear boundaries and expectations. Only in a space where emotions can be expressed freely and received with understanding can children build the safety and trust needed for inner stability. Even if the first stage was compromised in earlier experiences, the second stage offers a renewed opportunity for growth. Clear boundaries actually reinforce freedom. They deepen the sense of trust and pave the way for internalized autonomy.

Initiative emerges from feelings of competence, safety, and trust. In the Theater's daily routines, children practice initiative in everything from signing in to arranging their shoes and backpacks. At first, adult guidance is essential. Once children gain confidence, educators step back, observing rather than directing. Snack time, toileting, and meal preparation are all self-managed. Setting the table, cleaning up afterward, and preparing for naps are also carried out by the children. Older children assist younger peers, not by doing tasks for them, but by supporting them to do it themselves.

Each group also follows a rotating duty schedule. On occasion, we jokingly ask, "Shall we give someone else a turn today? You look tired." But the children almost always decline. They are eager to serve and take pride in their responsibilities. Their initiative regularly surprises us adults.

We regard children as fully capable individuals with their own thoughts and practical intelligence. The root of difficulty often lies not with children, but with adults who avoid autonomy, resist reflection, or remain passive. The child's growth catalyzes the parent's transformation. Our parent education program is designed to help adults understand child development more clearly and adopt a posture of humility and shared learning. As transpersonal psychology teaches, true maturity involves the integration of self with others, with community, and with life itself. This understanding does not arise from textbooks. It grows through acts like drying dishes, folding blankets, and working together.

We also observe that AI plays a meaningful role in the family-school connection. Through intelligent feedback systems, parents can track their child's emotional and developmental rhythms. This helps them participate more mindfully in the evolving parent-child relationship. AI does not replace human connection. It becomes a second-order observer, equipping adults with insight and timing to better support their children.

This is what we mean by generative education. It does not seek linear progress. It attends to how life unfolds through relationships and resonance. Within this system, parental growth is not merely about learning better techniques. It becomes a deep generative process. Parents revisit their own childhoods, repair old wounds, and find themselves in the very act of supporting their children. As Maturana and Varela remind us, the persistence of life depends on a system's ability to respond, not merely adapt. In the Generative Theater, the family is the system. Growth is generative. Every act of collaboration and attentive listening becomes an act of transformation. We are not planting knowledge. We are cultivating the seeds of life.

Education Awakens, Not Shapes

Some readers may wonder why we emphasize integrated psychological-educational counseling when our primary focus lies in the generative development system for children.

In the Generative Theater, we have always held that a child's development is not a linear progression of learning outcomes. Rather, it is a dynamic unfolding of body, mind, and spirit. To understand education in this light requires an integrative perspective, one that sees learning not merely as knowledge transmission, but as a holistic manifestation of character, emotion, cognition, and life intention. Education, in its deepest sense, is a mirror through which the self learns to reflect and refine itself in relation to the world. It is a sacred unfolding of potential, not a race to mastery.

Through our practice, we have found that the development of character and psychological resilience, though not immediately measurable in academic terms, is fundamental for sustained learning and social adaptation. To support children in navigating formal education without losing their personal developmental rhythm, we created innovative programs such as psychological mathematics, psychological language arts, and psychological English. These are not designed to teach content per se, but to cultivate intrinsic motivation and autonomous learning capacity. They are vessels through which children begin to grasp not only the external structures of knowledge, but also the internal architecture of their desire to learn.

Education of the future will not be about teachers transmitting information while children passively receive. Instead, children will become the subjects of their own learning, unfolding through lived experience. As Carl Rogers advocated in Freedom to Learn , true education springs from freedom and initiative, not from obedience and indoctrination. This philosophy underpins our integrated psychological-educational counseling system, a playful space centered on self-guided learning. Here, children do not merely absorb content. They discover how to become the guides of their own learning process.

What Is Integration?

Integration means that different dimensions of life are able to communicate and empower one another, forming an organic whole. It is not the piecing together of fragments but a fluid, generative process, a co-evolution of systems through structural coupling and synchronized renewal. In our theoretical framework, integrated education is a practical application of the autopoietic system, founded on dynamic symbiosis between the individual and their environment. Structural coupling signifies that growth is not one-directional reception of knowledge but a mutual unfolding between child and world.

What Is Integrated Education?

Integrated education consciously nurtures emergent abilities in a child, fostering inner connections across domains and gradually forming a whole being who is independent, autonomous, and creative. We identify three core dimensions:

- Spiritual: determining one's values, beliefs, and life vision, offering a sense of direction.

- Psychological: organizing emotions, relationships, and self-awareness, forming the internal structure of being.

- Physical: grounding all experiences, feelings, and cognition in embodied action.

These are not sequential layers. They operate as a generative network where each element influences the others. This interdependent model reflects the core of autopoiesis, the ongoing co-creation of cognitive structures and behavioral patterns through interactions between the self and the environment. Education, therefore, becomes the co-design of a child's own growth. It is the dance of experience and reflection, the shaping of interiority through exterior encounter.

In the Generative Theater, we emphasize experiential integration and situated cognition. Children grow through dynamic encounters, facing challenges, resolving conflicts, collaborating, and reflecting. These become the basis for cognitive structures that are both personal and relational. According to situated cognition theory, knowledge does not emerge in isolation within the brain. It unfolds through interactions across culture, community, body, and environment. It is an improvisational dialogue, shaped by presence and participation.

Autopoiesis offers a deeper systemic perspective. Individuals are not passive subjects of environmental conditioning but active participants in the generation of meaning. The educational process does not follow a linear trajectory of input and output. Instead, it involves perturbation, response, and structural reconfiguration. In the generative space, new ways of thinking and acting continually emerge. Education becomes the architecture of self-generating systems. Every child is a self-organizing entity, requiring an environment that nurtures emergence rather than molds from the outside.

Crucially, the fundamental arenas for this education are family and school. And for these arenas to function authentically, adult systems, parents and teachers, must awaken. A triadic relationship of trust and support must emerge:

1. Each behavior of the child is an expression.

2. Parental responses become emotional mirrors.

3. Teacher interventions initiate structural transformation and integration.

This triad must be continuously maintained and renewed. It is not a chain of control, but a living system of interaction. In the Generative Theater, we invite parents and educators to truly see the child, not to rush into correction, but to witness.

In today's education systems, entrance exams and standardized testing dominate the priorities of families and schools. Development becomes fragmented training. Children often grow weary, anxious, aggressive, or emotionally numb. Many no longer express themselves, struggle with solitude, and fail to collaborate. These symptoms point to a deeper failure, the failure to see the child as a whole person. As a result, integrated psychological-educational counseling was created.

It supports children's development while guiding parents and teachers in self-understanding, reshaping beliefs, and co-creating environments that allow for individual emergence. Its focus is not on what to teach, but on how to accompany. And the essence of accompaniment, as transpersonal psychology teaches, is presence, a state of consciousness that embraces the moment, empathizes with experience, and welcomes uncertainty. This is what we call the generative space. Within this system, a new developmental triangle emerges between child, parent, and counselor:

• The counselor offers psychological and developmental insight to help adults see the child clearly.

• Parents, through understanding, release control and anxiety, creating a softer and more stable support field.

- Children, in turn, feel safer to express and explore, deepening trust in self and world.

This triangular structure is iterative, support, response, generation, renewed support, evolving into a self-regulating, continuously renewing relational network. This is what we mean by an autopoietic educational relationship. It is not static or closed. It evolves dynamically, allowing each individual to unfold at their own rhythm. Children are not shaped by prescription. They define themselves through interaction and feedback.

We emphasize the vast potential of artificial intelligence in generative education. Rather than fear AI as a replacement, we explore how it can enhance self-directed learning, self-expression, and self-formation. In our system, AI is not a controller but an activator. It provides abundant resources and responsive feedback, enabling broader and deeper connections. Since AI operates through human-given instructions, it trains decision-making and consciousness itself. Our pedagogy embeds AI tools intentionally, to help children build storylines, create characters, and explore visual imagination, expanding perception and expression where art and technology meet.

The true value of AI lies not in replacing human thought but in awakening the creative will at the heart of the human spirit. This reflects the autopoietic logic of structural generation. Machines do not dictate how we grow. They serve as tools and mirrors on the path of deeper self-becoming.

Many parents and teachers wish for children to become excellent. But real education helps them become themselves. When growth is founded solely on the expectations of others, the resulting personality will be distorted, high achieving but without agency, obedient yet uncreative.

We have observed that children pass through multiple phases of independence. These are often misinterpreted as rebellion. In truth, they are attempts to seize opportunities for becoming. When adults misread these moments and respond with control or suppression, they disrupt the child's rhythm and diminish their capacity for exploration and vitality.

Integrated psychological-educational counseling is not a tutoring program or therapy room. It is a generative space for growth. Here, the child is their own teacher, the counselor a fellow traveler. Children learn freely using pointing pens, story cards, tactile boards, and everyday objects. Language and math become windows into understanding the world, not tools for examination.

We have seen a five-year-old recreate the geometry of their home using shape cards. A three-year-old composed a cleaning song while setting the table. These sparks of wisdom emerge not from instruction but from a responsive structure that supports becoming.

As a street artist once said, I just release what was already there. Children are the same. What we provide is the system that allows their becoming to unfold.

True integration is not chiseling children into ideal forms. It is awakening their capacity to engage with the world, to respond to life, participate in community, and dwell with ease within themselves. This is our deepest understanding and commitment to education.

- It is not sculpting. It is awakening.

- It is not indoctrination. It is activation.

- It is not control. It is coexistence.

And this is the ultimate meaning of integrated psychological-educational counseling within the Generative Theater educational system.

Move in Rhythm with the Child's Soul

Integrated psychological-educational counseling serves as a vital platform, offering both children and parents the opportunity to experience temporary hardship in exchange for enduring ease. It reflects a commitment to long-term growth, where the path of becoming is nurtured with patience and care. This system is grounded in three core aims: to foster holistic and integrated development in children, to root learning in lived and embodied experience, and to weave together classical traditions, psychological insight, and technological innovation into a generative educational system.

Human beings are born with innate differences. Education exists not to flatten those differences, but to recognize and refine them. Whether a child is exceptionally gifted or possesses more modest abilities, education is essential. Discipline and effort are not optional. In fact, the more natural talent a child has, the more urgent the need for proper guidance. Without it, potential may wither or be misused. Wealth, on its own, cannot deliver wisdom or virtue. Assuming that affluence makes education unnecessary is a grave error. For those called to lead, education is not merely a benefit. It is a moral responsibility.

In this model, early academic success is not treated as a primary objective. Instead, it is regarded as a natural outcome of a deeper developmental process. Children who engage in mathematics, English, and language arts within this system gain foundational skills that support both long-term learning and social adaptability. These outcomes emerge through a series of carefully structured practices:

First, each child begins from a personal baseline. This respects individual readiness. Learning advances not by comparing one child to another, but by comparing each child to their own potential. This individualization reduces anxiety and makes learning a source of joy.

Second, independent learning habits are cultivated. Children work through thoughtfully designed, self-guided materials without direct instruction. They are required to concentrate, apply themselves, observe examples, and manage their time. Counselors step in only when support is necessary, creating space for reflection and self-correction. This fosters confidence and achievement.

Third, children are taught to delay gratification. Working at their own pace, they often develop a strong desire to continue. At moments of peak interest, counselors may encourage them to pause, teaching the value of moderation and sustainable motivation.

Fourth, children establish personal goals. There are no standardized timelines. Each child proceeds at their own level, free from pressure or comparison. In this freedom, they learn how to map their own academic journeys.

Fifth, focus and critical thinking are developed. Because guidance is gentle and non-directive, children learn to trust their own reasoning. Mistakes are seen not as failures, but as moments of insight. The absence of criticism opens a space for curiosity and perseverance.

Sixth, creativity is awakened. When independent thought and initiative are honored, creative impulses emerge naturally. Creativity is a human birthright. It thrives in environments that are open and non-prescriptive. Integrated counseling consciously preserves this space.

Seventh, children strengthen their ability to self-regulate. They study different subjects, often side by side, yet each at their individual level. Over time, they internalize the understanding that learning need not be synchronized. Self-regulation arises naturally.

Finally, children absorb the capacity to love and care. Each counselor is trained in psychological guidance and meets children with genuine concern. This care is not performed. It is lived, and it extends to the family as well. In such an atmosphere, children naturally embody empathy and relational trust.

These practices form the foundation for a child to become independent and self-possessed. Western educational traditions, particularly those rooted in classical and humanistic thought, have long emphasized the formation of character alongside the acquisition of knowledge. Thinkers from Plato to John Dewey recognized that education must nurture moral awareness, civic responsibility, and personal integrity. In many modern systems, however, these values have been overshadowed by a narrow focus on standardized performance. Integrated counseling restores balance by placing emotional development and ethical awareness at the heart of academic learning. This cultivates a deeply rooted sense of purpose and an authentic commitment to personal and social well-being.

True growth cannot be separated from experience. Real learning engages the whole being: body, emotion, mind, and action. Laozi reminded us that observation deepens through repetition and return. Thus, education must become a practice of returning to what matters and making it meaningful through context. The Generative Theater honors this by transforming experience into expressive learning, not by emphasizing memory, but by cultivating reflection and embodied wisdom.

At the philosophical level, the system draws deeply from classical models and systems theory. Most fundamentally, it is rooted in the logic of autopoiesis. The child is not an empty vessel. Rather, the child is a self-organizing, self-renewing life form. Education becomes a living interaction between child and environment, a generative process in which both are co-created. This concept is known in systems theory as structural coupling.

Theater is the central practice of this model. Through drama, children translate life into action. They role-play, move, express emotion, and learn by doing. Every character they play expands their perspective. Every rehearsal becomes a rehearsal for life. Every reflection that follows awakens deeper self-awareness. Theater is not an extracurricular activity. It is a developmental mirror.

From the standpoint of phenomenology, learning is not input from the world but a co-creation of world and self in the present. A child's experiences in school, in drama, in family life, all reflect this world-self coupling. Education must honor this reality. Knowledge does not arise from passive reception. It is generated in context. Failure, repetition, and emotion are all part of this cycle. Learning proceeds through a generative loop of experience, perception, reflection, and renewed experience.

Transpersonal psychology offers the consciousness framework to support this integration. It challenges us to ask deeper questions. Who is this child? What is the meaning of this life? Growth is not merely social development. It is a spiritual unfolding. Rather than treating behavior as problems to fix, we listen for the inner call. We guide children toward their deeper identity and sense of purpose.

To support this vision, artificial intelligence becomes a significant ally. AI can detect emotional and cognitive patterns, analyze learning styles, and suggest tailored learning trajectories. It can generate dynamic theater scripts, support simulations, and encourage empathy and creativity. In this setting, AI is not simply a tool. It becomes a reflective partner. When children engage with AI, they also engage with their own internal language. The instructions they give reveal their clarity of thought and depth of awareness. AI amplifies human learning rather than replacing it.

We believe the future of education depends not on increasing control, but on deepening trust. We trust life's ability to generate itself. We trust that when children are held within a thoughtful, intentional system, they will grow. The Generative Theater is this system. It stands where the classical and the contemporary converge, where psychology and theater meet, where humanity is free to evolve.

To honor our classical heritage, we look to the seven liberal arts, which form the foundation of Western education. These arts are divided into two branches. The first, called the trivium, consists of grammar, logic, and rhetoric. These disciplines teach language, reason, and the art of expression. They are essential for developing clarity of thought and communication. The second, known as the quadrivium, includes arithmetic, geometry, music, and astronomy. These disciplines provide insight into structure, pattern, beauty, and cosmic harmony.

In our system, these seven arts are reimagined through experiential learning. Grammar becomes the art of storytelling and the construction of narrative, giving children a voice. Logic is approached through collaborative inquiry and problem-solving games. Rhetoric is expressed in drama and performance, where persuasion is lived. Arithmetic and geometry are made tangible through spatial reasoning and real-world application. Music trains emotional sensitivity and awareness. Astronomy opens children to the wonder of the universe, cultivating awe and reflective thinking.

This approach to classical learning does not stop at skill. It aims at wisdom, discernment, and the freedom to imagine and create. It is deeply rooted in tradition, yet fully alive in the present.

Our instructional approach is heuristic. We teach through discovery, conversation, and meaningful experience. We do not fill children with facts. We invite them to seek truth. This aligns with Platonic philosophy, which teaches that real learning is remembering. Before birth, the soul has already touched truth. The material world awakens what is forgotten. Learning becomes remembrance, not acquisition. Transpersonal psychology affirms this: knowledge arises from beyond the ego. It speaks to a larger consciousness.

Our Generative Learning System treats the world of appearances and the world of ideals as parts of a whole. The sensory world is fleeting. The ideal world is eternal. Education must guide learners in turning their attention from the surface of things to their essence. The highest aim in this journey is the Good. Only in encountering the Good does one see clearly. This movement from sense to essence is the true foundation of generative learning.

Moral development is essential in this process. Morality is not innate. Right action emerges from right understanding. People choose wrongly not because they desire evil, but because they misunderstand the good. Moral education is therefore the cultivation of wisdom. It is the shaping of judgment and the training of restraint. Educators must model discipline through their lives, not only their lessons.

Even technical subjects such as geometry, astronomy, and mathematics must serve moral ends. They should not exist only for speculation. They exist to develop reasoning and support human flourishing. Health, likewise, is not just a gift. It is a habit. Strength can be cultivated even in the weakest. Practice and discipline are powerful teachers.

The philosophy of Aristotle offers further grounding. He taught that matter contains potential, which becomes actual through form. Husserl phenomenology echoes this, describing development as the realization of possibility. In our system, we go further. We suggest that growth is driven by an inner force, a first movement, a self-arising dynamism that seeks to become.

Aristotle also held that sensory experience leads to memory, and memory to reasoning. From sensation to generalization, the mind moves toward universal truths. This is the scientific path to knowledge. Transpersonal psychology complements this by describing the soul in three parts: (a) nutritive, which connects us to the plant world; (b) sensitive, which links us with animals; and (c) rational, which defines us as human. Each corresponds to a domain of education: physical, emotional, and intellectual.

Instincts must not be denied but guided. Humans, like animals, have drives. But unlike animals, we possess the power of reason. The role of education is to help children balance these forces. Nature must be shaped by habit, and habit guided by reason. When this triad is in harmony, the child becomes a person of character.

Our Generative Learning System follows this classical wisdom. We affirm the child's nature, cultivate habits through environment and rhythm, and direct reason through careful pedagogy. This is the path not only to learning, but to becoming. In this light, the Generative Theater is more than a school. It is a living philosophy. It is an invitation to grow into what one already is, and what one is still becoming.

Symbols as Mirrors of Becoming

(Suggested totemic image: a life tree spiraling outward from its center. Its trunk is solid and steady, growing from the roots upward into a crown of layered spiraling branches. The crown remains open, curving and flowing skyward like a blossoming flower of consciousness. Suspended among its branches are luminous points representing the body, emotion, thought, and spirit, symbolizing the dynamic symbiosis of the inner human structure.)

The totem of the Generative Theater is not a closed geometric shape. It is a spiraling tree of life. It symbolizes education as an open, nonlinear living process. Each child is like one ring of this tree, not a loop of repetition but an ascent, expansion, and deepening within a spiral of becoming.

The roots of this tree are grounded in the soil of relationship. A child's growth does not begin in isolation, but through structural coupling with family, educators, and the environment. Parental understanding, pedagogical guidance, and environmental nourishment together form the soil. Only when relationships are stable can life truly take root.

The trunk of the tree is formed layer by layer through experience. Each experience is not a static deposit of knowledge, but a structure of understanding formed through a cycle of perception, action, and reflection. The tree trunk does not grow upward in a straight line but adjusts its direction with the shifts in wind, sunlight, and water, never losing its upward inclination.

The branches represent the unfolding of multiple intelligences.

Some branches grow into bodily wisdom developed through movement, play, and dramatic practice. Others become emotional vessels formed through relationships, failure, and empathy. Still others unfold into cognition, creativity, soul, and spirit. These capacities are not mutually exclusive. They coexist and collaborate, forming a multidimensional spectrum of life's potential.

The crown of this tree is unfinished. It is not a bonsai pruned to shape, but a living system still growing, changing, and transforming. This reflects our understanding of education, not as designing goals for children to reach, but as creating an environment that activates their innate generative drive. As transpersonal psychology affirms, to become oneself is not to be shaped by others, but to unfold one's own potential under the right conditions.

This life tree is not a static symbol. It is a dynamic vision of becoming. It stands in the present while rooting itself in the past and extending toward the future. Its roots lie hidden beneath the surface, made of unspeakable emotional experiences, unreadable behavioral codes, and unnamed vibrations of life. These unseen layers nourish the trunk so that growth is not merely an accumulation of skills but a deep unfolding from within. We understand that the visible height of a tree is always determined by the invisible depth of its roots.

Each spiral of the tree is not a mechanical repetition but a witness to inner transformation. Like the dramatic exercises in the Generative Theater, every repetition differs with changes in bodily state, emotional intensity, and the responses of others. Every rehearsal is an act of generation. Children are not simply playing roles. They are generating them. They are generating themselves, generating meaning through action, understanding through expression, and selfhood through relationship.

There is also an essential dimension in this tree: time. Generation never occurs in an instant. It requires the sedimentation and resonance of time. Education does not accelerate ripening but accompanies growth. Like tree rings, it cannot skip steps. We care more about who the child is now than who they should be in the future. Every present struggle, joy, or hesitation becomes the raw material for future personality. We believe that allowing a child to be a process is more fundamentally valuable than forcing them to become a product.

The luminous points in the tree represent its inner vitality. They may be a moment of shared empathy, a solitary listening to one's inner voice, or the renewal of belief after falling. These lights hover throughout the system, symbolizing the child's ongoing process of self-integration across emotions, body, language, thought, and spirit. Educators and parents are the ones who pause, observe, and respond to these sparks.

Ultimately, this tree is not only a symbol for the child. It is a metaphor for the entire educational system. Every educator who truly respects life becomes a guardian of this forest. They do not force growth or trim for uniformity. They listen to the rhythm of growth, breathing with it, attuning to it. What they protect is the generation of life itself, the awakening of spirit, and the path by which each child becomes their own.

Thus, the Generative Theater is not merely a teaching method or a curriculum framework. It is a way of understanding the human being. A person is a tree that can grow, a life that tells stories, a theater that is still in the making.

This life tree stands amid the winds and rains of the world, yet its roots hold firm and its will remains flexible. It lives with becoming as a verb and generation as a direction. It does not ask for height. It asks for depth. It does not seek achievement. It seeks unfolding.

And we are ready to live, take root, and grow together with each child beneath this tree.

It is not a symbol, but a process. It is not a doctrine, but a generation. It is not a picture of knowledge, but a metaphor for life itself.

Six Silent Years That Shape a Life

Speak then of children, whose souls are like gardens at dawn, awaiting the warmth of time, the waters of experience, and the winds of wonder. In the system we have come to call Generative Theater, the development of potential is not the training of a single skill but a comprehensive unfolding. It encompasses perception, cognition, emotion, relationship, creativity, and action.

We do not regard potential as a hidden treasure waiting to be unlocked. Rather, we understand it as a generative structure that gradually emerges through interaction with the world. Each child carries within them a pathway toward creation, expression, and growth. Our task is to provide a supportive, responsive, and open environment in which this potential may flourish through lived experience.

Within Generative Theater, drama becomes a crucial gateway. It is not the practice of theatrical technique, but a passage into life itself. Here, children simulate the world. They play at being kings, princesses, pilots, animals, or machines. These are not merely games. They are profound psychological exercises. Through role-play, children encounter otherness, understand the world, explore emotion, and build the self.

When a child says, "I do not want to," or "I am afraid," in the safety of the theater space, the true self reveals itself. And when that same child steps forward, embodying an unfamiliar role, they are not pretending. They are reaching, understanding, empathizing. These are not skills imposed from without. They arise naturally from the generative cycle of enactment, sensation, reflection, and re-creation.

We care deeply for the texture of experience. Potential does not emerge through coercion. It is sculpted slowly by experiences that are bodily and emotional. As phenomenology affirms, consciousness never exists apart from experience. The goal of our pedagogy is not for the child to know, but for the child to encounter being.

In the integrated psychological counseling of Generative Theater, the development of potential is understood as a process of autopoiesis. We draw upon the core logic of our system, structural coupling, experiential cycle, and systemic renewal. In real relationships with others, with environments, with knowledge and inner capacity, each child co-creates their unique structure of ability. This structure is not born of talent. It is born of sustained experiential support.

The involvement of artificial intelligence offers new possibilities. AI does not replace the thoughts of teachers or children. It acts as a systemic observer and feedback generator. It helps us detect rhythms, interests, difficulties, and emotional patterns. In personalized learning pathways, character simulations, and scenario design, AI serves as a partner. It sharpens our observations and reminds us that no child should be seen through the lens of an average.

We discard the myth of the success template and avoid misinterpreting talent. The aim is not to produce prodigies. The aim is to help each child become themselves. We believe intention, openness, patience, and inquiry are the soil in which generative growth takes root.

- Every child holds a passage to the unknown.

- Every image formed in the mind is energy toward creation.

- Every role enacted is an expansion of the structure of life.

- Educators in Generative Theater are companions, creators of contexts, guides of structure, and witnesses of transformation.

- We do not plan success for children. We accompany them through the process of becoming.

- We do not impose a direction. We walk beside them as they discover their path.

- We do not write their scripts. We invite them into their own theater.

- Each child is their own director, actor, and playwright.

- Every unfolding of potential is a reverberation between life and the world.

We also learn from tangible stories. A young man who plays piano with his feet, born without arms. A girl whose reactive strength and maturity of expression astonish the world. Karl Witte, the German educator who cultivated early philosophical depth and wisdom through emotional training in daily life. These are not miracles. These are the results of early, systematic, and ongoing support.

In the nineteenth century, the pastor Karl Witte raised his son, also named Karl, from a frail infant into a university student by the age of nine, a doctor by fourteen, and a jurist by sixteen. His strength lay not in inborn genius, but in the emotional education he received from his father from the very beginning. As the elder Witte said, it is not talent that determines a child's path, but the educational journey of life. This aligns profoundly with the insights of Montessori education.

Karl Witte believed intelligence may be innate, but its development is subject to decline. A child with an IQ of 100, if educated from birth, retains full potential. Begin at age five, and only eighty percent remains. Wait until ten, and perhaps not even sixty percent survives. This underscores the urgency of timely intervention, especially in the early years of language development.

These stories teach us that potential is not bestowed from above. It arises from structured support, ongoing relationships, and emotional attunement. With a generative system in place from the start, every child, regardless of initial conditions, can develop a structure of self through the cyclical engagement of body, emotion, and knowing.

Once, I participated in a living community that embodied the generative spirit. It resembled the Israeli kibbutz. A collective founded on shared vision and mutual care, its members pooled income and redistributed resources equally. All were required to undergo continuous training and learning, even if unwilling at first. They practiced openness and acceptance.

Most began with only elementary or secondary education. But through sustained systemic cultivation, they created schools, hospitals, psychological services, and social institutions. The average member achieved graduate-level education, and most administrators emerged from within. This was no accident. It was the fruit of intention, structure, engagement, and renewal.

Generative Theater aspires to bring this logic of potential to early education. Through structure, intention, experience, and renewal, we help each child form their unique path of development.

We also think of Susan Boyle, who stun ned the world with a single performance. Though overlooked in youth, she held to her love of music, and in a moment of being seen, released her potential into the world.

Music shows us that potential often lies in the subtlest moments. Ryuichi Sakamoto built musical worlds from forests and natural sound.

Such works embody the fusion of experience, sensation, and expression. They mirror the integrative creations of Generative Theater through voice, movement, role, and space.

A child's growth is a melody in the making. We must listen carefully. When we honor their rhythm, accept their emotional shifts, and accompany their exploration of the unknown, their potential awakens unseen. We cannot rush the song. We cannot play it for them. Each note must rise in its time, to complete the music of their life.

We believe that every child is an unfinished symphony, holding infinite possibilities within. And it is the mission of integrated psychological-educational guidance to become the accompanist, not the composer. To stand beside them in patience and love, and help them write the symphony that only they can hear.

If we do not listen for their music, who then shall hear it?

Space Breathes Freedom

From the vast deserts of the farthest East to the stillness of the western shores, I walked not to arrive, but to listen. From Ürümqi to Chengdu, from Shanghai to the frostbitten hush of Moscow's markets, my path wound across lands not to chase destinations, but to search for a sense of home. In minus thirty -nine-degree dawns, I bartered with gestures for raw poultry, returned to Shanghai with hunger in my chest and hope in my palms, then one day arrived, almost unknowingly, in a quiet corner of Silicon Valley. There, in a modest university, a single term stirred something deep within me—transpersonal psychology.

On the surface, I had wandered far. Yet every journey outward was a journey inward.

I was seeking a question that lived inside my body before it reached my lips.

Who am I?

Since the age of sixteen and a half, I had lived among others, always sharing, always entangled. My childhood bed was pressed beside my parents'. My college years unfolded without a door to close behind me. I yearned for a space that was not merely empty, but mine. A space where silence could echo without interruption. I did not long for isolation. I longed for belonging. I longed to feel whole.

And so, it began. A realization emerged: space is not just physical. It is shaped by memory, touched by emotion, constructed through relationships. My longing for a room became a longing for rootedness. My drift across cities became a meditation on sanctuary. The child's sense of space is born in that same yearning. A need not only for room, but for resonance.

Years later, I often heard Western critiques of Chinese wet markets, especially regarding animal welfare. The cages, they said, were cruel. In the West, animals are measured by spatial rights, protected under law. Yet I watched closely and noticed that even in large enclosures, birds huddled together, wings pressed, seeking closeness. It was not expanse they craved. It was contact. It was comfort.

When I began shaping the Generative Theater, I visited many kindergartens. Some schools were architectural marvels: sleek, luminous, expansive. Yet in these vast classrooms, children ran with a kind of restlessness. Rules and design could not anchor them. The space was abundant, but the spirit was scattered.

Then I entered a school small in footprint, but rich in rhythm. One hundred children shared limited ground, yet tranquility hung in the air. Nap mats lay low on the floor like soft boats rocking in silence. Children napped shoulder to shoulder, breathing in gentle unison. During breaks, they read, puzzled, played. No child sprinted. The room embraced them like a cradle.

I began to wonder: Might smaller, cocoon-like spaces answer a deeper need? The womb, our first chamber, is not wide but warm. Not grand but intimate. Could the child's body remember that primal closeness, and long for it still?

Back in our center, I noticed how children nestled into a reading nook no larger than a closet. Five at most could fit. Cushions were scattered. A canopy hovered. No one spoke of rules. Yet the children flocked. They squeezed in not to read, but to be. To exist. To be held. One afternoon, I crawled in myself. I exhaled.

We redesigned our architecture, not to impress, but to embrace. The open floor plan gave way to small "home units," each guided by a dedicated mentor. We transformed the counseling room into the "Companion Corner," a space of soft shadows and slow time. We capped class sizes at fifteen, then divided further into intimate pods. Shared areas became ceremonial rather than constant. Activities unfolded within their home spaces: science here, drama there, culture tucked gently in the corner. Tatami mats remained for communal naps, binding warmth to presence.

This transformation was not decorative, it was foundational. In theater, space is not background, it is story. A single chair becomes a throne. A threadbare cloth becomes a sky. A doorway is not a line. It is a threshold. Small spaces do not confine. They invite. They say,

"Here you are safe." They whisper, "Here you may begin."

In our theater workshops, space is never static. A blanket shelters a kingdom. A table becomes a marketplace. A circle of breath marks the entrance to the sacred. Children do not simply use space. They awaken it. They converse with it. They belong to it.

Months passed. The air changed. Running softened into walking. Shouting softened into humming. Children still burst across outdoor fields, but inside, calmness grew roots. Their nervous systems began to sync with the boundaries offered. As Montessori once taught, the outer world's order cultivates the soul's inner music.

Space is not only built with beams. It is woven through stillness, sculpted with care, anchored in trust. A child's sense of space does not bloom from quantity, but from quality. It is not about how much space surrounds them, but how deeply that space receives them. Not about spectacle, but sanctity. Not size, but soul.

And so, we return to the question that started it all: What is space if not the first stage upon which the child learns to become?

Boundaries Grow the Self

I have now spent over two decades immersed in the interwoven worlds of drama and psychology. In those years, I have come to understand one truth with deep clarity: adulthood is difficult not because of external obstacles alone, but because of the internal burdens we carry, too many fears, too many anxieties, too many silent negotiations with ourselves. We fear being disliked, we dread being hurt, and so we either please, attack, withdraw, or blame ourselves. It becomes nearly impossible to remain authentic. Even with the help of therapy, progress can be limited. The problem does not lie in the method, but in the blurriness of one's self-boundaries.

For years, I have asked myself: what truly brings about transformation? The answer, I believe, lies not in treating symptoms but in reshaping the roots. We must begin not with damaged adults, but with children, offering them a kind of education that differs fundamentally from what is currently dominant. We help children build confidence and self-respect, and at the same time, help parents shift how they perceive their children. This was how I embarked upon the path of Generative Theater, a path from which there is no return.

Through our work in Generative Theater, we observed that children's understanding of boundaries arises through the gradual construction of selfhood. This understanding does not stem from imposed moral rules, but grows naturally through bodily experience, emotional resonance, and theatrical practice grounded in real-life situations. Within our self-generative system, these experiences unfold in spirals. Children perceive rules within context, test boundaries through action, gain clarity through expression, and integrate their understanding through reflection.

Generation is not the output of indoctrination. It is the process through which the self becomes itself in the interplay between inner order and the external world.

This is precisely the ontological meaning of phenomenology in education. We no longer regard rules as abstract commands but return to the original experience of how human beings live in the world. Children are not beings who need to be taught rules. They are generators, actively constructing their way of understanding. We invite them to enter space through the body, enter relationship through emotion, and enter rules through language, not as a form of judgment, but as a lived narrative.

In this generative system, drama is not merely a tool of narration or performance. It becomes an interactive field of consciousness. Through characters, children build themselves. Through stories, they sense others. Through boundaries, they learn to coexist. AI, in this setting, becomes our most gentle partner. It does not replace. It enhances.

In the AI-supported classroom, the child's agency is not lost. On the contrary, it is amplified. Children learn to ask, to discover, to reflect. With AI-generated scenarios, they simulate conflict. With AI-guided semantic tools, they express emotion. With AI memory structures, they revisit experience. The aim is not to replace human connection but to help children learn how to articulate the world more clearly, and to understand that the self arises through the cycle of instruction and response.

Knowing, Being, and Doing, this triadic cycle lies at the heart of our generative system. In the formation of boundaries, children move from knowing what rules are, to becoming selves shaped by those boundaries, to practicing coexistence with others. These are not external standards applied to children. They are scripts that emerge through relational experience. The educator becomes a guide, a supporter, and a co-participant within this theater of becoming.

Just as every child in the theater has their own rhythm, emphasis, and storyline, so too do their boundaries form in rhythm with their growth. When we understand and support that rhythm, it becomes a structure they can stand upon to face the world.

In our first pilot class, there were four children. Among them was Xiaobao, a mischievous boy of three. He touched everything. He ran everywhere. I found myself growing uncomfortable. The truth is, all the children were like this. So, my team and I began boundary training. We taught them not to touch items on the table, not to enter the kitchen uninvited, not to throw trash randomly.

One teacher said to me, "Didn't you say we shouldn't say 'no'? Now we are only saying 'No.'" My face flushed. Yes, I had said that during our orientation session. But the truth was, without the word "no," we could not teach at all. The children had not yet developed the social learning required to stay safe or participate meaningfully. I was afraid they would fall or get hurt. So, we proceeded with boundary training.

I began to ask myself: Why do we say "no"? And how should we say it?

After just one day, by the third day, things changed. The children stopped touching everything. Xiaobao still ran around, but he no longer hit the writing table or tried to open the kitchen door. With teacher guidance, he began helping move chairs and pass out cups, and he engaged in counting games. We changed our "No" to "Stop," using crossed arms and clear gestures to reinforce the boundary.

I was surprised by how quickly the children adapted. Within a day, there was stability. I began to reflect: what made this "no" different from the usual adult "no"? Why was it effective? What makes a "no" ineffective?

I turned inward.

Let the children's behavior be the mirror of what we taught. I asked myself again and again, why do we dislike saying "no"? Why do we hesitate even when we must set boundaries? What are we afraid of? Then it struck me. It all comes back to boundaries and rules.

If we establish clear expectations early on, then future interactions do not require endless negotiation or hesitation. We know what is acceptable and what is not. Relationships become less confusing, less strained.

It is not the word "no" that people resist. It is the unpredictability of sudden prohibition. It is not the clarity of a boundary that disturbs us. It is the shifting terrain that might explode without warning. Like landmines hidden beneath polite smiles.

Boundaries offer certainty. Certainty provides peace. Through that peace, we find security. And through that security, the self is given space to grow.

Boundaries are not shackles. They are more like riverbanks that allow life to flow forward. With boundaries, the water of life knows where to go and how to move. Without them, the water disperses, loses momentum, and eventually vanishes. I have always believed that the foundation of growth is not in one's capacity to learn, but in one's clarity of boundaries. Especially for young children who have not yet mastered language or the understanding of self and other, boundaries are like gentle and steady beacons, guiding them through the fog of development.

When we speak of boundaries, we can roughly divide them into two types. The first type refers to visible boundaries. These are boundaries we can observe, describe, and regulate through examples such as space, time, and rules. Crossing national borders without permission may trigger conflict. Walking into a golf course uninvited could lead to injury. These boundaries can be shown, explained, and enforced. The second type is more subtle. These are invisible boundaries, encompassing privacy, power dynamics, bodily autonomy, and psychological space. Though these lines are harder to draw, when crossed, emotions surge like tidal waves. Such boundaries must be respected. And where necessary, they should be clarified through mutual understanding. I deeply believe that everything in the world deserves to be treated with respect. The lack of respect for boundaries is what leads to ecological imbalance, climate crises, and species extinction. Families mirror society. Without boundaries, emotions become volatile, and relationships rot. A parent-child relationship that establishes clear boundaries forms a solid foundation for love and trust, one rooted in equality.

Rules Launch, Not Cage

1. Boundaries and rules are neutral. They are not inherently good or bad:

    Many parents mistakenly believe that setting boundaries is a form of repression. One parent once said, "I gave birth to my child. Of course, they should listen to me." But upon deeper understanding, I saw that he longed desperately to be respected. His desire for control was driven by fear of losing it. Children are independent beings, full of thoughts, emotions, and choices. The more we try to control them, the more they resist. The increasing issue of child-to-parent violence stems from this very absence of boundary. Only with clear boundaries can love remain untwisted.

2. Boundaries clarify one's role and position in a relationship:

Two people form a system, and confusion leads to misunderstanding. Add a third person and it grows even more complex. The saying "Three monks draw no water" reflects this lack of boundaries. Boundaries are like maps. They tell us where we stand and where we need to go.

3. Boundaries make responsibility clear:

    In relationships, vagueness is dangerous. What is allowed? What crosses the line? Many avoid setting boundaries out of fear of conflict, but in doing so, they only create more confusion. Clear boundaries lead to honest communication and fewer conflicts.

4. Boundaries bring stability:

    People differ in gender, age, and experience. We cannot naturally understand each other. Establishing boundaries is a process of reaching consensus. It brings clarity out of vagueness. It brings peace to shared space and solidity to relationships.

5. Boundaries reduce children's confusion and anxiety:

    Young children have not yet developed mature language or self-awareness. For them, boundaries are a form of unspoken language. When they know what is allowed and what is not, their sense of safety naturally arises. That safety gives them the confidence to explore the world.

6. Boundaries stimulate neurological development and unlock potential:

    Around the age of two, children enter a phase of sensory and motor sensitivity. Structured boundaries at this time act like a womb, providing containment and security. Within this safe structure, their neural networks, sensory integration, and creativity can flourish.

One more essential distinction lies in demarcating and defining boundaries. Demarcating refers to drawing clear distinctions between people. For example, you are you, and I am I. Your belongings are not mine to use. Your body must be respected. Defining boundaries refers to setting specific operational rules within life's various areas. These can be categorized into six aspects:

1. Material Boundaries

   Every item has ownership and rules of use. Books on a shelf can be read but must be returned. Toys are to be used in designated spaces. These help children understand what belongs to whom and how things should be handled.

2. Spatial Boundaries

   Each space has its purpose. Kitchens are for cooking, not playing. Bedrooms are for resting, not dancing. While these functions can be renegotiated, such changes must come with mutual respect.

3. Temporal Boundaries

   Time is a shared resource. A single kitchen cannot accommodate five people at once. Schedules must be set. Similarly, time spent caring for children should be mutually discussed and fairly divided, not evaded or sacrificed.

4. Responsibility Boundaries

   Children are not incapable of responsibility. More often, it is adults who, out of love, rob them of the chance to participate. Educational duties, household chores, caregiving plans all need clear divisions of responsibility to prevent confusion and conflict.

5. Psychological Boundaries

   These are often invisible but frequently violated. Some dislike noise, others dislike being touched, some are sensitive to criticism. Without psychological boundaries, actions become wounds. People who cannot say "No" often fear disappointing others. But long-term suppression leads only to self-destruction. Psychological boundaries require honesty with oneself and respect for others.

6. Spiritual Boundaries

The quality of one's inner life determines the clarity of one's path. Everyone needs personal time, space, and rhythm. Many children today are addicted to screens and emotionally dysregulated because their spiritual boundaries have been disrupted.

How to Set Boundaries: Five Attitudes We Uphold

1. Express "No" with firm calmness, without emotional outbursts.

   Children do not fail to understand. They fail to receive when met with anger.

   Only when we express rules firmly and gently can they internalize what those rules truly mean.

2. Provide positive alternatives clearly.

   Boundaries are not only about what is forbidden, but also about what is allowed. Children need to know what they can do instead. Boundaries should not be chains, but guides for exploration.

3. Speak to children while making eye contact.

   Eye contact is a bridge of emotion. Look into their eyes, speak slowly, and use simple, clear language. Then ask them to repeat what they heard to ensure they've understood. Never assume understanding. Words can often mislead.

4. Hold to your principles. Do not waver.

   Children test boundaries as part of their development. If we waver, the boundary becomes meaningless. They are not trying to make life difficult. They are checking if the rules are real.

5. Praise specifically and in the moment when they succeed.

   Instead of vague praise like "You're great," be precise. Say, "I'm touched that you sat and drew quietly while I was in a meeting. That helped me a lot." Specific praise nurtures true confidence.

And thus, in Generative Theater, we believe:

- Boundaries are one of the deepest expressions of love.

- A household with clear boundaries is not a cold, rule-bound place. It is a living, respectful, and safe ecosystem. In such a space, children learn not just to coexist, but to become themselves.

- Their bodies relax. Their emotions stabilize. Their eyes shine with clarity.

  Because they know where they are, how far they can go, and how to dance with the world.

One day, I was invited to give a lecture. Before it began, I witnessed a scene inside the school that stayed with me:

- "Leo, stop running!" Kathy, the mother of three-year-old Leo, shouted anxiously.

  Leo continued running as if he hadn't heard her.

- "Did you hear me? Where did your ears go? If you don't stop and bump into someone, the police will take you away. Do you understand?" Still, Leo showed no sign of stopping.

- Kathy's voice softened, now filled with desperation. "Sweetheart, I'm begging you. Please stop running. You're making me dizzy. I really can't take this anymore."

- She turned to me and said, "Teacher, you see? I'm exhausted. I work all day and barely have the energy for him. I'm at my limit. I just can't do this anymore."

- Her eyes brimmed with fatigue and defeat. I said, "May I try?" She agreed.

- I called out to Leo, and interestingly, he ran straight to me. I looked him in the eye and gently placed my hands on his shoulders. In a calm but firm voice, I asked,

  "Why are you running?"

- He replied, "Ultraman."

- "Ah, you want to be Ultraman?" I understood. "Yes. Ultraman runs everywhere," he said.

- "Leo, Ultraman does run, but is Ultraman supposed to run inside the room?"

He said nothing.

- I continued, "Let's think again. Ultraman can go outside to run and do Ultraman things. But inside, we walk."

- I slightly pressed his shoulders downward, signaling him to lower his energy.

Leo looked at me and said, "Okay."

As I continued talking with Kathy, I kept an eye on Leo. He played with the other children and didn't run again. Occasionally, he glanced at me, and I would affirm him by saying, "Yes, Leo, good job walking. Well done." Kathy was amazed at how quickly Leo listened to a stranger. But the reasons were quite clear.

First, Kathy had been shouting. Loud voices can easily overwhelm a child that age. Second, she relied on blame and threats to control him, exposing her own helplessness. Without realizing it, Leo likely interpreted the situation as "I've won." Lastly, Kathy gave up and almost broke down in tears, which only reinforced his resistance.

In reality, children are quite capable of following adult requests if the rules are clearly established and communicated in advance. Why is this so? Because everything in the natural world runs on patterns. The sun, the moon, and the stars follow their orbits. Plants grow in seasons. Without order, chaos ensues.

Human development mirrors this natural rhythm. To function harmoniously, boundaries and rules are needed so that people, tasks, and objects all fulfill their roles. But it is up to us to define, guide, and uphold these rules—never to control but to structure.

Types of Rules

There are two categories of rules. The first are independent rules. These help people, objects, and systems function without confusion. The second set supports the healthy enforcement of boundaries, especially in human relationships. These rules encourage respect, cooperation, and accountability, ensuring that boundaries are not violated.

Independent Rules

There are four types of independent rules :

1. Legal Rules: For instance, traffic laws dictate that we use crosswalks and stop at red lights. Administrative rules say people work Monday to Friday and rest on weekends. Skipping work requires responsibility.

2. Organizational Rules: Schools have codes of conduct. Students must attend a set number of classes and take exams. Libraries, museums, and other institutions also have their own codes.

3. Daily Routines: Waking up, eating meals, and going to bed at set times all fall under personal routines. Disrupting them can affect health. Milestones like eating independently or walking to the store also belong in this category.

4. Contextual Rules: Indoor spaces require walking. Outdoor areas allow running. In the kitchen, where dangers exist, rules dictate how and which tools to use. These must be taught consistently.

Children must be reminded of such rules in daily life. Because their self-awareness and cognitive abilities are still developing, they often lack understanding of respect and safety. Rules give structure and set the foundation for learning larger societal norms as they grow.

Rules That Reinforce Boundaries

Boundaries are ideally co-created. But in reality, people may compromise out of politeness, lack awareness, or simply forget. This blurs boundaries. When this happens, additional rules help restore clarity and protect mutual freedom.

For example, if a father has agreed to spend time with his child from 7 to 8 p.m. but breaks this agreement, he violates both a time and responsibility boundary. A rule might then require him to apologize or take over a task, like bathing the child, to reaffirm commitment.

Or, if a child is meant to read in the reading corner but moves into the kitchen, they've crossed a spatial boundary. A rule should clarify consequences, such as a temporary pause in privileges. Rules must match a child's age and ability. Otherwise, they become hollow and ineffective.

There are important principles and steps for establishing rules; for example, a respectful tone is crucial. Consider the following principles:

1. Maintain focused eye contact.

2. Use clear and specific language.

3. Stay firm but calm.

4. Affirm good behavior promptly.

5. Avoid bribing or compensating.

6. Do not act out emotionally.

7. Build trust with your child.

8. Create a warm family atmosphere.

9. Adults should remain emotionally regulated.

These principles may seem simple, but they are foundational. Children learn rules best from adults who also follow them. Once internalized, rules provide the foundation for stable cognitive development. For younger children, extra support may be needed:

1. Break rules down into actionable steps.

2. Repeat and rephrase.

3. Practice regularly.

4. Revisit and reinforce over time.

Rules are not only for children. Adults must follow them too. They model the behavior children emulate. Establishing a family-wide system of shared rules is not easy, but it is worthwhile. Wishing you success as you build a space of clarity, trust, and shared respect.

Feelings Are Maps to the Soul

In 2009, an incident at Virginia Tech University in the United States shocked both the Chinese and American communities. A 25-year-old Chinese doctoral student suddenly and violently attacked a fellow student at a campus café, without any prior argument or provocation, resulting in a tragic outcome. This event left many people stunned. How could a seemingly outstanding young scholar lose control so completely? And this was not an isolated case. Similar acts of extreme behavior have repeatedly occurred on college campuses over the years.

I have long pondered why such emotional turmoil lies hidden in the hearts of those who appear so accomplished. Through years of observation and reflection, I have come to believe that beneath these outbursts lie emotions that were repressed, ignored, or misunderstood since childhood.

It was this realization that led me to establish the Generative Theater Center for Children's Psychological Drama Education, a space dedicated to helping children express, understand, and integrate their emotions from an early age. We believe that every emotion a child experiences is a key to growth and understanding.

Example 1:

- In one theater class, a four-year-old boy playing the role of the Sun God suddenly stopped and retreated quietly to a corner. I knelt beside him and asked, "What's the matter?"

- He said, "I don't want people to see me mess up."

- I asked, "Are you feeling a little worried?"

- He nodded. "My sun might fall down."

- I responded, "Then let's act out a story where the sun falls. Would you like that?"

- His eyes lit up. "Yes!"

- He stood up again, returned to the stage, and performed with renewed imagination and confidence.

Example 2:

- During a parent sharing session, a mother described an evening when, overwhelmed by work stress, she yelled at her child. Her child neither cried nor argued back. After a moment of silence, he said:

- "Mom, are you too tired?"

- In that moment, she embraced her child and cried. "He understood me. But I hurt him because I couldn't control my emotions."

- From that day on, she committed herself to learning how to better understand and guide emotions.

We tell children: It is okay to cry, to be angry, to be afraid, but please tell us why. When you can say the reason, we can help you find an answer. Over time, the children learn to articulate their feelings. Their bodies relax. Those who once avoided eye contact begin to look adults in the eye.

In 2016, a television show invited celebrities to look into the eyes of their loved ones for three uninterrupted minutes. Many wept. It had been so long since they had faced each other so openly. Emotions long buried began to stir. Three minutes may not seem long, but it is enough to awaken forgotten feelings. Behind every emotion lies an untold story.

1. The Limits of Emotional Expression

   We are taught from childhood to express positive emotions such as joy, calm, and gentleness, while suppressing the ones labeled negative like anger, sadness, and anxiety. But these so-called negative emotions do not disappear. They are buried and may later erupt as illness, violence, or addiction.

2. The Authenticity of Emotions

   Human development requires a balance between reason and emotion. Yet modern society leans heavily toward reason, casting aside emotional richness. When emotions are misunderstood and suppressed, they pass from generation to generation as unresolved trauma, eventually erupting into uncontrollable turmoil.

Emotions Are Layered with Complexity

A simple feeling of sadness might mask shame, anger, disappointment, or vulnerability. Recognizing and naming these emotions is the first step in understanding ourselves.

Emotions Are Energy

Each emotion carries its own energy level, as noted in Salingerbert's Emotional Energy Scale of 1951. Emotions are not good or bad; they are forces of movement. By understanding their intensity and flow, we learn to manage our inner states.

Emotions Are Silent Language: They Ripple, Spread, and Resonate

Emotions require no words to be felt. Their presence pulses through our interactions.

Experiment 1

- Sit still. Close your eyes. Recall a moment of deep sadness. Identify where that sadness sits in your body.

- Now, have someone gently press down on your arm. You may notice how easily it drops.

Experiment 2

- Now, recall a joyful memory. Notice your physical shift. When your arm is pressed again, it may feel steadier.

This energy shift affects not only people but also plants and animals. We once conducted a rice experiment. Children placed equal amounts of cooked rice in three bowls. One bowl was told "thank you" each day. The second was ignored. The third was insulted daily. After a month, the first had fermented slightly but retained a sweet smell. The second had decayed. The third had rotted and stank. This simple experiment gave children a powerful understanding of how emotions shape the world.

In the Generative Theater system, emotions are not problems to be solved but the beginning of creative expression. Through embodiment, symbolic play, and role enactment, children do not merely manage emotions. They explore, reconstruct, and transform them.

We create emotional spaces within the rules of the dramatic role. For example, a child may cry, but the character must have a reason. Or the child can express anger, but through the character's voice. Children learn not to fear their emotions, but to use them as a wellspring for self-expression and imaginative creation.

At the heart of the Generative System lies this core belief: Emotions are not problems to be eliminated. They are gateways to life's deeper understanding. Our task is not to suppress emotions, but to learn how to dance with them.

If love were a kingdom, then emotion would be both its herald and its flame. It breathes and withdraws, it wounds and heals, it breaks apart and mends together again. Let us speak plainly of this most elusive force, emotion, not as a storm to be weathered nor a fault to be fixed, but as a current that runs through every chamber of the human soul. Emotions are subjective. They are neither right nor wrong, neither good nor bad.

People often say, "I feel great today" or "I'm in a terrible mood," and media outlets routinely categorize emotions into "positive" and "negative." But this binary classification is a fundamental misunderstanding. Emotions are personal experiences, shaped by our unique developmental environments and value systems, not moral judgments. For example, a child raised in the United States may feel comfortable seeing unconventional clothing styles, while a child raised in China might feel uneasy about the same. The difference lies not in the clothing, but in the individual's subjective experience.

Responses to stress also vary. Some people thrive under pressure, while others may feel overwhelmed by even minor challenges. This further demonstrates that emotional reactions are deeply personal and shaped by individual perception.

While emotions themselves are neutral, their consequences can be constructive or destructive. Prolonged suppression of anger or anxiety can lead to cardiovascular problems. Depression and sorrow, if left unexpressed, may develop into psychological disorders or even life-threatening conditions. On the other hand, joy and calmness can enhance immunity, promote well-being, and improve relationships. Thus, what society labels as "positive emotions" are in fact those that tend to yield favorable outcomes. The impact stems from the consequences of emotion, not the emotion itself.

To understand the truth of any situation, we must first understand its emotional landscape. Because certain emotions are deemed socially unacceptable or personally painful, many people employ defense mechanisms such as rationalization, sarcasm, humor, or self-mockery to mask their true feelings. Yet, each time we ignore or bypass our emotions, we suppress the truth of our experiences. The deeper the emotion is buried, the further we stray from reality. Eventually, we may find ourselves living in a self-constructed illusion. Only by facing our emotions and allowing them to flow can we return to the heart of what actually happened.

Emotions are bridges between people. Despite our varied beliefs, backgrounds, and stories, we all share a common emotional language: joy, anger, sorrow, serenity. These emotions transcend cultural identities and help us connect deeply with others. Through this shared language, we find empathy, recognition, and a sense of belonging.

The flow of emotional energy is the source of vitality. Every emotion, when allowed to flow naturally and be expressed appropriately, becomes a force of meaning and motivation. Emotions move like rhythms within us. When this energy circulates freely, we feel whole and alive.

Suppressed emotions do not fade with time. Repressed feelings are like sediment gathering in the well of the soul. Over time, they obstruct our ability to perceive clearly and distort our view of the world. The saying "the size of your heart defines the size of your stage" reminds us that if emotions remain unexpressed, our inner space contracts, and our creative vitality diminishes.

Emotional experience transcends gender. Society often stereotypes women as emotionally expressive and men as rationally restrained. But the capacity for emotional experience is a shared human trait. Women may verbalize emotions more readily, while men often process them through behavior or internal regulation. This difference in expression is frequently misread as women being overly emotional, when in truth, men possess equally rich emotional worlds.

Common emotional escape strategies include:

1. Intellectualization: Using logic to avoid emotional engagement, appearing calm while resisting real feeling.

2. Anger: Exploding with rage to mask discomfort or helplessness.

3. Rationalization: Applying reason to avoid acknowledging pain, thus leaving emotions unprocessed.

4. Avoidance and suppression: Minimizing, joking about, or ignoring emotions, only to have them retreat deeper.

5. Displacement and outburst: Redirecting negative emotions onto others or objects, such as yelling or breaking things, without resolving the root cause.

6. Neglect: Ignoring emotions entirely, which diminishes sensitivity over time.

7. Emotional detachment: Cutting off emotional engagement, leading to numbness or dissociation.

8. Pseudo-spirituality: Using practices like meditation to temporarily feel calm, but doing so to escape reality rather than confront it, thus masking rather than healing emotions.

The "Cellar Bank" and Emotional Accumulation

The "cellar bank" is a metaphor for the place where we store unresolved emotions deep within ourselves. These buried feelings eventually surface in various forms, impacting our health and behavior.

Common signs of accumulated emotional energy include:

- Anxiety, tension, depression, withdrawal.
- Guilt, self-blame, insomnia, hypersomnia.

- Obsessive thoughts, compulsive behaviors, fear, possessiveness.

- Aggression, passive-aggression, addiction, compulsive caregiving.

These are symptoms of the cellar overflowing with unresolved emotions. How can we avoid storing emotions in the cellar? The key is to:

Understand what emotions are and where they come from.

- Recognize and express them in real time instead of denying or repressing them.

- Create a supportive environment where emotions can move safely and be transformed.

On "Sharing Emotions" Versus Genuine Expression

Contemporary culture often encourages us to publicize our emotions and private lives, under the banner of transparency. But when this "sharing" is merely for attention and not grounded in self-awareness, it becomes another form of avoidance. True emotional expression is conscious, intentional, and transformative. It is a path to healing, not a performance.

Emotional Education in the Generative Theater

In the Generative Theater system, we do not see emotions as problems, but as gateways to growth and transformation. Children simulate, express, and explore emotions within dramatic contexts, building a sense of safety and authenticity within themselves. For example, in one drama class, children played the role of a small animal afraid of the dark. When fear emerged in the character, the teacher did not rush to comfort or correct the feeling. Instead, they asked, "Why do you think it's scared?" and "What would you do if you were it?" These questions helped children build an emotional vocabulary and understand their own internal experiences through projection.

In this environment, emotions are not dismissed or judged. They are seen, heard, and transformed. Emotions become a shared resource for creation rather than a private burden.

Incorporating principles from transpersonal psychology, the Generative Theater recognizes emotions not only as psychological phenomena, but as bridges to deeper spiritual insight and self-transcendence. Emotions, in this framework, are catalysts for personal awakening and relational healing.

- This is why we affirm:

- True growth begins with emotional awareness.

- True companionship allows emotion to flow.

- True wisdom emerges when we learn to listen to the voice within.

- True presence is born when we dwell in the truth of feeling.

- True transformation arises when we embrace emotion not as chaos, but as teacher.

When the curtain falls, when the silence returns, when the story ends, shall we not ask ourselves: Did we feel with depth? Did we see with clarity? Did we let the heart speak, not in haste, but in truth? For in that answer, we shall find the soul's quiet reckoning and the measure of our becoming.

The Body Speaks First

Dr. Herold Fuchs, an American psychologist, once remarked that a hug can dissolve sorrow, strengthen the immune system, and breathe new life into a weary body, renewing vitality and restoring youthfulness. Within a family, daily hugs can reduce conflict and deepen relational bonds.

The Principle of Embrace

Before birth, a child resides in the mother's womb, what may be called the original home. The womb is warm, soft, finite, and filled with rhythm. Enclosed within the thick walls of this sanctuary, the fetus lives in safety, a cradle of ordered movement. The child senses unchanging protection, develops trust, and intuitively believes that hopes will be fulfilled. Amid the mother's breath, heartbeat, and gait, the child encounters rhythm. Through the stillness of the head and ongoing interactions, the child begins to sense the self.

In The Fidgety Child, the author notes how a mother's swaying allows the fetus to experience the limits of the womb. These alternating sensations, of tension and release, create rhythmic engagement. Through this pattern, the child perceives connection, and intimacy begins.

After birth, the world becomes bright, cold, and without familiar boundaries. The rhythm disappears. The child is thrust into a boundless reality. In such moments, embrace becomes a way to restore boundaries and security. Within the hug, the child rediscovers containment and trust.

Types of Embrace

In the Generative Theater approach, four types of embrace have been identified, each selected based on the child's age, emotional condition, and physical tension. Before offering an embrace, connection must first be established.

Usually, the process begins with brief conversation. The adult observes expressions, speech, and resistance. For children less expressive with words, questions like "Are you feeling a little scared?" or "Have you been drawing a lot today because you don't want to do anything else?" can help gauge the child's state. If the child responds with, "I'm scared," the adult may open their arms and say, "Come here. Let me hold you." In that gentle embrace, exploration begins. Some children may remain silent. A light touch on the arm helps to detect physical stiffness. If present, a firmer embrace may be needed, particularly when emotions such as fear or anger dominate.

Once, while visiting a traditional kindergarten, a child showing intense resistance was brought to a quiet room. Though he said nothing, he watched closely. I joined him in stomping to release tension, affirming, "You're really angry. That's okay." After some release, I offered a firm hug. The child began to cry. His tears signaled the flow of emotion. Many children appear calm but carry unresolved emotions.

The goal of embracing is to facilitate emotional circulation, reduce inner pressure, relax the body, and ease anxiety, fear, or anger. While embracing, the educator also explores the emotional origin, supporting healing and mental development.

1. The Firm Embrace

   For children who show strong resistance, remain silent, cry silently, act sluggishly, or exhibit hyperactivity—often from environments lacking boundaries or filled with fear—a long, firm hug can stabilize them and restore trust. While holding them, the adult may say softly, "It's okay to be angry. You can cry. I'm right here."

2. The Semi-Firm Embrace

   Best for children who hold internal anger without strong external resistance. If the child's body stiffens during the first hug, continuing may help dissolve defense mechanisms. During arrivals and departures, this embrace can nurture routine and trust.

3. The Encircling Embrace

   As emotional intensity fades and awareness of boundaries increases, children still accumulate pressure from daily stress. This embrace helps them reconnect with safety and support. Even if they cannot verbalize their feelings, they soften in body and spirit.

4. The Everyday Embrace

   Fear of separation is deeply rooted. Embracing is a way to answer this longing for closeness. Generative Theater encourages habitual hugs to offer ongoing emotional nourishment.

Assessing the Effectiveness of Embrace

To assess the effectiveness of an embrace, consider the following:

- Observe body relaxation. Is the child softer, more at ease?

- Watch for willingness to act. Do they respond to small requests, like fetching tissues?

- Test through repetition. If resistance remains, continue gently until tension releases.

- Conclude with affirmation. Speak kindly, "You did very well. I love you. Next time, let me know how you feel so I can help." Look into the child's eyes to ensure they feel calm.

Through embracing, emotion flows freely. That which words cannot express begins to transform into lasting safety. In Generative Theater, embracing is seen as a return to the original rhythm of being, like reentering the sanctuary of the womb. It becomes the child's inner home, a familiar and longed-for place of safety, and the harbor of belonging that we gently rebuild for them.

Add some transition text here. Tell the reader that you're about to present two cases as well as why you are about to present these two cases.

- Case 1-Jasper

In the days leading up to Thanksgiving in 2019, during a Generative Theater workshop held at Tianjin Ruide Kindergarten, I encountered a five-and-a-half-year-old boy named Jasper. Exceptionally perceptive and quick-witted, Jasper simultaneously exhibited significant emotional instability. I first met his mother in another parent's living room. With no reservation, she scolded Jasper at the top of her voice, attempting to control him through forceful suppression. She confessed that arguments with her husband were frequent, often arising from trivial matters, and during moments of emotional breakdown, she would pin Jasper to the sofa to "calm him down." This approach, however, proved entirely ineffective.

1 boundary training protocol. We selected a method of deep containment embrace to help reestablish his sense of security.

Each time Jasper transgressed boundaries or acted out aggressively, he was gently led to a quiet space. There, I would hold him, not tightly, but firmly enough to offer embodied support. Jasper resisted with intensity, screamed, and used hostile language, shouting, "I'm going to call the police on you." I maintained a grounded presence and whispered, "I know you're feeling upset and angry. I am right here.

You are safe."

These episodes often lasted two or three minutes, and sometimes longer. Gradually, Jasper's body softened, his speech became coherent, and his emotional expression evolved into communicative engagement. Following each of these embrace sessions, we created a symbolic reentry ritual through theater. Jasper returned to the group in a designated role, such as Forest Guardian or Theater Mediator, symbolizing his reclaimed agency and capacity for behavioral transformation.

Within three weeks, Jasper had developed the ability to follow rules, ceased his physical aggression, and began asking teachers for help. He transformed from a child perceived as unmanageable to one who was gentle and collaborative, even supporting peers in group tasks. His mother, visibly moved, said, "For the first time,

I feel that my son is truly loved."

- Case 2-Eli

In November 2019, within the same experimental program, we welcomed a thirteen-month-old toddler named Eli. He exemplified the profile of a highly dysregulated infant: hyperactive, light sleeper, and unable to form consistent relationships. His mother, worn and emotionally depleted, confided, "I'm at my breaking point."

After assessing Eli's condition, we implemented a regimen of rhythmic supportive embrace, which was paired with Generative Theater techniques such as mirror play and rhythmic movement. We incorporated three daily holding sessions, each lasting fifteen to twenty minutes. During these sessions, Eli was gently swayed while being held, accompanied by vocal rhythms and breathing patterns that simulated the intrauterine experience.

By the third day, his eyes had begun to focus more clearly. Mealtimes became less chaotic, as he stopped spilling food.

He initiated contact with educators, began imitating peers, and participated in theater activities. During story segments, he used physical expression to depict scenarios such as the boat rocks or the wind is coming. His mother, tearfully watching his transformation, said, "This is the first time he has fallen asleep without crying."

Eli's evolution from a preverbal and emotionally dysregulated infant into a socially responsive child demonstrated the profound efficacy of the Generative Theater framework combined with somatic co-regulation practices.

An embrace, in this pedagogical context, becomes a quiet act of revolution. It is a compassionate response to emotional isolation and existential disconnection. In Generative Theater, the embrace transcends its surface function of emotional comfort. It becomes the point of entry for relationship restoration, self-regulation, and the foundational processes of social integration.

This brings to mind the work of Jane Chen, a Chinese-American innovator who, while pursuing her MBA at Stanford University, co-developed the Embrace Warmer, a portable, low-cost neonatal device that does not require electricity. Designed to replicate the thermal fluctuations of the womb, the Embrace Warmer has helped save over 300,000 low-birthweight infants globally.

Chen's contribution speaks not only to technological ingenuity but also to a rediscovered human intuition, the healing significance of warmth, rhythm, and embodied connection. Generative Theater echoes this ethos. Through the multidimensional integration of body, emotion, and relationship, children learn to reorient themselves to the world, return to inner coherence, and develop authentic selfhood.

Authentic education is not a project of domestication or control. It begins where all life begins, in the safety and rhythm of an embrace.

Conflict Gives Birth to Connection

Liam and Noah

"Teacher, Liam and Noah had a fight." A child came to report this incident. This was highly unusual. Within the Generative Theater Education System, we place great emphasis on conflict transformation, and children typically engage with each other in ways that reflect an understanding of emotional regulation and mutual respect. Physical altercations are extremely rare, so I immediately sensed there must be a deeper story.

I approached Liam and Noah, who had already ceased their physical interaction. I crouched to their level and placed a hand gently on each of their shoulders to create a sense of safety and connection. Then I invited them to share what had happened.

Reconstructing the Scene

Effective conflict resolution begins with contextual reconstruction. It is only through understanding the sequence of events and the intentions behind each action that we can access the deeper truth.

Noah said, "I was lying on the ground, and he got on top of me."

Liam responded, "I didn't! He was the one who lay on me. You nearly crushed my bones!"

Noah insisted, "You were definitely on me."

To clarify, I asked, "Who was really on top of whom?" Several children who had witnessed the situation interjected. They explained that Liam had first leaned on Noah, provoking Noah to respond physically, which then escalated into mutual aggression.

I turned to Liam. "Did you climb on top of Noah?"

He replied, "I was just playing with him."

"You were playing. So, what happened exactly?"

Noah answered, "I was lying on the ground first, and then he lay on top of me."

"Why were you lying on the ground?"

"I was watching the sunlight make shadows."

His sincerity and focus on this simple beauty struck me.

"Liam, why did you lie on him?"

"I wanted to see the shadow too."

In that moment, their honesty and innocence revealed the misunderstanding. What seemed like a conflict was, in fact, a miscommunication about shared curiosity.

Noah added, "But you were hurting me. I felt like you were going to crush my bones."

Liam quickly retorted, "That's impossible. You're too heavy to be crushed!"

Noah fired back, "Of course not!"

"So, what should happen now?" I asked. The boys fell silent. I offered a suggestion.

"Liam, maybe you should apologize."

"No. I just wanted to play with him."

This moment revealed a critical insight. Liam's intention was relational, but his method of engagement lacked awareness of boundaries. I then proposed a playful solution.

"Liam, you wanted to play with Noah. Noah also wants to play with you. How about you let Noah lie on top of you this time?"

"No! He'll crush me!"

"You almost crushed me earlier," Noah replied.

I moved slightly as if to lie Liam down, and he backed away.

"Then what do you think we should do?" I asked gently, giving him space to think.

After a pause, Liam said, "I'm sorry."

Without hesitation, Noah replied, "I accept."

They embraced briefly and then ran off hand-in-hand, laughing and playing as though nothing had happened.

This incident illustrated that, with mindful facilitation, children can resolve conflict swiftly and genuinely. Unlike adults, they do not cling to resentment. Their emotional elasticity is remarkable.

Uncovering Deeper Psychological Dynamics

In a post-session debrief, we examined the deeper psychological context. Liam's father had been traveling for work, and his mother was experiencing heightened emotional distress. This created in Liam a stronger-than-usual need for physical closeness and emotional reassurance. Lacking the verbal tools to express this need, he sought proximity through action.

Noah, in contrast, is a highly sensitive child who values personal space and respects bodily boundaries. When his sense of physical sovereignty was violated, he reacted instinctively.

Generative Theater does not merely address behavior. It is a psychodynamic framework that seeks to illuminate the internal states behind external actions. We approach every conflict as a doorway into the child's emotional world. What may seem like a trivial altercation can, in truth, reflect unresolved attachment needs, communication challenges, or developmental stressors.

In a follow-up theater session, we designed an improvisational exercise focused on the embodied experience of personal space. Children explored movements representing "approach," "rejection," and "optimal proximity." In a key moment, Liam said to Noah, "I want to be close to you, but I don't know how." That vulnerability was the beginning of authentic relational growth.

A Framework for Conflict Facilitation

Not every conflict should be resolved by adults. Some are necessary developmental experiences through which children learn social rules and relational nuances. Over-intervention leads to dependence and impedes the cultivation of emotional resilience.

However, when adult intervention is warranted, the following eight-step framework can be applied:

1. Bring the children involved together. Include any witnesses if necessary.

2. If the environment is emotionally or physically unsafe, relocate to a calmer, more private space.

3. Reconstruct the incident through verbal narrative and physical reenactment.

4. Listen to each child without judgment. Remain aware of your own implicit biases.

5. When the full picture is established and all parties have been heard, ask them what they think should be done.

6. If they cannot propose a resolution, offer suggestions but avoid imposing them.

7. If they resist your suggestions, explore the underlying emotional or developmental reasons.

8. Facilitate reconciliation and provide closure.

Conclusion

Human beings, regardless of age, inevitably encounter conflict. Conflict is not inherently harmful. Rather, it is our mode of response, whether through avoidance, authoritarian imposition, or empathetic inquiry, that shapes whether it becomes a source of harm or a path toward growth.

Within the Generative Theater Education System, conflict is not treated as a behavioral disruption, but as a generative opportunity embedded in the relational field. This approach draws on systemic thinking (Capra & Luisi, 2014), which understands the child as an open, self-organizing system whose emotional, cognitive, and social development emerge from continuous interaction with their environment (Maturana & Varela, 1980).

Rooted in the principles of drama therapy (Emunah, 1994; Jennings, 1998) and transpersonal psychology (Grof, 2000; Wilber, 2000), our method interprets behavior not as a target for correction but as an expressive signal revealing the child's inner dynamics. Each push, withdrawal, or silence becomes a symbolic gesture to be witnessed and held, not suppressed. As Siegel (2012) notes, emotionally attuned interactions can reshape the architecture of the developing brain, thus turning conflict into an instrument of transformation.

Montessori (1967) reminds us that children's development is rhythmically shaped through interaction with a structured, supportive environment. From this view, conflict becomes not a deviation from growth but a necessary friction through which relational ethics and identity are sculpted. Maslow (1971) similarly conceptualized growth as a dynamic process of self-actualization, advanced not through perfection, but through authentic and challenging encounters with others.

This dialogic process is also rooted in the generative cycle of Knowing, Being, and Doing. In every conflict, children come to know their inner world, experience their relational being, and practice new forms of engagement. The theater thus becomes a sacred rehearsal space for enacting not only roles but realities. They begin to embody what it means to pause, reflect, and act in relational integrity.

Conflict is no longer feared but welcomed as a threshold. It reveals hidden needs, activates embodied truths, and invites co-regulation. Treated with care, curiosity, and structure, conflict becomes the soil in which empathy, discernment, and mutual regard grow.

So, we ask: What is the true aim of education? Is it silence or expression, conformity or consciousness, obedience or understanding? The children answer not in words, but in presence, through every repaired rupture and every return to connection. In those gestures, education lives.

Choice Gives Rise to Responsibility

- "If you skip your nap, you won't be allowed to go outside."
- "If you don't finish your meal, there will be no cake."
- "If you misbehave, I'll call the police."
- "Good kids listen. If you don't, Mommy won't love you anymore."
- "Study hard or you won't get into college. Be like your father—he's successful."
- "Do well in school. Our family's honor depends on it."

- "You did great. Now we can feel proud."

These statements are deeply familiar to many. They were woven into the fabric of my upbringing, shaping a conflicted inner world. I didn't want to obey, but I felt I had no choice. Noncompliance meant missing out on playtime, forfeiting treats, or worse, being punished or rejected. Simultaneously, I carried the weight of guilt for wanting something different. My desires clashed with expectations, and I felt ashamed for not being a "good" child.

This internal conflict haunted me for years until I chose to confront it head-on. I came to realize that I had been caught in a loop, struggling to be myself while fearing the consequences of authenticity. My sense of selfhood had been constrained, my autonomy eclipsed by an unresolved tension between obedience and individuality.

I began to ask: How many other children live inside this same paradox?

The Sense of Selfhood

Selfhood refers to an individual's experience of being an agent in the world, capable of making decisions and assuming responsibility for them. It includes the ability to form opinions, take action, own outcomes, and refrain from displacing blame. A person with a well-developed sense of selfhood is typically more confident, emotionally secure, open to others, and resilient in the face of challenge.

Transpersonal psychology expands this view by emphasizing the importance of integrating higher states of consciousness into the personality structure (Walsh & Vaughan, 1993; Scotton, 1996). Selfhood is not static. It is an unfolding process, deeply interwoven with relational and embodied experiences (Kasprow & Scotton, 1999). Children begin life with a powerful trust in their own perceptions, as described by Montessori (1967), showing natural curiosity and expressiveness.

But over time, this authentic self-expression is gradually curtailed by adult expectations and social conditioning. Children are instructed to behave, to please, and to conform. Phrases like "If you don't..., then..." become habitual structures that teach fear and compliance, muting the child's intrinsic guidance system.

The Absence of Selfhood

Lacking selfhood can manifest in various forms:

1. Indecisiveness

   - During a Christmas charity event in 2017, I watched children from disadvantaged backgrounds struggle with a choice: one gift for themselves or one for their mother. Many were overwhelmed. Some cried. It struck me how such a simple decision could trigger so much distress.

   - The phenomenon extends to adults as well, where to eat, what to study, whether to move, whom to marry. The terror of making the "wrong" decision points to an inability to integrate risk, imperfection, and loss. This inner fragmentation is noted in depth psychology and systems theory alike, often linked to the suppression of autonomy in early development (Siegel, 2012; Firman, 2002).

   - Children who grow up in environments where adult opinions conflict or shift unpredictably become hypervigilant. They rely on external cues to navigate behavior, watching for approval and avoiding disapproval. In doing so, they lose access to their own compass.

2. Oppositional Behavior

   - In authoritarian cultures, the "exploratory drive" in children is often punished. Curiosity becomes disobedience. Noncompliance is seen as defiance. The phrase "I'm doing this for your own good" becomes a veil for control.

   - Developmentally, children pass through two crucial stages, the "individuation burst" around 18 months and the integrative period of adolescence. Without appropriate support, children may resist not out of clarity but desperation. They might reject authority, lie, or feign autonomy, but beneath the surface, their inner world remains fragmented. As Emunah (1994) notes, genuine agency arises not from defiance but from attuned relational encounters in therapeutic and educational play.

3. Blind Compliance

- On the opposite end, some children become outwardly obedient, overly cautious, and desperate for approval. They avoid making waves, lose touch with personal desire, and defer entirely to authority. Their seeming calm masks a deeper loss, the erosion of internal agency. Later in life, they may avoid responsibility, fear decision-making, and attribute outcomes to others or to fate.

What Is Responsibility?

Responsibility is the capacity to acknowledge the connection between one's actions and their consequences. It is not about self-blame, nor is it about projection. Rather, it reflects an integration of awareness, ownership, and intention.

Within the transpersonal frame, responsibility is linked to the emergence of the witnessing self, the ability to observe one's own mental, emotional, and behavioral patterns with clarity and compassion (Wilber, 2000; Grof, 2000). This witnessing enables transformation. It allows for evolution.

How Can We Cultivate Responsibility in Children?

The Generative Theater Education System cultivates responsibility through embodied and structured opportunities for choice. Rather than enforcing compliance, educators present real scenarios where children must make decisions and experience the natural consequences.

From an early age, simple options foster this development:

- "Would you like to put on your shoes yourself, or would you like me to help you?"

- "Do you want to clean up now or after your snack?"

Effective choices should be:

1. Age-appropriate and understandable.

2. Defined clearly in terms of outcome.

3. Safe emotionally and physically.

4. Open to exploration, feedback, and repair.

Language must remain neutral and warm. Avoid statements such as "If you don't do this, you are a bad child," as such phrasing fosters shame rather than agency. Neutral wording supports the child's developing internal will.

With each real opportunity to choose, children build an inner architecture of accountability. They begin to believe: "I can make a decision," "I can live with my choice," and "I am capable of learning from what happens." This is the root of a healthy, dynamic self, what Capra and Luisi (2014) describe as a self-organizing, living system. It is also aligned with the developmental arc described in psychosynthesis, where choice and responsibility support the integration of higher potential (Assagioli in Battista, 1996). Through such education, we do not threaten or punish. We create conditions where the self may become what it already is.

In everyday parenting and educational contexts, adults often, out of anxiety or fatigue, resort to issuing commands or veiled threats to elicit compliance from children. Statements like "If you don't eat, no dessert for you," or "If you keep making noise, we're not going out," are common. While such tactics may produce short-term results, they convey a problematic message: that obedience leads to reward, rather than inviting reflection and understanding. Over time, this erodes a child's internal sense of judgment and diminishes their capacity for authentic responsibility (Synkova, 2021).

Here are two examples of ??? ... Tell reader what you are about to present

- Example 1:

   Coercion: "If you don't eat, you can't have dessert." This conveys punishment and control.

   Threat: "If you don't eat, you won't grow tall." Even when gently phrased, it leverages fear.

Choice: "You have two options. If you choose not to finish your meal within the agreed time, there will be no dessert this afternoon. If you do finish your meal, you may have dessert."

- Example 2:

  Coercion: "If you don't do your homework, you won't watch TV."

No room for autonomy.

Threat: "If you don't do your homework, you won't get into a good school."

Invokes long-term fear.

Choice: "You may choose not to do your homework now, which means missing

TV time later. Or, if you finish your homework now, you will be able to watch

TV afterwards."

Although these two examples may appear similar on the surface, the psychological stance they embody is quite different. Coercion and threat come from frustration and control, often framed as ultimatums. True choice, however, stems from a place of trust, clarity, and openness. When offered real options with genuine outcomes, children experience agency and begin to internalize accountability. Threat-based approaches, whether harsh or subtle, tend to activate fear and resistance, limiting emotional flexibility (Farmer, 2007).

Children's sense of self is an emergent, evolving phenomenon. Maria Montessori described this early consciousness as a "spiritual embryo," while others have called it an "organic psyche"—a naturally self-organizing form of awareness (Firman, 2012; Montessori, 1967). Without interference, this self unfolds like a sapling in rhythm with its own growth. Coercion, manipulation, or fear-based strategies, by contrast, stunt or distort this unfolding.

This recognition is foundational to Theater in Education (TIE), which, as Redington (1979) and Pr endergast & Saxton (2009) describe, invites experiential learning through symbolic play, fostering moral agency and relational awareness.

Two stories illustrate how structured choices can support a child in developing responsibility through experience.

A Story from Fremont: The Lunch Decision.

One afternoon in Fremont, I visited neighbors who had recently moved to the area. Their family included six children—five boys and one girl—all homeschooled by their parents. The father, an engineer, and the mother, who had studied educational psychology, created a vibrant, structured home-learning environment.

As we discussed the themes of boundaries and responsibility, the mother shared a moment involving her five-year-old son, Caleb. During lunch, he refused to eat and insisted on skipping to dessert. Rather than scolding him, she met him at eye level and spoke softly:

"Caleb, you have two choices. If you don't eat your lunch during our agreed time, you will not have dessert this afternoon. If you do finish lunch in time, you will get dessert."

Caleb listened closely. When she asked him to repeat the options, he did so clearly. That day, he did not eat his lunch, and he accepted that dessert was not served. The next day, he made the same choice. On the third day, however, he finished his lunch and said, "I realized I'd rather eat lunch than end up with nothing."

This was a meaningful moment of experiential learning. As Walsh and Vaughan (1993) note, the development of consciousness must integrate personal meaning and lived experience. Caleb was not coerced; he was invited into choice. In doing so, he became a participant in his own growth.

This sequence also embodies the generative cycle of Knowing, Being, and Doing. Caleb first came to understand the available options and their consequences (Knowing), emotionally experienced the results of his choice (Being), and ultimately made a different decision grounded in understanding (Doing). This progression is central to the Generative Theater model.

A Studio Moment in Pleasanton: The Right to Make Noise.

On occasion, I accompany my son to my wife's movement and drama studio in Pleasanton. Her work integrates somatic education with creative play, guided by principles of generative learning. These sessions resemble what Ada (2021) refe rs to as process-based theater education: the child is both creator and subject.

After lunch one day, the children entered a free-play period, during which they were asked to use soft voices. Mateo, a six-year-old, repeatedly spoke loudly despite reminders. I approached him calmly and knelt to his level.

"Mateo, you have two options. You may continue speaking loudly, and if so, you will stay inside during the outdoor play session. Or, if you choose to lower your voice, you will be able to go outside with the others."

He looked at me seriously and chose to keep speaking loudly. I acknowledged his decision and walked away. When it came time to go outside, he lined up with the group. I gently reminded him, "Remember what you chose earlier?" He began to cry. I looked into his eyes and said, "This was your choice." He nodded and returned inside.

The next day, Mateo was the quietest child in the room.

This simple event again reflects the Knowing-Being-Doing cycle. Mateo understood the expectation and options (Knowing), faced the emotional reality of his decision (Being), and modified his behavior accordingly (Doing). This experiential arc affirms Bruce Scotton's view that education must aim for the realization of selfhood, not mere obedience (Scotton et al., 1996).

Theoretical Reflection: The Nature and Limits of Choice

True choice is not a behavioral strategy but an existential offering, a space of freedom in which the child's self may come into being. Mariana Caplan (2009) writes that the goal of generative education is not to manage behavior through options, but to deepen a child's self-sensing and personal meaning.

However, when choice is used manipulatively, its essence is

lost. Packaging punishment or reward within a false choice elicits fear, not agency. As Elmer, MacDonald, and Friedman (2003) argue, children confronted with conditional choices often develop either submission or reactive defiance. This aligns with findings from Brainstorm Productions (2020), whose live theater education programs emphasize emotional safety and authentic engagement over compliance.

Real choice is defined by clarity, equity, and the ability to bear its consequences. It is neither unrestricted liberty nor covert control. As Davis (2003) suggests, choice becomes a mirror reflecting and shaping the relationship between soul and environment. Similarly, Prendergast and Saxton (2009) stress that applied theater enables children to enter liminal spaces where they can safely test roles, explore values, and experience agency.

Children are not passive recipients of order but active constructors of their own internal rhythm. Within the framework of Generative Theater, we continuously ask what the child is generating in this moment. We examine how their choices reflect their growing selfhood and how rules transform from instruments of control into invitations for presence.

We hold that choice is not a hidden form of punishment but an open invitation to become. Rules are not limitations but musical structures. Responsibility is not a burden but the pulse of development. A simple moment, like finishing lunch or choosing to quiet one's voice, becomes a profound act in the theater of selfhood.

Chapter 3: What I Wish to Say Before You Grow Wings

Before you begin this chapter, I would like you to understand that this chapter is different because I didn't write it. These pages belong to the parents, who each wrote a letter with love for their children. EXPLAIN THE ASSIGNMENT.

I still remember the first time I gave this assignment. One mother sat silently for a long while. Then she finally asked me, her voice trembling, "Can I write about the things I did wrong?"

I nodded and said softly, "Of course. This letter is for your child, and it is also for you."

When she read it aloud, the room fell completely quiet. No one moved. Some cried. Some stared off into space. Some clenched their hands together. From that day on, I kept inviting parents to write letters. Not because the letters had some measurable benefit, but because they opened a doorway.

Writing became a moment of generation. During the process, parents began to look back. They started to see the parts of themselves they once tried to ignore. They began to recognize the child they once misunderstood. And they began to see, often for the first time, how much love had been there all along, trying so hard to be expressed.

In the framework of Autopoietic Psychodramatic Education for Children, we speak often of Knowing, Being, and Doing. This cycle is not theoretical. It begins in raw experience. Letter writing is one such experience. It begins in emotion, draws from memory, and finds meaning through reflection. It pulls life from the past and sets it gently into the present, where it can be held with care.

Many people believe that only children grow. But every child's growth is mirrored by a parent's quiet, unseen transformation. When a child enters preschool, the mother begins her first year of motherhood in a new way. When a child turns three, the father may only just be learning what it means to truly listen. When a child cries out, "I don't want you anymore," it is often the wounded child within the parent who feels the sting.

So, when you read these letters, I hope you see more than children being lovable. I hope you feel more than the sweetness of hearing "Mama, please don't grow old."

I hope you see the parents too. The ones who struggled. The ones who failed. The ones who stayed. The ones who began learning again. These parents chose to stop shouting. They chose to stop blaming. They chose to sit with their fears and write with honesty. A sentence. A look. A letter. A gesture of love in its truest form.

This is the heart of the Generative Theater. It is not a method. It is not a tool for correcting behavior. It is a practice of courage. A process of growth rooted in the soil of love.

It is inspired by transpersonal psychology. It carries the symbolic wisdom of drama. But more importantly, it invites real people to appear fully as they are. Whether you are a parent, a child, or someone still learning to be human, this space welcomes you. There are tears in these letters. But behind every tear, there is hope.

Each letter is a lamp. It lights the path forward for the child and gently lights the hidden corners of the parent's heart.

- If you are a parent, you may see yourself in these words.

- If you are a teacher, you may remember why you began this work.

- And if you are simply a visitor to this chapter, perhaps this is life's way of inviting you to write a letter to your own younger self.

This is why this chapter matters.

Not to display emotion. Not to be moving for its own sake.

But to remind you.

Love can be awakened.

Love belongs not only to children.

It belongs to the adults who are still trying to become whole.

And once love begins to generate, it continues.

I hope that after reading these letters,

You will believe again in the beauty of human connection.

You will trust that education is about people before anything else.

And you will remember that you too deserve gentleness.

Welcome.

From me,

A companion to children and the parents walking beside them,

Still learning every day how to love more truly.

Fourteen amazing letters are presented next. Letters written by fathers, mothers, grandfathers, and grandmothers to their much-loved children .

Elena

Dear Elena,

Thank you for coming into this world and showing me, in your own gentle way, that life is not about rushing forward. It is about walking together, side by side.

Because of you, I've learned to slow down and listen closely to the quiet rhythm of a new life. Watching you grow, day by day, fills me with wonder. I often catch myself smiling as I see you putting on your own clothes, running to the bathroom on your own, flushing the toilet, and gently closing the lid. You help me wipe the table, pass me the cloth, and sometimes bring me the broom without being asked. After finishing your meal, you even pat your chair and say, "Let me tidy this up."

But what moves me most deeply is the way you care for me. When I am feeling low or when something in me grows heavy and quiet, you come to me with such knowing. Without needing words, you walk over, place your tiny hand on my back, and give a soft, gentle pat. Then you ask me, "Mama, are you feeling a little sad?" In that moment, I feel as if you stepped out of my own heart, as if you are a mirror of my soul. At just three years old, you already know how to hold space for someone else. You understand care in a way many adults still struggle to learn.

I am not a perfect mother. Sometimes I feel tired, sometimes frustrated. Sometimes I speak too fast, or my words come out too sharp. But you never turn away from me. Your love stays, simple and full. You remind me that love does not need to be earned, and it does not disappear when we fall short. Real love just stays, right where it is needed.

Do you remember what I used to say to you when I was resting after your little brother was born? I would tell you, "No matter what happens, Mama will never stop loving you."

Today I want to say it again, and I want you to feel it even more deeply. No matter who you become, no matter how big or complicated the world may feel, as long as you lift your head and look around, I will be here. Always.

Thank you for choosing to be my daughter. Because of you, I have been given the gift of learning how to love someone with my whole being. Because of you, I get to grow again, right alongside you.

With all my love,

Mama

Leo

Dear Leo,

Thank you for being with us this past year in the Generative Theater.

Your presence and growth have gently led our entire family forward, step by step.

You are like a clear mirror, quietly reflecting parts of ourselves we had not noticed before. Grandpa says you helped him rediscover the courage he had when

he was young, the kind of courage that stands up without hesitation. Grandma says

you reminded her that a promise is not just something you say but something you live,

a way of showing love with responsibility.

Your dad often says he has learned from you how to let go of the things he used

to hold on to, and how to meet each new difference with a more open and patient heart. And I, your mom, have been learning quietly too. Every time I see the way you look at me, the way you wait for me and lean on me with trust, I learn a little more about what

it means to be truly present.

You, too, have been gathering light from each one of us. You have learned how

to walk your own path with steadiness, and how to meet hard moments with grace.

You have learned how to embrace life with joy, and how to care for others with a kind and gentle heart and because of you, this year has been filled with a kind of love that feels vivid and alive. As we move into the days ahead, may we continue to be each other's light, growing together in love and strength.

With all our love,

Grandpa, Grandma, Dad, and Mom

Evie

Dear Evie,

You are already five and a half years old, and it feels like time has flown by. Every time I see a newborn with those soft little hands and feet, I remember the day

you came into this world. I remember how tiny you were, how your hands and feet

grew little by little, how your height stretched inch by inch. You were once that little

baby who needed to be carried everywhere, and now you are a big girl, so tall that

my arms can barely hold you anymore.

From the moment you were born, I began asking myself how I needed to grow

in order to truly become your mother. As I raised you, I felt like I was walking through my own childhood again. It has been both astonishing and deeply moving. With you,

I've come to notice all the tiny details of growing up. I used to rush through things,

but now I am learning to slow down and be more present. I used to be the one who

was cared for, and now I'm learning how to care for others. I used to be rigid, and now

I am slowly becoming more gentle. I still have a lot to learn. I used to live in worry

and fear, but now I am trying to face those emotions, understand them, and grow

from them.

You have taught me that growing up is not just something children do. It is something families do together.

Most of the time, I don't feel like I'm teaching you anything. It's you who are teaching me. You are teaching me how to be with you, how to be with our family, and how to be with myself. You are teaching me what it really means to love. And yet, I know I don't always get it right. Sometimes my emotions come too quickly. Sometimes I speak too sharply. Sometimes I react in ways that hurt you. And I'm sorry. I know I made you sad. Will you accept Mama's apology? I promise I will keep trying, step by step, to become a warmer, more dependable mother for you.

Thank you for letting me be your mom. Thank you to our whole family for walking beside me as I try to grow into this role. With all of you near me, I feel truly lucky.

I love you more than words can say.

With all my love,

Mama

Little Duo

Dear Little Duo,

Today marks a gentle milestone. It is your final day of the semester at Generative Theater, and soon your winter break will begin. The New Year is just around the corner.

I wonder if you are already quietly looking forward to it in your heart.

These past five months with you have been filled with moments that make my heart glow. You have grown taller, but more than that, you have begun to grow like a seedling in spring. Each day you seem to stand a little straighter, shine a little brighter, and reach a little further toward your own light. The way you have developed new habits, and the clarity with which you now express yourself, has truly amazed us.

At three and a half, you already know how to put on and take off your clothes all by yourself. Before bath time, you move through each step with such ease and confidence that sometimes you are even quicker than I am. Every morning and afternoon, as we walk to and from school, I see you walking ahead of me with your little backpack bouncing behind you. You move with the joyful rhythm of a young deer, full of energy and trust, completely at home in the world. Watching you like this often brings a quiet warmth to my heart. You remind me that life is not a race but a dance, and that wonder lives in the small, unnoticed corners of each day.

These three and a half years have not only shaped you but have shaped us as well. While you are growing into yourself, your father and I are learning how to grow alongside you. You comfort us when we are tired. You soften us when we forget to be gentle. You ground us when we drift too far from the truth of what matters. Your presence brings clarity. Your questions bring meaning. Your joy reminds us that we are alive.

Thank you, Little Duo, for choosing to walk this path with us. You have taught us that love is not in grand gestures but in quiet mornings, warm hands, and shared glances. Because of you, we wake each day with a little more intention, a little more care, and a deeper understanding of what it means to be a family.

We will always be here with you. We may not always get it right, but we will always try. With every step you take, we will be there, close by, learning how to be the kind of parents your light deserves.

Happy New Year, my love. May every day ahead bring you joy and curiosity,

and may you always feel how completely you are cherished.

With all our love,

Mom and Dad

Edmond

Dear Edmond,

Four years ago, on a quiet day, you came into this world with soft hair and a calm breath. From the moment you opened your eyes and looked into our home, I knew my life was no longer just my own. From that point forward, every step I took would be alongside you.

You are a smart and kind-hearted little boy. Sometimes you are as playful as a breeze, full of energy and surprise. But more than anything, you bring constant joy and laughter into our home. Even at your young age, you often say, "I am the little man of the house." When your father is away, you come close to me and gently say, "I'm here. You don't need to worry." Those words touch me in ways I cannot fully express.

One of your favorite things is gathering everyone after dinner for "family cleaning time." You lead us all, asking each of us to help wipe the table, organize the toys, take out the trash. I often watch your small body lifting a trash can almost taller than you, and in those moments, I see more than a child. I see a young tree standing tall, growing stronger every day.

You are not only growing, Edmond. You are helping all of us grow too. Because of you, your father has learned how to be more patient and how to truly listen. He is beginning to understand what it really means to be a parent. As for me, you are not only my child. You are my teacher. You show me, through your actions and your heart, what love means, what responsibility looks like, and how important it is to stand beside someone with kindness and care.

Thank you for coming into our lives. Thank you for the gift of this bond and for the happiness you bring us every single day. You have made our lives more complete. You have brought real warmth into my world.

I hope you always hold onto the lightness and honesty in your heart. I hope you grow with strength and courage. And no matter where life takes you, I will walk beside you, just as you have quietly stayed near me.

With love always,

Dad

Eliott

Dear Eliott,

Hello, my love.

This is the second letter your mom and dad have written to you. Time has quietly passed, and we have entered a brand-new year. Among all the changes this year has brought, nothing touched our hearts more deeply than the simple joy of holding your warm little hands each morning and evening on our walks to and from school. Even on the coldest winter mornings, the moment your small fingers gently curled around mine,

I could feel a quiet light glowing inside me. You are the softest sunshine in our home, quietly melting away our tiredness and warming every corner of our winter.

There are moments when I am not the best version of myself. Sometimes I lose patience, speak too quickly, or let my emotions get the better of me. After those moments pass, I feel regret and often wish I had done better. But you, with your big heart, always forgive me without hesitation. You smile, you hug me tightly, and you say, "Mommy,

I still love you." That kind of kindness and grace is rare, and I am truly grateful. You

have already taught me so much with your gentle ways, and I find myself learning from your softness, your forgiveness, and your care.

Thank you, Eliott. Because of you, I found the courage to walk back into the classroom and begin learning something I had long dreamed of but never dared to start. Through you, I realized that real growth does not mean being perfect. It means learning to accept myself in the process, to stay true to who I am, and to stop worrying so much about what others think. You are like a mirror, helping me see a more honest and braver version of myself.

In this new year, I wish for you to grow strong and happy and peaceful. I hope our family will continue to hold hands as we move forward together, learning side by side, becoming better with each step. Thank you, Eliott, for choosing to be our son. Thank you for giving us the chance to become your parents.

With all our love,

Daddy, Li Jiang

Mommy, Wu Ji

Theo

Dear Theo,

Today, you are four years and five months old. That also means we have been lucky enough to spend four years and five months with you, sharing this journey as a family with your mom, dad, grandpa, and grandma. Thank you for growing so beautifully inside your mother's body and arriving into our lives with such energy and light. It is your presence that fills our days with joy and hope. Every step of your growth brings countless moments of happiness.

Over these past years, we have cared for you, but just as often, we have felt cared for by you. In your own quiet way, you always show us love and concern. While your mom and dad are busy with work, you go about your school days with independence and confidence. We trust you because you've learned how to care for yourself and how to understand others. That trust brings us great peace and helps us focus on our own responsibilities with ease.

You often offer the sweetest words of praise after we complete something, and your words always make us feel warm and supported. When you say grandpa's or mommy's cooking is delicious, your kind voice melts our hearts. And when mommy loses a soccer game or a round of chess, your soft "It's okay" is one of the most comforting things in the world. You may not realize it yet, but you are a great encourager.

Even when you are sick, you face it with so much courage. You take your medicine, drink lots of water, eat your vegetables, and do your best to take care of your body. The way you handle discomfort with such optimism and determination teaches us something powerful about bravery.

In everyday life, you fill our home with laughter and play. You invite us into games, help us rediscover the fun of childhood, and remind us how important joy can be. You bring love and care to every corner of this family.

Dear Theo, thank you for taking care of yourself. Thank you for taking care of all of us. And thank you most of all for your constant effort, your spirit, and your presence.

We love you more than words can say.

With all our hearts,

Mom, Dad, Grandpa, and Grandma

Peng

Dear Peng,

This is the very first letter I have ever written to you. As I sit down to write it,

my heart feels full. There is so much I want to say, and all of it is about you.

I still remember the day when your dad came home from work and rang the doorbell. You ran to open the door, unlocked it by yourself, and even picked up the broom to keep the door open carefully. Watching you in that moment filled me with such warmth and tenderness. You are already five years old now, and you can do so many things all on your own. You brush your teeth, wash your face, apply lotion, wash your hair, fold your clothes—every little task you take on, you do it with focus and care. Sometimes, when I watch you fold your clothes, I feel like you do it even better than I do.

There are times when you want to do something by yourself, but I hesitate or hold you back because I worry. I am sorry, my dear. I will try my best to give you more space to explore and take on things on your own. I want you to feel the pride and confidence that come from doing things by yourself. I believe in you, and I promise to stay close as you grow, little by little, day by day.

What I am most grateful for is simply that you came into our lives. You brought with you so much joy and gentleness. You are the most precious gift in our family. Because of you, we have learned how to love more deeply, how to be more patient, and how to keep growing together. You have made our home feel more complete and full of light.

Your dad, your grandparents, and I all love you very, very much. You are our little sun, lighting up each and every one of our days.

With all my love,

Mommy

Zhang Ping

Isla

Dear Isla, my sweet girl,

Hi, my love.

Today, I am writing you this letter as part of your Thanksgiving project, and I find myself sitting here with a heart full of emotions. There is so much I want to say to you, so much I feel, and yet, I think the best way to begin is simply with an apology.

I am sorry, my dear. I'm sorry for the times I took over too quickly, thinking I was helping you, but in truth, I was taking away your chance to contribute, to care, to show your love in your own beautiful way. I was so eager to care for you, to make everything perfect, that I forgot you also long to give, to help, to love with your own hands and heart. I see it now, and I want you to know that I am learning. I promise to give you more space to grow, more chances to shine.

I still remember our conversation last night, when I asked you what you were thankful for. Without missing a beat, you said, "Thank you for making food for me. Thank you for going to the bathroom with me. Thank you for watching cartoons and playing games. Thank you for always being here." And in that moment, I realized that to you, love is presence. Love is shared time. Love is simply being together. Your words reminded me that showing up for someone with your whole heart is more powerful than any grand gesture.

I also told you what I'm grateful for. And what I meant with every word is this: I am thankful for you. More than anything else in my life, I am grateful that you came into this world and chose me to be your mother. You are my greatest joy, my deepest blessing.

From your very first babble to your earliest, wobbly steps, from the tears you cried in my arms to the laughter that fills our home when you giggle uncontrollably, every single moment has etched itself into my memory. These memories live in the quiet corners of my heart. They are sacred. They are mine and yours.

And then there are the little things you do that I will never forget. The way you run toward me from across the room, arms wide open, ready to leap into my embrace. The way you gently place your tiny hand on my stomach when I say it hurts, whispering, "Mommy, does it still hurt?" The way you rush off to get a blanket when I say I feel cold, carefully tucking it around me, and lying next to me in silence, just to keep me company. And when I'm sad, the way you quietly play by yourself, pausing every so often to glance over at me, asking in your softest voice, "Mommy, are you feeling better now?"

These are the things that stay with me. These are the moments that teach me how to love. Sometimes, Isla, I truly believe you are wiser and more compassionate than I ever was at your age. You are tender. You are forgiving. You are kind in a way that makes me want to be better.

Thank you, my daughter. Thank you for being in my life. Thank you for your patience, your affection, your light. You are the sweetest gift I have ever known. Because of you, I am learning to slow down. I am learning to grow. I am learning what it really means to love.

I hope that as you continue to grow, your heart remains just as gentle and free. I hope

you laugh easily, cry when you need to, and keep showing your love the way only you can.

And I hope that no matter how far you go or how big the world becomes, you will always know where home is.

With all the love in my heart,

Mommy

Claire

Chenchen

Dear Chenchen,

Hello, my sweet one.

Another year is drawing to a close. You might ask, "Mama, where does time go?" It slips past us like the wind and flows quietly like a stream, becoming warm memories and shining moments we carry in our hearts.

This year, like a little bird, you took your first steps out from under our wings into a wider world. I remember the day you put on your backpack, how we decorated your magic notebook together, and got your supplies ready for your first day of kindergarten. I held your tiny hand as we rode the 804 bus to school. On the way home, I picked up your favorite fruit and waited at the gate for you. That moment, when I saw your face, was one of the happiest moments in my life.

You came home filled with stories. You talked about your teacher, Dr. Liu, and your classmates, sharing all the exciting things you were learning and discovering. It felt like you were describing a magical kingdom you were exploring day by day. You made new friends and met teachers who adore you. You sang, danced, painted, and listened to stories. Your laughter has grown louder, your eyes have grown brighter, and your heart more open. Through you, we have seen how beautiful the world can be when seen through a child's eyes.

On weekends, what we look forward to most is simply spending time with you. We eat breakfast together, build puzzles, dig in the sand, play with train tracks, and make up silly games. I remember how happy you were playing arcade games at Universal Studios, and how you told me that the sand by the river smelled like sunshine. I remember when you played teacher at home, giving us serious lessons just like your real teacher. These memories are treasures I will always keep. And this year, something even more special happened. You became a big brother.

Thank you for being so kind and thoughtful while Mama was carrying your baby sisters. You would say, "Mama, you rest, I'll play by myself." You gently placed your hand on my belly, whispered to the babies, kissed them, and gave them all your love in the most natural way.

You came with us to the hospital and watched them come into the world. You helped hold them, made bottles, handed us tissues, brought diapers, and said, "When I grow up, I'll take care of them like you take care of me." You even said you wanted to get a phone so you could fill it with cartoons for them to watch. All your sweet ideas live in my heart.

We know it is not easy being a big brother. Their cries often take away from the time we used to spend just with you. You have learned to wait and to understand. You still feel sad sometimes and need to cry. When you say, "Mama, I miss you. My heart is with you," my eyes often fill with tears. Thank you for showing us your feelings. Thank you for reminding us that you need love and that you are also giving so much of it.

Chenchen, you are incredibly precious to us. We love everything about you. We love your joy, your tears, your strength, your gentleness, your playfulness, and even your little temper. Our love for you never changes. You are never alone. No matter how far you go, we will always be right here, waiting for you with open arms.

To your teachers, you are a bright student. To your friends, you are a joyful companion. To your little sisters, you are their hero. But to us, you are simply and forever our one and only Chenchen. As the new year begins, let us keep walking together with love and hope.

With all our love,

Mama, Papa, Grandpa, Grandma, and your two lovely sisters

Aurelian

Dear Aurelian,

In the blink of an eye, you are now four years old. Over these four years, we have shared countless gentle and precious moments together. As the new year approaches, you stand on the edge of a new chapter in your growth. I often realize how quickly time passes only when I find more and more clothes that no longer fit you. Quietly, you are growing into a little man standing tall in the world, no longer the tiny baby cradled in my arms.

Thank you for choosing to come into our family. Thank you for your smiles and your hugs that tell me you love us. Thank you for holding me close on stormy nights and using your soft voice to explain thunder and clouds, offering your little arms as reassurance by simply saying, "I'm here." Thank you for quietly dragging a stool over to stand beside me while I wash dishes or fold laundry, your small hands working beside mine in quiet companionship. And thank you for the time when the elevator doors suddenly closed, and although I could sense your nervousness, you comforted me first by whispering, "Don't worry, Mama."

In so many small moments, you brighten my day without even realizing it. At the supermarket, you help me line up the groceries and count the change. When I feel a little low or quiet, you come running and ask, "Mama, are you feeling sad?" and offer a drawing or a warm hug. Even when I make a small mistake, you gently suggest,

"Maybe we can try a different way next time."

You are still so small, yet already such a kind and steady presence. You have brought joy to your grandparents, hope to your father, and the courage to grow once more to your mother.

I know sometimes you doubt yourself. You ask in a small voice, "Did I make you upset?" and your eyes fill with tears over a tiny mistake. Sweetheart, I want you to know that you are already doing so well. None of us are perfect, and the way you are, just as you are, is exactly what I love most.

Thank you for walking with me into this colorful world. You have taught me to slow down, to listen to the wind, to feel the weight of sunlight. You've helped me believe again that love is something worth spending a lifetime learning.

In the new year, I hope you keep exploring and loving the world with your kind heart and bright eyes. And always remember, no matter where life takes you, there is a place called home that will be waiting for you.

I will always love you.

With all my heart,

Mama

Lin Chen

Sophie

Dear Sophie,

Come here, sweetheart. Let Mama hold you for a moment.

Another year has quietly passed. As I pick up my pen, I want to write down the little pieces of this past year and give them to you in this letter. Looking back, I can truly see how much you have grown. You are taller now, your vocabulary has expanded, and most of all, your heart has become even more tender and thoughtful. You shine like a warm little sun, bringing light and joy into my life.

When you first started preschool, there were still some tears and emotional ups and downs. But soon, like a little seed taking root, you adapted gently, and your unique rhythm and light began to blossom. You started listening closely to stories, making new friends, and slowly learning what it means to follow rules, to care for others, and to love.

People often say that daughters are like little coats of warmth wrapped around their mothers' hearts. When you were younger, I didn't quite understand what that meant. But now I do. You truly are that soft, warm little coat that rests against my heart and makes me feel safe no matter how cold the world gets.

There was a time when the elevator in our building displayed stories about the "Twenty-Four Paragons of Filial Piety." Every day, you would pull Grandma over to read one out loud. Then I'd hear you whispering the words to yourself, "We should always honor our parents." In that moment, I realized something important: inside your tiny body lives a heart that already knows how to respond to the world with love.

"Mama, be careful, you might cut your hand."

"Mama, hold on, don't fall. I'll help you."

"Mama, don't be scared. Let me blow on it and make it better."

You say these things so naturally. And each time, my heart melts and my eyes begin to sting with tears. Of course, there are moments when you get upset and pout, telling me you don't want to play with me anymore. But I know those are just passing clouds. Deep down, I know that Mama is still your favorite person in the world.

Am I right?

Sophie, you are a gift sent to me from above. You've filled my days with laughter, and in your quiet way, you've helped me grow. Because of you, I've started to truly reflect on what patience means and what real presence looks like. Because of you, I want to become a gentler, braver version of myself.

The road ahead is long, and we will walk it together. Sometimes your little hand will hold mine, and sometimes I'll hold yours. But no matter what, our hearts will always stay close, always connected.

I will love you forever and ever.

With all my love,

Mama

Aven

Dear Aven,

Hi there, sweetheart.

Before anything else, Mom and Dad want to thank the universe for the gift of you. We still remember that morning, September 13th at 7:50 a.m., when you arrived in our arms for the very first time. You were so small and perfect, and in that moment, our hearts overflowed with a joy we had never known before. That was the day everything changed. Your presence filled our lives with laughter, purpose, and light.

This is the very first letter we've written to you since you turned three, and we hope these words stay with you as you grow. We hope they bring a smile to your face

and remind you of just how deeply you are loved. You have brought so much joy into

our lives. We want you to keep growing with that same laughter in your heart, and the same courage in your step.

In our eyes, you are endlessly wonderful. You are thoughtful, kind, sometimes

a little mischievous, and always shining in your own special way. You surprise us every day with your curiosity and creativity. Your birth was not just a moment. It was a miracle that forever changed the shape of our lives.

You love books and stories, and we've seen how deeply you connect with the worlds you discover inside them. This love for reading and learning is something beautiful, something that will carry you far. Keep asking questions. Keep imagining. Keep expressing what you think and feel. Even if your words aren't perfect, it's the courage to speak that matters most. We're here to grow with you, not to judge you.

We want you to always feel free to be fully and wonderfully yourself.

We're also so grateful for your kindergarten. It has become a place where you learn about independence, friendship, kindness, and the quiet rules that help people live and play together. Every day, you come home excited to tell us about the songs you sang, the games you played, the stories you heard, and the friends you made. Your joy is contagious. Your confidence is blooming, and we see it sparkling in your eyes.

Because you are doing so well, we find ourselves growing too. Ever since you came into our lives, we've tried our best to give you every bit of our love and time. We read with you. We play with you. We explore the world together, one small adventure at

a time. You've taught us how to slow down and pay attention to the little things, how to be patient and present. You've softened us. You've strengthened us. You've changed us.

Thank you, Aven. Thank you for being our child. Thank you for choosing us. Thank you for filling our lives with meaning, for reminding us that the ordinary can

be extraordinary when seen through your eyes.

We love you, always and completely.

Mom and Dad

Qianqian

Dear Qianqian, my precious girl,

As I sit down to write this letter, my heart begins to beat a little faster. It is not from anxiety, but from a feeling so deep that it lingers at the edge of words. I want to say everything just right, and I hope what I write will be honest enough to reach you. We have never exchanged words this formally before, and perhaps that makes it feel a little new.

But I imagine you, in some not-so-distant future, reading this letter word by word, like we are holding hands across time.

I often think of you as a newborn, soft as a cloud, your eyes still closed but your tiny fingers already holding mine tightly. That moment was our first true embrace, and in it,

I realized there would never be anything in the world more important than you.

When you were just two and a half months old, I fed you one night. Afterward, you lay in my arms, eyes barely open, and smiled. It was a small, mischievous, satisfied smile, like a baby fox who had found a secret joy. I could not stop looking at you. My heart burned with warmth. The entire universe seemed to fall silent, leaving only that tiny smile shimmering in my soul. The next day, I excitedly told Grandma it was your first smile.

She beamed with joy. We both knew that smile was not just a reflex. It was your way of saying, "I like being with you."

At six months, Grandma crinkled a plastic bag by accident, and you burst into laughter, throwing your head back with delight. I remember thinking, how could any child's laughter sound this magical? You were our little sun, radiating joy and light. Grandma called you her "happy fruit," but to me, you were more like a piece of my heart.

Still, my love, I have not always been gentle. You were so full of energy, always moving, and often refused solid food. I was overwhelmed, exhausted, and frustrated. I did

not know how to be a good mother. I did not know how to manage my emotions. Sometimes I lost my temper over the smallest things. I yelled. I even spanked you once or twice. Watching you cry made me ache inside, but I did not yet know how else to cope. I was drowning in fatigue and self-blame.

I remember especially when you were two and a half and we moved into a new apartment. It was just the two of us. I was handling all the chores alone, caring for you around the clock. One night the bathroom pipe burst and water flooded the floor. I had to clean up, take you to the hardware store, and fix the pipe by myself. I still remember how helpless and worn out I felt. You did not understand what was happening, you just followed me quietly, and I was too tired to notice your needs. I snapped often. I shouted too loud.

There was one night when you refused to cooperate in the shower. I broke down.

I held you and cried, sobbing, "Why is there no one to help me?" That moment, I truly felt alone. You cried too, scared by my outburst. I felt like a child who had been forced to grow up overnight, craving someone to say, "You are doing your best."

I remember when you hid the remote-control batteries. I lost it. I yelled and kicked. You sobbed, your little heart breaking. But then, with red eyes and trembling lips, you walked over and quietly pulled the batteries from your sleeve. You said, "Mama, I found them." That image is seared into my memory. You were so small, yet you chose to forgive me, to comfort me. I have never felt more ashamed or more grateful.

Because of you, I began to change. I joined a reading group, learned about emotions, started understanding myself, and tried to understand you. I became less reactive. I replaced anger with gentleness, and blame with hugs. You were the reason I found a way back to myself.

Now, you have grown into a sensitive, thoughtful little girl. Your eyes reflect not just curiosity but a quiet pride in who you are becoming. I remember when we went to the grasslands. You were the only child who walked the entire way without a stroller. You laughed with abandon as we flew down hills together on the slide. I felt so proud of you.

You help carry things, hold water buckets, and always want to ease my burden. "Mama, you rest. I will do it," you say. Your tiny hands reach out with so much care.

Every gesture of yours flows into me like a gentle stream, soaking into my soul.

One moment I will never forget is when you chose to stay overnight at your cousin's house. You walked away with your little water bottle, so determined. Later, I heard you cried before bed. My heart broke, but I was also moved. You were learning to grow, to leave my arms little by little. It hurt sweetly.

Lately, you have been asking about death. Maybe it is because I told you about Grandpa. When I said, "Mama's father passed away," you furrowed your brow and said, "Then you must be sad. I am sad too, because I have never seen Grandpa. I really want to meet him." You were so serious. My heart cracked open. Grandpa may be gone, but he is watching you from the stars, loving you in his own quiet way.

You also miss your dad. You hate to see him leave so soon after arriving. You hold back tears every time he walks out the door. I see how much you miss him, even when you try to be brave. Your father is trying too. He is learning to be a better dad, and I think you have noticed. Just like me, he is growing because of you.

You once said, "I am Mama's little angel." And yes, you are. You live inside my heart, lighting up every shadow. You once told me, "I do not want to grow up, because if

I grow up, you will get old." You worry that my voice will not sound the same when I am old, and that someday you might lose me. Every time you say things like that, I cry. Your words, your love, I hold them all close, and I never want to forget.

These years with you are the most beautiful time of my life. I write this not just to remember the past, but so that one day, you can read it and feel all the love I sometimes struggled to say. I am not afraid of getting older. I am only afraid of missing a single moment with you.

I often call you Qianqian or Zhu Xiaoqian, but no matter what I call you, my love for you never changes. It is constant. It is forever. Wherever you go, however you grow,

I will always love you, without conditions or end.

They say children choose their parents. Thank you for choosing me. Thank you for entering my life and making me your mother. Because of you, I have come to understand love, responsibility, and resilience. I have stumbled, stood up again, cried, and then reached for you with open arms.

I know life will not always be easy. But as long as we walk together, heart to heart, hand in hand, we will not fear the storm. Because of you, I want to be softer, stronger, and more loving. I will take what you have taught me and become someone who can love

herself fully, so I can love you even better.

Thank you, my precious girl, for choosing to be mine.

This road we walk, you and I, is filled with light. And it is beautiful.

I love you, always.

Your mama who loves you more than words can hold.

Before You Begin This Chapter

This chapter is the one I always find myself unable to rush through. I have read every letter here many times, sometimes in the quiet light of morning, sometimes long after midnight. And each time, something in me pauses. My eyes begin to sting, and my heart feels as if it's been gently touched by something deeply human. It might be a child softly saying, "Mama, don't be afraid," or a parent whispering on the page, "I don't know how I became that version of myself." These words stay with you. They show, moment by moment, how love does not arrive all at once. It grows. It struggles. And it finds its way into the ordinary days where most of us live.

At the beginning of this work, I used to wonder whether the real focus of the Autopoietic Psychodramatic Education system was the child. But as the journey deepened, I began to understand something else. Transformation never belongs to children alone. Time and again, parents would come into the space carrying questions like, "How do I discipline my child?" or "How can I fix this behavior?" And yet, after just one class, or even a single act of witnessing their child with more care, they would say something quietly surprising: "I think I'm learning how to love again."

That's the quiet truth that lives in this work. It is not only about teaching or guiding a child. It is about remembering something inside ourselves. And often, it is the child who reminds us who we were before the world made us forget.

This, to me, is the meaning of autopoiesis. Not as a theory or technique, but as a lived process. It is something that unfolds between people, in relationships that are not perfect, but willing. It happens when we see each other more clearly, when we allow ourselves to soften instead of tighten, when we grow a little more generous with the parts of ourselves, we used to hide.

That is why these letters matter. Not because they are polished or poetic, but because they are honest. They are written by parents who were brave enough to put their real voices on the page. Each letter carries the texture of a life being lived. Each one is a small light that flickers in the darkness and says, "I am here. I am trying."

What comes next in this book are the handwritten notes and daily reflections of the facilitators. In them, you will begin to sense another kind of presence. A quiet companion who does not instruct or intervene, but who stands near, observes closely, and listens with an open heart. There is love in these pages too, though it may not call attention to itself. It exists in the background, steady and unspoken.

So, take your time here. Read slowly. Let yourself be moved.

These are not just stories of children learning to grow. They are stories of adults learning how to begin again. And that, perhaps, is the truest form of education we can offer one another.

Welcome into this chapter.

Welcome into the theater of becoming.

Chapter 4: Counselor's Notes

The following 18 stories are written by my fellow counselors. They are stories about their experiences working with children, etc. ... Explain "who" the writers are. Are they your coworkers? What were these writers asked to write about? Help the reader understand what it is they are about to read. Do that in a brief intro paragraph here as you did at the start of your Ch. 3.

Your Hand in Mine | *by Ying Zhou*

September marked the beginning of a new school year. During this time, many parenting blogs and newsletters were filled with discussions about separation anxiety and the tears that often accompany a young child's first days at preschool. I had heard countless stories from friends who said their children cried for days when they first started school.

At Fountainhead Montessori Adult Education, (or FMAE), we also welcomed a new semester. After a two-week break, I found myself quietly wondering how the children would transition back. Would they feel unsettled? Would they struggle with the shift? Would emotions run high again? But when the first day came, what I saw completely surprised me.

The children were more grounded than I had imagined. Even the younger ones, though a few shed some tears when saying goodbye to their families, quickly settled in with the help of our gentle facilitators. After just a short moment of comfort, they naturally turned toward the environment and rejoined the rhythm and flow of their familiar activities.

That day, the entire atmosphere at FMAE felt peaceful, warm, and joyfully familiar.

The facilitators reintroduced the environment, reviewed classroom agreements, and gently reminded the children of our shared routines. Most of the children remembered everything with such clarity, as if they had never truly been away.

Their presence stunned me in the best way.

I began to understand that perhaps what FMAE offers is more

than just a school. It feels like a second home. It is not a cold, impersonal classroom, but a space where emotions can rest and relationships can grow. These children are not being "watched over," they are being seen, understood, and supported. For them, returning to FMAE feels less like a transition from freedom to rules, and more like returning from one loving place to another.

At the heart of it, I believe this is because the system at FMAE provides children with something deeper than a daily routine. It gives them a sense of inner order and belonging. They are not just receiving education. They are living within an organic way of being. They experience, they practice, they absorb, and then they carry those experiences back home.

I saw this most clearly in my daughter, Xiaoyuer.

This past holiday, I was deeply moved again and again by the quiet ways she had grown. I saw her love, her discipline, and the sense of care she had begun to carry with her.

Scene 1:

At her great-grandfather's house, Xiaoyuer noticed the garden full of flowers on the balcony. She would always ask to water the plants. We helped her carry the water, but she insisted on doing the pouring herself. As she watered, she'd say softly, "They've grown taller." In that moment, I realized she wasn't just playing. She was caring. She was building a relationship with another living being.

At FMAE, the first lesson begins with nature. Children are invited to learn by caring for plants, by witnessing life up close. It isn't just a task. It is a gentle philosophy of education that teaches children to find themselves between the sky and the soil.

Scene 2:

At mealtimes, Xiaoyuer often says, "Mama, let's be grateful together." She recites our gratitude words in both Chinese and English. The pronunciation isn't perfect, but the sincerity in her voice takes my breath away.

At FMAE, gratitude is not a lesson to be memorized someday in the future. It is something lived in the present. The daily pre-meal rituals gradually sink into a child's heart, helping them grow from the inside out. Gratitude, in this space, is not taught. It is caught.

Scene 3:

One afternoon while we were playing, she climbed onto my lap and said, "Mama, let's have a chat."

I asked, "What do you want to talk about?"

She paused, then answered with seriousness far beyond her years, "Let's get to know each other."

I was curious. "Get to know who?"

She thought for a moment and replied, "Get to know me."

I nearly teared up.

That is what it looks like when a child grows in a space of safety and emotional presence. She wasn't waiting to be asked. She was initiating a connection. She was using language to reach into her inner world and invite me there. That kind of self-awareness in a three-year-old is something truly rare and precious.

Scene 4:

Another time, I was impatient and asked her to do something. She looked at me calmly and said, "Mama, I don't feel good. I might get angry."

I froze.

She had noticed my energy before I did. And then, she surprised me even more by asking gently, "Mama, why are you angry?"

That moment left me speechless. My three-year-old had the emotional sensitivity to check in with me. Her empathy stopped me in my tracks. She had become my mirror.

Xiaoyuer joined FMAE at just one year and eight months old.

In just a little more than half a year, she learned how to express her emotions, care for others, and explore independently. And in that same stretch of time, my husband and I began to reflect, shift, and grow alongside her. Her changes encouraged us to reexamine the ways we live, love, and relate.

I am especially grateful for the parent workshops at FMAE. They are not just about learning techniques or tips. They are more like mirrors that help us see ourselves with clarity. They offer us a space to understand our children more deeply, and in the process, to re-learn how to be the kind of adults who can hold them with both strength and tenderness.

At FMAE, it is not only the children who grow.

Parents grow too.

And it is this shared evolution, this process of mutual becoming, that I believe holds the true essence of family education.

To be able to live and learn alongside my daughter in the FMAE system, to grow into better versions of ourselves together, is the deepest joy I have known.

Eyes Wide, Play Begins | *by Lushan Qi*

During this week's outdoor activity, I experienced a game that moved me more than I expected. It was a warm and thoughtful adaptation by our FMAE team, inspired by a simple children's song called Looking for a Friend. The game is gentle in its structure, but powerful in its emotional reach. The children gather in a circle and begin to sing: Looking, looking, looking for a friend, I've found a good friend, and their name is ... At this moment, the facilitator calls out a child's name, and all the other children rush over, cheering, to surround that child in a gentle group hug, and say together, [Name], I love you.

Even imagining such a moment is enough to bring a smile. That afternoon, as the song began, I felt something soften inside me. At first, I thought the activity was only for the children, so I stood quietly on the side, simply watching. As they sang, the children giggled and tried to guess who would be next. Every time they ran, every hug they gave, every time they shouted "I love you," the air around us seemed to shimmer with warmth.

Then suddenly, I heard my own name being called.

"Teacher Liu Shan!"

In that moment, the children ran toward me, laughter in their voices, arms wide open. They wrapped around me softly and said, "Teacher Liu Shan, I love you." I stood there in the middle of them, surrounded, held by so many tiny hands and open hearts. It felt like I had fallen into a dream filled with sunlight. And without thinking, I answered, "Thank you, I love you too." That reply wasn't planned. It wasn't shy or unsure. It was simply what my heart had to say.

It was in that moment that I truly felt how natural it can be to express love. There was no hesitation. No calculation. Just feeling, flowing freely. What moved me most was realizing that it was the children who had given me this gift. Their openness reminded me that love doesn't always need a reason. It only needs a place to land, and once it lands, it begins to flow.

Later I noticed something else.

After being chosen, some children didn't want the moment to end. They would eagerly volunteer to call out the name of the next friend. They didn't want the love to stop. They wanted it to continue moving from one child to the next. Xiangxiang chose Xuanxuan, and Xuanxuan chose Liuliu. Ruyi walked hand in hand with Dudu, and then chose Dudu's name with a gentle smile. Their hearts were connecting, their love finding paths to flow through.

At FMAE, we hold one principle very close: every child's name will be called. No one will be left out. Because in our eyes, every child matters equally. Every child deserves to be seen, to be held, and to be loved.

In his book The Growth of the Mind, Stanley Greenspan wrote, "Children must gain emotional satisfaction through human interaction… television and computers will never fulfill this need." Our mentors often remind us that games like this are not just play. They are ways of filling up a child's love reservoir, slowly but surely.

When we participate together, when we speak love aloud, that love becomes real. It moves beyond vocabulary and becomes a living current among people. A sense of community is quietly formed in these moments, not through instruction, but through the lived experience of saying and receiving "I love you," again and again.

I feel deeply grateful to Dr. Jiawei Liu, and to this team full of heart.

They don't just design games. They plant seeds. In every blade of grass, in every word spoken with care, they are creating a space where love can be practiced.

What touches me even more is that in this garden called FMAE, we adults are also learning. We are relearning how to feel, how to express, how to pass along emotions that are tender and strong all at once.

In a world that seems to be moving faster every day, FMAE feels like a quiet, truthful piece of land. It has its own rhythm, its own way of being. It doesn't rush. It doesn't compare. It simply stays beside the child. In this place, we grow alongside them. We express our feelings through play. We respond with presence. We all grow a little at a time.

That afternoon, I stood in the sunlight, gently held by a circle of children who whispered "I love you" again and again. In that moment, I knew something for certain. The world is made tender by love. And it is love that brings us back to what is most true.

Memory Travels Far | *by Baocheng Zhang*

At FMAE, each month unfolds around a theme that is carefully interwoven into the children's daily experiences. This April, we turned our attention to the idea of remembrance. We explored what it means to honor the past, to understand where we come from, and to feel the quiet presence of those who came before us.

On the day before our local remembrance holiday, the children gathered in the garden. The teachers had prepared a small altar with flowers, candles, and fruits. Each element was introduced with intention, not as decoration but as part of an old and meaningful way to remember. One by one, the children stepped forward. They bowed gently and offered words of thanks to their ancestors. Their voices were soft, yet the sincerity in the air was unmistakable. Even the youngest children grew still, as if something in them recognized the weight of the moment. This was not a performance. It was presence. They may not have understood the full meaning of remembrance, but something had already taken root within them.

Some families, especially those with very young children, may not always be able to visit ancestral burial sites. Yet we believe that these lessons should not be delayed. When a child someday stands beside a grave with a parent, the moment will not feel strange. It will feel familiar. They will recall a quiet ceremony in a garden, and within them, they will know that love and memory are never lost. They are carried.

After the ceremony, we gathered to ask a question together. Where do we come from? Teachers shared stories of origin, blending mythology with imagination. The children listened with wide eyes. Then they created their own first people using clay. One child gave their figure wild grass for hair. Another molded eyes so large they seemed alive. Through storytelling and play, the children stepped into the mystery of beginnings. In doing so, they began to feel that they, too, are part of something much older than themselves.

Later, each child drew their own family tree. They added parents, grandparents, and great-grandparents, carefully filling the page with names and faces. One afternoon, my daughter ran to me with her drawing. She said, very quietly, "Daddy, I want to show you how I grew." I smiled and asked, "How did you grow?" She pointed at the branches and said, "First there was Nana and Grandpa, then you and Mommy, and then me." Her voice was steady. Her eyes sparkled. In that moment, I saw how the past had come alive in her drawing, and how her heart had opened to those who came before her.

Living in the Bay Area, we are surrounded by layers of history. At FMAE, we believe that education should be rooted in that history. Last year, our children visited a local heritage museum where they learned about the early days of public education. They touched old desks, read letters from long ago, and looked closely at photographs of classrooms that came before their time. This year, we walked through historic neighborhoods. The children sketched arches, windows, rooftops, and traced the shapes of memory onto paper. They were not just copying buildings. They were listening to stories held in brick and tile.

What we have learned through all of this is simple. Children are not disconnected from the past. They only need a language that speaks to them. That language often comes through story, through ritual, through the act of creating and sharing. It is found in silence, in art, in play, and in presence.

Our hope is that this sense of rootedness will remain with them. Even if they do not yet understand the word legacy, they are already learning to be grateful. They are learning to listen. They are learning to remember. And they are learning to carry memory forward, not through instruction, but through quiet and lasting experience.

Perhaps one day, when they are grown and walking along their own paths, they will pause for a moment. In that pause, they may feel something soft and glowing deep within them. It will be the memory of a garden, a small offering, a voice that once said, with love, we remember.

This Place Feels Right | *by Liu Ye*

This week, for the first time, we were never late. Not even once.

Every morning still felt like a little whirlwind. Getting dressed was a mix of laughter and a bit of chaos. It reminded me of watching a scene from Crayon Shin-chan, full of little stumbles, giggles, and last-minute dashes out the door. But underneath the noise, something was shifting. There was a rhythm forming, one that felt steadier than before.

Compared to the previous two weeks, I could feel myself beginning to settle. The anxiety I once felt each morning had softened. I had started to understand the flow of FMAE, its quiet rituals, its steady pace. Even the playful teasing from the older students no longer made me tense. I could smile back with ease, and something inside felt more grounded.

On Wednesday, we celebrated six birthdays. The children were buzzing with anticipation, already talking about the cake and singing happy birthday before breakfast had even ended. Before the party, they lined up in their small shoes to wash their hands and use the bathroom. Among them were twin sisters, Zuo Zuo and You You, just two years old. That day, their mother came along too.

These two girls were always so capable. Their handwashing routine was almost a little ceremony. They wet their hands, added just enough soap, rubbed thoroughly, rinsed carefully, and each picked up her own towel. Never the wrong one. Every move was deliberate, every glance full of quiet confidence.

But with their mother nearby, something shifted. She watched closely, perhaps too closely. Worried they might not wash properly, she reached out to help, gently urging them to hurry. The girls, without a word, pushed her hands away. Their faces were firm, their eyes a little hurt.

I realized in that moment that their independence had already begun to take root. What they needed was not help but trust. When adults interrupt their rhythm with worry or impatience, it doesn't make them feel loved. It makes them feel small.

True independence is not about doing everything perfectly. It is about being given space to try, again and again, until it becomes their own.

Later in the week, I met another child who left a deep impression on me. Huahua, just over two years old, wore a wool coat with small buttons near the collar. Two of them had come undone. She looked down, her tiny fingers trying again and again to close them. The fabric was thick, the buttons small, and her hands still clumsy.

I knelt beside her and gently asked, "Would you like some help?"

She didn't look up. Her voice was steady. "No, I can do it."

So, I waited.

Three minutes passed. Then five. Then eight. Her fingers kept slipping, the button always just out of reach. But she didn't give up. She didn't get frustrated. Her face stayed calm. Her hands kept trying.

And then, there it was. A quiet click. Then another. She stood up, looked at me, and smiled. "See? I did it."

In that moment, I wanted to cheer. Not because she had managed the buttons, but because she had shown such quiet strength. Her patience. Her focus. Her willingness to keep going without needing applause. This was what growth looked like.

At FMAE, we don't rush children to the finish line. We don't take over. We wait beside them, holding space for each tiny victory. Every time a child says, "I did it," they are building something far more important than a skill. They are building a sense of self.

This week, I found myself settling more deeply into my own role. I came to FMAE as a learner too. Every day has been exhausting, but not in a draining way. It is the kind of tired that feels worthwhile. I have started to notice my own patterns. My own emotions. There are moments when I catch myself before reacting. Moments when I breathe and choose to be softer.

It is not always easy. But it is beautiful.

This work, this journey of standing beside children as they grow, is also a journey back to myself.

And now, with week four ahead, I am ready to keep going.

Holding the Invisible | *by Yuling Wang*

Xiaoyou is a quiet child, with a kind of stillness that feels almost like a mystery. He often stands motionless, like a little tree rooted in place, watching the world around him without saying a word. Sometimes, even when snack time arrives, he remains lying on the floor. Other times, when the other children have already begun reading aloud, he stands in front of his green backpack, as if waiting for a breeze that never comes.

One day, after lunch, I was sweeping the floor with him. He held a small broom in his hands like it was a new toy, swinging it around with excitement. At first, I assumed he didn't know how to sweep, so I crouched beside him and gently demonstrated how to hold the broom and sweep.

Instead, he turned the dustpan into a pretend broom, playing and tossing the tools into the air. His eyes sparkled with mischief. I wasn't sure how to respond. At that moment, Teacher Yueyue walked by and softly said to me, "You can bring more strength into your presence."

I paused. Strength? I didn't quite understand what she meant.

Before I had time to reflect, Xiaoyou suddenly became quiet. He began sweeping carefully, with full concentration. It turned out that he knew exactly what to do. He was simply testing me.

Later, when I talked to Teacher Yueyue, she explained that Xiaoyou already understood the task. What he needed was not a lesson in technique. He needed a stronger, steadier presence from me. Without clarity and firmness, he would feel unsure and ungrounded. He might even stop trusting me.

That conversation stayed with me. The moments I had thought of as misbehavior were really a mirror reflecting my own uncertainty. It was the first time I realized just how deeply a child's sense of order can be shaped by the strength we bring to a moment.

Another day, after naptime, I went to gently wake Xiaoyou. As usual, he was the last one to open his eyes. I softly touched his arm and cheek, stretching his name into a calm and gentle call. When he opened his eyes and looked at me, I picked him up, gave him a warm hug, and said, "Good afternoon."

Pointing at the clock, I said with a kind voice, "When the minute hand reaches 26, we'll begin folding our blankets. Did you hear that?" He nodded. I crouched down again, held his face in my hands, looked into his eyes, and asked, "Do you remember what time we start folding?"

"Twenty-six," he whispered.

I stood up and began to clean, but I kept an eye on him. Right at 26 minutes, Xiaoyou got up and started folding his blanket on his own. I nearly clapped for him.

That moment helped me understand something important. When we speak with calm certainty, when we look a child in the eye and truly believe they can do it, they begin to believe it too. They begin to grow from the inside. They begin to root themselves.

At FMAE, we often talk about "strength." I've come to see that it's not about volume or control. It's about an internal steadiness, a kind of presence that is both gentle and firm. It's the ability to express yourself clearly, without emotional noise.

Looking back at that moment with the broom, I realized I was not grounded. I was unsure if I should let him play a bit longer. I felt anxious about what would happen if he didn't cooperate. I even felt a little frustrated. All of these emotions swirled together and weakened my voice, my posture, my presence. I didn't believe in myself. That is what it means to lack strength.

When we are firm but kind, clear but warm, children respond. They settle. They feel safe. Not because they are being controlled, but because they know exactly where the edges are.

I've come to understand that safety does not come only from physical comfort. It comes from the way we stand in the world. And for children, our posture becomes their anchor.

How do we build this kind of strength? For me, it started with clear boundaries and well-defined expectations. Not to restrict children, but to build a world where they can explore with confidence. Every time we express a rule with calm and clarity, we are really saying, "You are free to grow here, and you are safe within these walls."

This work is ongoing. At FMAE, I practice every single day. I pay attention to my voice, my tone, my timing, my posture. I try to offer something real in every interaction.

Growing alongside children takes courage. It takes deep honesty and a willingness to keep learning. But it is a path I am grateful to walk.

I will keep going, keep reflecting, and keep offering the kind of strength that helps children feel seen, safe, and deeply supported.

Just a Little Is Enough | *by Yue Zhuang*

The morning sun was cool with the light touch of early fall. As I stepped into the classroom, I found the children gathered around the bean-bags, giggling and bouncing with excitement. I picked one up, smiled, and said, "Let's play spaceship." Their eyes sparkled instantly.

"I'm a little astronaut."

"I want to fly to the moon."

We imagined the beanbags were rocket engines and began to race through the room. Some children climbed on top and got pulled along. Others spread their arms, steering through imaginary stars. Footsteps danced across the floor. Laughter filled the room. For a moment, the space around us truly felt like a launch pad reaching toward the skies.

After the game, they collapsed on the mats, breathless and joyful. One child crawled onto my back and whispered that he was catching the next ship home. I pretended to faint from exhaustion, still caught in their laughter.

Later, just before nap time, I returned from finishing a few errands. The room had settled into a hush. Curtains drawn halfway. Light filtered gently through. Each child was tucked under their blanket, like tiny birds resting in their nest.

Then I heard a soft cough.

I walked quietly over and saw a little girl curled up, her blanket pushed off toward the foot of the mat. She was still asleep, her small legs moving in search of warmth. I bent down and gently pulled the blanket over her again, brushing her hair away from her face. She didn't wake. She simply leaned ever so slightly into the comfort of my hand.

In that moment, something inside me softened.

Perhaps she hadn't slept well the night before. Or maybe the shifting weather had unsettled her. I began walking slowly around the room, tucking blankets here and there. A few children stirred and blinked drowsily. When they saw me, they closed their eyes again. They didn't speak, but their trust was felt in silence.

It was then I realized how simple warmth can be. It doesn't require words or big gestures. Sometimes, it's just a hand that tucks the blanket a little tighter around you.

Later that afternoon, during snack time, those same children came to me in unexpected ways. One leaned close and rested their head on my arm. One curled their fingers around mine and whispered something. One pulled me over to admire a new drawing.

None of them asked, "Was it you who covered me with the blanket?" But their closeness was their answer. They had felt the care, and they remembered.

And I realized something else too. Children are not asking for perfection. They don't expect magic. What they long for is presence. A moment when we lower ourselves to their eye level. A moment when we notice that they are cold, tired, or just needing someone to see them. A moment when we choose, without hesitation, to reach out with a small act of kindness.

This is what I have come to understand through the heart of our work at FMAE.

We do not see education as a system of correction or performance. In our community, learning is not about fixing or managing a child. It is about witnessing. About being present enough, still enough, to meet a child where they are. To build a space where love and structure do not contradict, but quietly support each other. Where warmth and clarity create the foundation for growth.

This is what we call Autopoietic Psychodramatic Education. It is not a method but a living system. It believes that each child is already whole, already carrying the seeds of their own becoming. Our work is to hold a space where they can feel safe enough, seen enough, to unfold at their own pace.

And when they do, when they come back to you with a drawing, or wrap a small hand around your finger, or lean into your shoulder without a word, you know: something meaningful has taken root.

They are telling us, in their way, "I saw you too. And I felt loved."

Calm Is Its Own Power | *by Yixia Li*

It was just past noon, and the early autumn sun filtered softly through the windows at FMAE, settling across the long table and gently brushing Haohao's shoulder with a golden warmth. In the quiet rhythm of our "Transformers House," lunchtime felt like an extension of the sunlight itself. Calm, gentle, steady.

Some children were focused on their food, while others chatted in hushed voices, their conversations light and kind. I moved quietly through the room, making sure everyone had what they needed, while letting myself be drawn into the gentle hum of their stories. When something funny came up, I couldn't help but smile or laugh with them. I felt less like a teacher and more like a quiet guest at their table.

From time to time, I would offer a small reminder, "Let's check the time and finish up." And just like that, lunch would end with the same quiet grace it began.

But this peace wasn't something that belonged only to lunch. It was woven into everything they did, into the entire rhythm of the day.

I remember working on our Mindful Numbers activities that afternoon. I worried for a moment that the sounds from the Rainbow House next door might disturb our classroom. Children were changing shoes, heading outside, voices were bouncing down the hallway. But inside our room, it felt like a quiet lake.

Our children didn't look up. They were still. Focused. They were drawing, counting, arranging number boards, each child held gently in their own quiet space. I watched as the air seemed to fill with invisible threads of concentration. It was as if each of them was weaving something unseen, something inward and strong.

Nap time was the same. When the time came, they would quietly lie down. The children who drifted off quickly were soon fast asleep. The others, even those who stayed awake, didn't stir or whisper. We never interrupted them. We trusted that even lying quietly was part of growth.

Sometimes boys from the Rainbow House would come through to use the restroom. Still, the calm in our classroom held. The children had already found their own sense of balance and didn't lose it easily.

This peace lived in every part of their day.

When it was time to put away chairs, they waited for the child in front of them to finish before moving. When they lined up for outdoor play, no one pushed ahead. If they had something to say to the counselor, they ran up to her side and matched her pace. During free play, they gathered in small groups, shared toys, made plans, and worked things out among themselves.

Each of these moments felt like watercolor—soft, unfolding, full of quiet life.

I remember one afternoon, Haohao and Xixi had a small disagreement. I thought it was over. But Haohao gently reached out and took Xixi's hand and said, "We're not done yet."

I leaned in and asked, "Is there more you want to say?"

He looked at her and asked with quiet seriousness, "Will I still be your friend?"

Xixi paused, then smiled. "Of course you are."

Then they ran off together, hand in hand, and I stood watching them with a lump in my throat.

This is what peace looks like here. Soft voices. Children waiting instead of rushing. Listening with care. Knowing how to hold stillness in both body and heart.

It is not something that is drilled or demanded. It grows in spaces where trust and respect are offered freely.

Each small action, each choice to wait, each soft word becomes a thread. Together they form something steady and whole.

There are days when I do not want to do anything but stand in the light and keep watching.

In Sync With Their Rhythm | *by Yan Wang*

One morning in March, sunlight poured through the windows of Tianjin Ruide Kindergarten, casting a soft golden glow across the wooden floor. It was my first day back, and the first thing I noticed was Tian. He stood quietly in the corner, his shoulders slightly hunched, his gaze drifting, like a little creature just waking from a dream, not yet sure how to return to the world.

The group activity had already begun. The other children were moving like a train, car by car slipping into rhythm. Tian hadn't caught the signal yet. He responded slowly, as if unaware of the things happening around him. When I gently hugged him or called his name, he would come back for a while. But soon after, he would drift away again, back into his own quiet pace.

Later, I spoke with Teachers Wenwen and Xiaoyan. They shared that there had been tension at home lately. Tian had been struggling with his mother and grandmother. His mother said he had become unusually stubborn, resisting everything like a kitten with its fur standing on end, ready to push back at anyone who came near.

Our director, Ms. Wang, came to observe and said something that stayed with me. She said Tian actually has a very strong inner sense of order. That simple sentence changed how I saw his slowness and resistance.

I began to watch him more closely. I noticed he had his own quiet logic. Every time he entered or left the classroom, he would loop around the floor marker before turning, even if no one reminded him. After playing with clay, he would quietly pick up the scattered bits on the floor. He was aware, thoughtful, and careful. But he always started later than the others. Just when the group was ready to move on, he would begin. He wasn't unwilling. His inner clock just ticked a little slower.

So, I tried to let go of my impulse to rush. I chose a gentler way to reach him.

Instead of standing above him with a stream of instructions, I knelt down. I gently held his face so our eyes could meet. I spoke slowly and clearly, one sentence at a time. "Tian, it's time to put on your shoes. We are getting ready to go outside. Is that okay?"

He blinked but didn't speak. So, I added with a smile, "I'll count to five, and then we'll do it together. Does that sound good?" He nodded. As I began to count, I saw him start to move.

One day, after he finished putting on his shoes, I heard him mutter to himself, "Tian put his shoes on fast." His voice carried a quiet pride. I leaned in and asked, "How did it feel to be quick today?" He answered seriously, "It felt good." I hugged him close and smiled, "I felt good too, seeing how quickly you did it." His eyes lit up. That light, born from being seen and affirmed, was the most beautiful thing.

From then on, whenever he froze again, I would kneel beside him and ask softly, "Do you want to feel good again, Tian?" Most of the time, he would nod and begin. It became our little agreement, a silent understanding between us.

Another day, he was slow getting ready for lunch. By the time he put on his apron, the others were already seated and giving thanks. He mumbled, "Tian played too long. The others didn't wait." I walked over and gently echoed him, "You feel like going slowly made you miss the moment to eat with your friends. Is that right?" He nodded. "So what can you do now?" I asked. "Put on my apron faster," he said, and he hurried to catch up. I placed my hand on his head and said, "That's wonderful, Tian. You moved so quickly."

In that moment, I could feel the change. He was not just hearing my words. He was feeling my care. He didn't need to be corrected. He needed someone who would enter his world and speak in his rhythm.

I began to change too. In the past, when he moved slowly, I felt anxious. Sometimes I just wanted to scoop him up and do everything for him. But now, I have learned to slow down, to speak with steadiness, to set aside my own worries and really listen to what he needs.

His pace no longer frustrates me. It moves me. Because in him, I see another kind of growth—steady, grounded, full of quiet strength.

I also began to understand what it means to be a guide. It is not only about correcting or directing. It is about discovering each child's rhythm and learning how to dance with it.

At Tianjin Ruide Kindergarten, we believe that every child grows at the pace of their own clock. Some move like seconds, fast and sure. Others move like hours, slow and solid. What matters is not making them match, but helping each one feel seen, trusted, and gently awaited.

Tian and I are still learning together. And this journey of gradually finding a shared rhythm has been the most meaningful gift I've received this spring.

What They Paint, They Feel | *by Yan Wang*

That afternoon, in the quiet of the companion room, I gently wrapped my arms around Weier. His body was stiff, his shoulders tense, and though he said nothing, I could feel a storm of emotion swirling just beneath the surface. Each time I tried to draw closer to what he was feeling, he would dodge the moment. His eyes darted away, his words wandered, and every conversation slipped through our fingers before it could really begin.

I tried to hold him a little tighter, hoping the pressure would help ground him. But Weier was tall for his age, and strong. He quickly wriggled out of my arms. I gathered my strength again and pulled him into a firm embrace. That was when it all exploded.

His face flushed deep red. His eyes locked onto mine with a kind of fury that almost crackled in the air. His arms swung wildly, trying to strike my shoulders. He was filled with anger, fully and fiercely.

And strangely, I felt a small sigh of relief inside me. He had found his feelings at last. He had touched the heart of what he had been pushing away.

I looked at him and said gently, "You're really angry right now, aren't you?"

Still breathing hard, eyes burning, he said, "When you held me so tightly, I saw all the people who used to hit me."

My heart clenched. He was not even in elementary school, and already he had memories like that?

I kept my voice steady and soft. "Can you tell me who they were?"

He looked down. "Too many," he said quietly. "I can't remember all of them. But I saw a lot of red."

A lot of red. That was what stayed with me.

I slowly loosened my arms, and as I did, the tension in his body began to fade. His face softened. His eyes no longer burned. I leaned close and said, "Would you like to draw all that red out, together?"

He nodded. He picked up his drawing pad and a pen, but then stopped and looked up at me. "This paper is too small," he said. "My red is really big."

Those words almost brought tears to my eyes. That little body holding so much red. I took his hand, and we walked over to the drawing wall.

He picked out a red marker, but the color was too light. With his permission, we switched to the wax crayons at Tianjin Ruide Kindergarten. He began to draw.

He drew his anger first. A big round belly full of fire. Flames on his head like a bright red hat. On his palms, he carefully added dozens of tiny red dots. "When I get mad," he told me, "my hands sweat."

Then he began to draw each member of his family. His older sister. His father. His older cousin. His mother. His grandfather. For each one, he drew two arrows. "This one is my anger at them," he explained, "and this one is their anger at me."

When he got to his father, he paused. "Dad has the most anger," he said. And he kept coloring, layering red over red, until his father's whole body was wrapped in it.

When he finished, he let out a breath. His whole posture relaxed. It was as if something heavy had finally been lifted.

Next, he drew a river. "This is where all the anger will go," he said. Then he drew some little grasses nearby. Suddenly, he frowned.

"Dad's anger is too much," he said. "If it all goes into the river at once, it will burn the grass."

"What should we do then?" I asked.

He thought for a moment. "We'll let it flow over three days. Just a little at a time. That way the grass will be okay."

He smiled. "Now, except for Dad, no one else is angry anymore." And with that, he picked up a white crayon and began carefully erasing the red from every family member. He wiped away the second arrow from each one too.

"They still have anger," he said, "but that's just for them to know. I won't draw it anymore."

And just like that, he was done. His face lit up with a smile that came from somewhere deep. It was the kind of smile that only comes when something long held inside has finally been let go.

Then, on the other side of the paper, he began a new picture. A soft, flowing river. A sun shining overhead.

"This river doesn't have any anger now," he said. "So, the water is white."

He drew it flowing into a field, where carrots and cabbage and peppers and eggplants were growing tall.

He looked at me and said, "They're all growing really big."

He was glowing now. His face calm, his eyes full of light. And all I had done was stay with him, listen, follow his story. It was his hands, his colors, his voice that took us on the journey. I was just the one who walked beside him.

We had spent nearly an hour drawing. When he finished, he turned to me and whispered, "I really like drawing like this. Can we do it again next time?"

That afternoon, Weier seemed lighter than I had ever seen him. He smiled often. He stayed close to me, not because he had to, but because he wanted to. That closeness came not from words, but from a bond that had grown quietly, gently, between our hearts.

This experience showed me how powerful drawing can be. I had used art therapy with adults, but never before had I given children the time and space to explore their emotions this way. Holding Weier was physically exhausting. He was strong, and I struggled. That was why I tried drawing instead. And it worked.

Later that day, I shared the experience with our team at Tianjin Ruide. Everyone was moved. We had all tried talking with Weier. We had tried hugs and encouragement. Nothing had worked before. But this time, through color and shape, a door opened.

I used the same approach with another child, a four-year-old named Xiaoming, who also held his emotions deep inside. After drawing, he lit up with joy and asked, "Can we do it again next time?"

What children need is not complicated. Their colors and lines are their words. Their crayons are bridges to their inner world. All they need is a little time, a piece of paper, a few colors, and someone who truly listens.

At Tianjin Ruide Kindergarten, we are finding more and more gentle ways to connect with our children. And drawing has become one of the quietest, kindest doors we can open.

It is a beautiful thing, to come so close to a child's heart. And I am grateful, every day, to be part of a place that lets us grow together like this.

After Fear, a Voice | *by Xia Li*

"Sometimes Mom hits me with Dad's stick. Sometimes she uses a different one."

Xiaozhou's voice was so soft it nearly disappeared into the air. His head hung low, as if the weight of those words pulled everything down with them.

I held my breath. My heart dropped.

"So … both your mom and dad hit you?" I asked gently, needing to be sure.

He gave a tiny nod, his voice barely audible. "Yes."

It wasn't just the words that hurt. It was the way he said them, like he had rehearsed them a hundred times in silence. There was no shock or anger in his tone, only quiet acceptance, as if pain had become a part of his everyday world.

I hadn't expected this. Xiaozhou had always seemed like such a calm and gentle child.

And it all began with something so small I might not have noticed, if not for what came after.

That afternoon, nap time had just ended. The room was warm from the heater, and the children's cheeks were rosy like apples fresh from the sun. Xiaozhou moved through the routine quietly, dressing himself, folding his blanket, placing it in the designated area, and heading over to get a drink of water.

As I turned around, I caught sight of him pouring the water he had just collected into the tiny basin under the water dispenser.

"Why are you pouring the water out?" I asked, puzzled.

He froze. He didn't respond. I looked closer and realized the cup wasn't his.

"Did you take someone else's cup by mistake?" I asked again, softly.

Still, no answer. His eyes flickered with fear, his shoulders trembled slightly. He stood there like a leaf just fallen from a tree, unsure of where to land.

It was such a small thing. A mistake that could be easily fixed with a few words. But he couldn't say them.

Later, we sat together in the quiet of the support room, and that's when I began to understand.

At home, even the smallest mistake meant punishment. No questions, no chances to explain. There was always a stick behind the door. Sometimes it was Dad's. Sometimes Mom would choose another. For Xiaozhou, silence was safer than truth. He had learned that explanations never led to understanding.

That afternoon, I asked his mother to stay behind for a conversation. I gently explained what had happened. As I spoke, her eyes turned red and tears streamed down her face.

She choked out the words, "I'm really not a good mother."

Her voice carried more than guilt. There was helplessness too, and sorrow, and a deep, aching shame. She told me about her husband's temper, about how he was raised by a father who also hit. Now he often lost control at home. Sometimes it was the stick. Sometimes it was a kick. She said she tried to stop him, but she couldn't. She couldn't change him.

"I was beaten badly as a child too," she whispered. "I know it's wrong to hit Xiaozhou, but sometimes I just can't hold myself back."

In that moment, I saw not just a mother, but a child who had once stood in a corner, eyes red, with no one to protect her. Many parents who hit their children carry the unhealed pain of being hit themselves. Inside them still lives that small, frightened version of who they once were, longing to be comforted, to be heard.

I didn't rush to offer advice. Instead, I asked if she would be willing to sit with us for a while longer and simply listen to her son.

Turning to Xiaozhou, I asked, "When Mom hits you, how do you feel?"

His eyes stayed low, but he answered, "I feel scared. I also feel really angry."

"Would you like to tell her that?" I asked.

He nodded.

So, I invited his mother to listen without interrupting, without defending. It was a quiet moment, almost sacred. Xiaozhou didn't say much, but every word came from a place of truth.

When he finished, I asked his mom if she had something she'd like to say.

She turned to him and said, "I'm sorry. I shouldn't have hit you. Will you accept my apology?"

Without a word, Xiaozhou threw himself into her arms. He hugged her tightly, tears pouring from his eyes, and whispered again and again, "I forgive you. I forgive you."

I asked him how he felt now.

"I'm really happy," he said through his tears.

I felt tears gather in my own eyes. A child's heart is so soft, so open to trust and love when given the chance.

A few days later, I called his mother to check in. Her voice sounded lighter. She said Xiaozhou had been more relaxed at home, less withdrawn. She told me she had begun taking a class on emotional growth and was learning how to manage her own feelings and connect with her son in new ways.

"I'm realizing that when I grow, he grows too," she said.

Her words moved me deeply. This wasn't just about healing a mother and a child. It was about restoring the tenderness in an entire home.

A child had been seen. A mother had chosen to change. And a family found its first steps back to love.

To that mother, and to every parent trying their best, I want to say: keep going. You're doing more than you know.

Respect Starts Small | *by Yan Wang*

It was our daily quiet time before nap. The classroom had settled into a gentle stillness, as if even the air had softened its steps. Sunlight filtered through the curtains and landed quietly on the children's small shoulders, illuminating the soft playdough in their hands.

In one familiar corner, little Zizi, just over two years old, sat curled up on a soft mat. His tiny hands were hard at work, shaping ball after ball of playdough. As he molded them, he spoke softly to himself, like he was having a private conversation with these colorful spheres, or perhaps planning some secret mission only he could understand. When he looked up and met my gaze, he whispered, "Teacher, I made so many balls." His eyes sparkled with a hint of pride and a great deal of tenderness.

April in Tianjin still held a touch of chill in the air, but the light had begun to feel more forgiving. Outside, the magnolias and peach blossoms were just beginning to bloom. Inside, the children gathered around the tables, lost in their creations. Time felt suspended. Lines of playdough balls stretched across the mats. Flattened "pancakes" lay next to pretend "cakes" and "french fries" in every shade of the rainbow. On a nearby table, one child was focused on forming a chubby little foot out of clay. Each piece held a universe of imagination. The classroom felt like a slowly awakening dream, and I sat within it, quietly watching as the children turned their ideas into reality with patience and confidence.

Just then, Youyou stood up and walked over to Zizi. He held one of his tools in one hand and pointed gently at a tool in front of Zizi. With a soft and hopeful tone, he asked, "Zizi, can I trade this for that one?"

Zizi looked up, then glanced down at the tool Youyou wanted. He paused, thought for a second, and said, "No."

Youyou did not protest. He did not walk away. He simply smiled again and pointed to a different tool. "How about this one?"

Zizi shook his head. "No."

Again, Youyou pointed. "No."

And again. "No."

Each time, Zizi paused and considered before answering. He remained calm, unshaken by the act of saying no, and free from guilt or hesitation.

Then, when Youyou pointed to a fifth tool, Zizi nodded. "Okay."

They made the exchange. Youyou walked back to his seat, content and cheerful. Zizi returned to his work without disruption, fully absorbed in rolling his clay balls once more. In that moment, time seemed to move more slowly.

Sitting nearby, I felt a quiet wave stir within me. These two young children had just shared a beautiful and respectful conversation. There had been no conflict, no tears, and no need for an adult to mediate. They had expressed their wishes honestly and listened to one another with genuine respect. It was a rare kind of balance, and an even rarer kind of order.

Many of us adults have long forgotten how to speak this way. We fear being turned down, fear offending, and fear being misunderstood. So, we swallow our truth and hide our real needs behind words like "It's fine" or "Whatever you want." But in these young children who have not yet learned to hide from the world, I saw something deeply human. I saw the courage to listen inwardly and the grace to acknowledge others.

At Tianjin Ruide Kindergarten, we believe that expression is a gift, and boundaries are a kind of quiet power. Saying no is not rude, and making a request is never a burden. Our children are encouraged to say what they want and what they do not want. They are heard, understood, and accepted. What we do as teachers is simply to hold space for their natural rhythm of growth.

That afternoon, the brief interaction between Zizi and Youyou showed me what trust and mutual respect could look like in its simplest form. Education is not always about giving direction. Sometimes it is simply about noticing, allowing, and deeply understanding.

The sunlight landed gently on their creations and found its way into my heart. In the small worlds of children, I saw wisdom that many of us spend a lifetime trying to remember.

I sat there quietly, breathing in the soft warmth and peace of the moment, and thought to myself how beautiful the spring light was that day.

Learning Happens While Playing | *by Shu Yi*

The April sunlight poured gently into the classroom, casting a golden warmth on everything it touched. This month's theme at Tianjin Ruide Kindergarten was "Knowing Our Community." But how could we spark a fresh sense of discovery in a space that already felt so familiar to the children? We decided to try something different. We invited them to bake cookies by hand and then take those cookies out into the community, offering them as small gifts to their neighbors, a sweet way of saying hello to the world around them.

So, we got to work. That morning, the classroom was filled with laughter and motion. The children sat around the tables, kneading dough, rolling it into shapes, pressing it flat with their palms. Their little hands moved across the dough with excitement and care. They had made cookies before, but this time it felt different. They knew these cookies weren't just for themselves. They were making them for others, for people who shared the same community.

Some shaped theirs like volcanoes. Others tried to create Baymax or made long, wiggly shapes like caterpillars. The younger ones simply pressed their palms into the dough, leaving behind perfect little round prints. Each cookie had its own name, its own story. As teachers, we could only smile. Whatever the shape, it was the heart behind it that made these the best cookies in the world.

We helped them chop cranberries and fold them into the dough. The children were so focused, we didn't want to interrupt. From time to time, a giggle would slip through, and it felt like the whole room was glowing. When the cookies came out of the oven, the smell filled the air. The children cheered, "It smells so good!" One of them whispered, "Can I have another one?" Another said, "I want to bring one home for my mom." We handed out small gift bags we had prepared in advance. The children picked out cookies for their families, carefully sealing each bag as if wrapping a special surprise for someone they loved.

The next morning, the sun was shining just right. Each child held a little bag of cookies and walked toward the neighborhood with light steps. Even before we reached the square, their laughter had already caught the attention of nearby passersby. At first, some children were shy, hesitant to speak. We gently reminded them, "You can introduce yourself." Slowly, their voices began to rise, one after another. "Hi, my name is Dodo. I made these cookies. I'd like to give them to you. It's nice to meet you." As neighbors accepted the cookies with smiles, the children's eyes lit up. They grew braver, their voices stronger, their smiles brighter.

But not every moment went smoothly. Xiaxia approached a young woman with his cookie gift, only to be gently turned down. He stood there, unsure, with confusion written across his face. We knelt beside him and asked, "Would you like to know why she said no?" Xiaxia nodded and, after a moment's pause, walked over to ask her. She smiled and said kindly, "My teeth aren't very strong, so I can't eat sweet things." Xiaxia let out a soft "Oh," and his eyes softened. "Then I'll give it to you next time," he replied with a little smile, and he turned to walk happily toward the next person.

In that quiet exchange, Xiaxia learned to face rejection with grace and to understand someone else's needs. It wasn't just about successfully giving away a cookie. It was about feeling seen, learning to listen, and learning how to manage the feelings that come with moments like these. That was the real gift.

On the way back to school, we came across a boy whose bicycle had fallen into a shallow roadside ditch. We stopped to help lift the bike out. Some of the children stepped forward too, offering a hand and asking if he was hurt. Once everything was okay, we continued our walk, laughter floating on the breeze behind us.

Xixi held a teacher's hand the entire way back. When we asked her why, she answered with great seriousness, "Because you're carrying a lot of cookies. If I stay close to you, I can help give away more." Her small cleverness made all of us laugh.

That day's walk through the community was more than just an outing. It was a practice in connection, in communication, in love. The children learned how to meet people safely, how to say their names with confidence, how to express what was in their hearts. They also learned how to handle rejection without anger, how to wait patiently when words failed, and how to offer help when someone was in need.

Through play, they found their voices. Through life, they began to feel the warmth of relationships. The cookies they carried may not have been perfectly shaped, but each one held a bit of courage and a soft, quiet kindness.

What a joy it is to witness the children of Tianjin Ruide Kindergarten building bridges, little by little, between hearts in the most ordinary moments of daily life.

Scissors Over Rock | *by Baochen Zhang*

The moment I heard the words "rock, paper, scissors," an old childhood memory came rushing back. I could almost feel the sun shining on the courtyard where my friends and I used to crouch down, hands flying through the air, bursting into laughter and shouts after each round. I hadn't realized a small smile had already crept to the corner of my lips.

At Tianjin Ruide Kindergarten, there's a warm little routine we follow during lunchtime. Once children finish eating, they can sit quietly in their seats and either chat softly or play simple games. Lately, their favorite has been none other than the joyful and familiar game of "rock, paper, scissors."

That day after lunch, Doudou was the first to finish. He cleared his dishes and sat back in his chair, his eyes gently drifting over to Dingding, who was still eating. His gaze was filled with quiet anticipation, as if to say, "Can you hurry up?" Not long after, Dingding finally put down his spoon, and Doudou leaned in with a whisper, "Want to play rock, paper, scissors?" "Sure!" Dingding replied with a big smile.

I was sitting nearby and could hear them clearly. "Rock, paper, scissors!" Their voices rang out, louder and louder with each round, full of laughter and bright eyes. Their cheeks flushed with excitement. At another table, a few more children had finished eating and started playing too. The whole room felt lit up by the rhythm of the game. It was cheerful, light, and filled with that special kind of focus that only children bring to play.

Seeing this, Teacher Tingting had a quick idea. When it came time to assign after-lunch cleanup tasks, she brought the game into it. "Who wants to wipe the table a second time?" she asked. The day's helper had already done the first round, and now anyone could jump in. Tongtong, Dangdang, and Honghong all shot their hands into the air. Their fingers pointed high with energy. "Let's settle it with a round of rock, paper, scissors," she said with a smile.

The three shouted together, "Rock, paper, scissors!" After one round, Dangdang won and proudly took on the job of wiping the table again.

Then came the third round of wiping. Tongtong and Keke raised their hands and played. Tongtong won. For the fourth round, Keke and Tiantian stepped up, and Tiantian won. The tasks kept going. Someone swept the floor, someone mopped, someone picked up leftover rice from under the table. Every chore was quickly and joyfully claimed in a matter of four minutes. The children were full of enthusiasm, and instead of chaos, the room felt surprisingly well organized.

I watched their little hands pick up rags and brooms with such ease. They moved around the classroom with intention, cleaning with real care. Soon the tables were spotless, and my heart was quietly moved. Children truly have a natural sense of rhythm. When you offer them something they enjoy, they pour themselves into it with joy and do it beautifully.

Rock, paper, scissors. What an ordinary little game. Yet in the hands of the children at Tianjin Ruide Kindergarten, it became something more. It brought not only joy but also a sense of order, shared participation, cooperation, and responsibility.

Play is never just a break from learning. It is, in many ways, the most real form of learning that children know. It's how they express their feelings, learn the rules of being with others, and grow their ability to connect.

The teachers at Tianjin Ruide Kindergarten are always trying to use games to guide the children. Not simply to make them obedient or cooperative, but to help them truly experience life through play. The goal is for them to grow into people who are loving, responsible, and proactive in daily life, not just students who perform well in a classroom.

When you go home today, try playing a round of rock, paper, scissors with your family. Maybe it will bring back some childhood joy. Maybe it will remind us all how even the simplest games can draw people closer and soften our hearts.

When Children Take the Lead | *by Sha Wu*

At Tianjin Ruide Kindergarten, there are two twin sisters who have become little stars in our community. Their names are Guoguo and Lele. They joined us hand in hand with their mother before they even turned two. Back then, they walked with that charming toddler wobble, cheeks full and round, their little bodies soft and cuddly, like two baby bear cubs learning to walk side by side. Every time I saw them from across the hall, I couldn't help but quicken my pace, crouch down, and pull them into a hug. I would whisper gently, "I love you. I like you just the way you are."

During those early days, when children are still learning what it means to be safe and cared for, we would often tell them, "You are safe here. We'll always be with you." It was through those tender phrases, and our steady presence, that the girls began to flourish. They adapted quickly to daily life at Tianjin Ruide. They could put on their own shoes, line up for handwashing, take off their diapers, eat with independence, and even use the potty all by themselves. Watching them run around the playground with such joy and confidence made something inside me quietly bloom. It felt like spring growing in my chest.

But soon, I began to notice something small.

Every child at Tianjin Ruide has two pairs of shoes: indoor shoes and outdoor shoes. Each morning, they switch upon arrival, and every afternoon before leaving, they change again. When their mother came to pick them up, Guoguo would always change her shoes promptly, then neatly tuck the indoor pair into the cabinet. Lele, however, clung tightly to her mother and refused to change her shoes unless Mama helped. If her mom encouraged her to try on her own, she would instantly pout and cry, looking heartbreakingly wronged, as if her whole world had collapsed.

At first, I did not intervene much. Lele was not part of my home-room group, and I thought it best to respect her pace. So, I let her mother help. But the more I observed, the more certain I became that Lele was fully capable of doing it herself. What stood in the way was not her ability, but the unspoken habits formed between her and her mom.

I began to feel torn. Each time she cried, my heart ached. Doubts crept in. Was I being too firm? Would she lose trust in me if I insisted? Was I mistaking rigidity for guidance?

Then one day, during a conversation with a counselor from our Huangpu campus in Guangzhou, I brought up my dilemma. As we talked, something shifted inside me. I realized that in giving in to her tears, I was unintentionally teaching Lele that tears and helplessness could influence adult decisions. That confusion blurred the lines between care and independence. It did not help her grow. It held her back.

That evening, I made a decision.

With her mother's support, I asked if she could stay a few extra minutes during pickup. When the school day ended, I gently brought Lele to the shoe room. This time, it was just the two of us. I knelt down beside her and said, "Lele, I know you want Mama to change your shoes, but I believe you can do it all by yourself." As soon as she heard my words, tears burst from her eyes. She tried to run to the door, sobbing loudly, calling out for her mother.

I held her gently, pressing my forehead to hers. "Mama is just outside," I whispered. "She and your sister are waiting for you." Her small arms wrapped tightly around my neck. I could feel her searching for safety. I asked quietly, "Why do you need Mama to help you change your shoes?" Through her tears, she answered, "Because when Mama helps me, that means she loves me."

My heart skipped a beat.

To Lele, Mama's help was proof of love. Deep down, she wasn't sure if Mama really loved her, so she kept using the act of being helped to find reassurance. And if I gave in right then, I would only reinforce that misunderstanding: that love needed to be proven through action, rather than simply felt and trusted.

I held her close and said softly, "I love you too, and I will always be with you. But this is something you are strong enough to do on your own." Little by little, I felt her body relax in my arms. Her sobs softened. After a few moments, she quietly slipped from my embrace, sat down on the bench, and began to change her shoes. Her fingers moved slowly but surely. Within a few minutes, she was done.

When she stepped out of the room and saw her mother and sister waiting, she ran to them and hugged her mother tightly. A calm, happy smile spread across her face.

In that moment, I knew I had done the right thing.

In the days that followed, Lele never again asked Mama to help her change shoes. She stopped associating that task with being loved. And our bond remained as strong as ever. She still loved holding my hand during free play. She still ran up for surprise hugs and whispered, "Teacher Shasha, I like you so much."

That tiny shoe-changing moment taught me something I'll never forget.

Tears do not always mean children cannot. Sometimes it is our hesitation that teaches them they are incapable. Real love does not mean doing everything for them. Real love means helping them discover what they can do for themselves.

We have to learn the difference. Emotions should be welcomed and accepted, but behaviors that hinder growth need steady boundaries. Standing firmly on the side of a child's development is one of the purest forms of love.

That moment taught me something about myself too. My uncertainty came from not yet fully trusting my own judgment. But confidence grows through action. Step by step. Just like children, we adults are learning too.

And sometimes, the most loving thing we can say is not yes. It is, "I believe in you."

Nature in the Rain | *by Yingying Wei*

"Learning from nature" is not just a slogan here. It is the gentle rhythm woven into the fabric of our daily life. It does not live far away in forests or mountains, nor does it require elaborate planning. It begins the moment a child steps barefoot into the soil. It begins when little hands reach down to touch a leaf or follow the quiet path of a ladybug.

At Tianjin Ruide Kindergarten, the very first lesson each day is a return to the arms of the natural world. The children plant flowers and vegetables, dig into the earth, lift stones with both hands. Through these simple, physical encounters with soil and seed, with insects and tiny rocks, they come to know names of plants, habits of bugs, and the secret meanings of growth and waiting. Their relationship with the earth is not a lesson to memorize. It is something personal, something close, something lived.

Then came the rain, adding a layer of poetry to that intimacy.

The drizzle began on Thursday afternoon, falling as gently as a feather. It drifted through the night like a lullaby, never loud, never harsh. By Friday morning, the sky was still whispering, and from the classroom window, I could see a thin layer of water glimmering on the wooden platform near the pond. For a moment, my heart paused. I wondered what the world looked like after the rain. If we took the children outside, what unexpected beauty might be waiting for them to discover?

I turned to the group with a smile. "We are going on an adventure," I said. Their cheers rang out as they pulled on their raincoats and boots. One by one, they leapt forward like little raindrops come to life, eager for the day's new mystery.

As we walked out, I asked softly, "Let's look closely today. What is different on a rainy day? Who has come out to play? Who is hiding quietly?"

We had barely stepped outside when their voices began to fill the air.

"The birds are gone. They must be hiding from the rain."

"But look, the butterflies are still flying. They're still looking for flowers."

"The grass is moving. That's the raindrops dancing."

"These raindrops are so pretty, like little glass beads."

"There are mushrooms growing now. The ground is so wet."

"Look over there. It's like a tiny river."

"Wow, the water is so deep here. It looks like a little ocean."

They walked, talked, splashed with their boots, reached up to catch falling raindrops, crouched to study droplets on blades of grass, and gazed upward into the soft gray sky. Every moment became a celebration of discovery.

I stood a few steps behind, watching them, and suddenly I remembered my own childhood attempts to write essays. I would sit at my desk, staring at a blank page, trying to imagine what it meant to walk in the rain or play in a country field. I could never find the words, not because I lacked vocabulary, but because I had never truly lived those pictures. They weren't mine.

But today, every word spoken by these children was their own unwritten poem. Their language was unpolished but honest, full of rhythm drawn directly from the world. These were not words from a textbook. They were born from real experience, from muddy shoes and wet hair and breathless laughter. This was how a child writes the world into memory.

During this little rainy-day adventure, the children touched water, chased butterflies, and tiptoed through mushroom patches. Without even noticing, they were developing language, observation, and critical thinking skills. They began to grasp cause and effect, before and after, not through lecture but through movement and play. And through it all, their imagination swelled like those soft mushrooms, rising quietly in the damp air.

As I walked with them, I felt something in myself change too. That faint resistance I often feel on rainy days, that quiet wish to stay indoors, it slipped away. In its place came a bright and open joy. I realized that even a rainy day could hold so much life, so much beauty, so much breath.

I Was That Child Too | *Geling Wang*

This week felt a little different for our small community. Wenwen was getting ready to leave Tianjin Ruide Kindergarten and travel abroad with her family for some time. She had already turned five. By the time she returned, she would be starting elementary school. So, for me, this wasn't just about saying goodbye to a child leaving preschool. It felt more like a send-off for someone graduating and stepping into a whole new chapter of life.

What made it even more special was that her older sister, Jingyi, had also been part of this place. She finished her time here last year. For a short while, the two sisters walked the same halls again, played in the same garden, and shared the same classroom memories. And now, their days together at Ruide were coming to a close. Over the past few days, they worked together, preparing something meaningful. They made cards for the teachers and children they loved.

Wenwen asked her mother to help her pick out beautiful stationery. On each card, she shared a heartfelt message. Jingyi helped write down her words. Wenwen then added colorful drawings and sealed the envelopes herself. One by one, she walked up and delivered each letter with a shy but sincere smile.

What moved me most was how personal every message felt. Wenwen didn't say the same thing to everyone. Each card reflected a specific memory, something she had noticed, something she had held onto. She wasn't just saying goodbye. She was truly seeing and honoring each person. And in return, some children quietly offered her their own little farewell gifts.

Jingyi did the same. Even though she is now in first grade and used to find writing difficult, she insisted on making several cards herself. Some were written in pinyin, others in neat Chinese characters. Her hands grew tired, but she didn't stop. Her mother wrote in the family notebook, "It turns out, when the heart leads, writing becomes easy." She was right. Writing wasn't homework this time. It was a way to express love.

Two of the cards stayed with me long after.

One was from Wenwen to a younger boy named Xiaolu. She wrote, "Dear Xiaolu, I know you might feel a little scared, but you don't need to. The teachers here are kind. They won't be mean to you. And you don't need to be afraid of me either. I grew up here too. I won't hurt you. I hope you grow up happy, wise, and playful."

Wenwen had only known Xiaolu for a few days. They hadn't spent much time together. But from just a few moments, she noticed something deeper in him. She saw a bit of fear and uncertainty. Instead of avoiding him, she chose to speak gently, as someone who had once been new too. When she wrote, "I grew up here too," my eyes welled up. It wasn't just a kind sentence. It was a quiet hand reaching out from one child to another. And her wish at the end, "happy, wise, and playful," touched me deeply. We had never said those exact words to her. Yet somehow, she knew. And she passed it forward.

Another card came from Jingyi to her old friend Tingting. She wrote, "I used to go to Ruide. You were always with me, and that made me feel warm. I will think of you often."

Just one simple sentence. But it held everything. That is who our children are. They feel deeply. They remember. And they give with open hearts.

These past few days, I often stood quietly and watched the sisters. They walked side by side, choosing their words, sealing envelopes, and delivering cards with care. Each act was a gentle goodbye. Each smile was part of growing up.

Thank you, Wenwen and Jingyi. You reminded me that what we are doing here matters. We are not just teaching children how to write, read, or count. We are planting seeds of tenderness, connection, and courage.

And I know I want to keep doing this work, right here at Tianjin Ruide, growing alongside the children, season after season, heart to heart.

Staying Through the Tears | *by Shihan Liu*

September arrived again, and with it came the quiet question that rests in many parents' hearts: how do we handle separation anxiety? At

Tianjin Ruide Kindergarten, though there is no fixed enrollment date, every new child and every family must eventually pass through that tender first moment of parting.

For the children, this first step into school brings two brand new challenges. The first is learning to be apart from their parents or familiar caregivers. The second is entering an environment where everything feels unknown.

It made me pause and ask: in all the ordinary routines of a day, what quiet and thoughtful designs are gently supporting these small hearts?

That morning, Xiaobei came in holding his mother's hand. It was only his second day, and they had arrived a little late, entering directly into the outdoor play area. All morning, he stayed pressed against her side, not letting go for even a second.

But after the playtime ended, we gently guided him through the regular morning routine. After the health check and sign-in, it was time for the daily goodbye ritual. Face to face, mother and child shared a long hug. Then Xiaobei whispered, "I'll be here at school, you don't need to worry. You can go to work, I won't worry either." His mother smiled and replied, "I know you're safe here at school, so I can go to work feeling at ease too."

It was only a short exchange. But it built something between them, a small bridge of trust. And once those words were spoken, Xiaobei let go, turned around on his own, and walked forward into the rhythm of the day. His steps were steady. His emotions were calm. You could almost feel the energy shift, as if the very act of saying goodbye out loud had smoothed the path ahead.

Separation anxiety is never just the child's experience. Parents feel it too. The hesitation, the tight chest, the worry they try not to show. And children, sensitive as they are, can sense that unease almost instantly. If those feelings go unspoken, they easily grow into a storm.

So, we try to make space for words. We help parents and children speak to each other with kindness. In those small moments of dialogue, the worry begins to soften, and the bond begins to deepen. When emotions are named and heard, safety begins to grow.

Before school starts, every new family receives a checklist of personal items to prepare. Unlike schools with matching uniforms, we encourage families to choose with intention. It might be a watering can, a small shovel, or a pair of little rain boots. We hope that parents and children will pick them out together.

Many families love the feeling of "new school, new beginnings," and they often buy everything brand new. But something that happened with Xiaobei offered me a different perspective.

During lunch on the first day, Xiaobei was seated beside an older boy named Xiaoze. When Xiaoze got up to get soup, he left his spoon on the table. Xiaobei spotted it right away and grabbed it, hugging it close. "This is mine," he said firmly, clutching it like a treasure. He couldn't let it go. For two full lunch periods, that spoon stayed on his mind.

At first, we thought he just liked the color or the shape. But later, his mother told us that there was an identical spoon at home. The same design. The same weight in his hand.

It made me wonder. If that morning in the garden he had seen the watering can he picked out with his mom, or at lunch held the spoon that reminded him of home, would the unfamiliar space feel a little more familiar? Would the new place feel a little more like his?

Objects are more than things. They carry memories. They hold comfort. They can remind a child of the people who love them most.

For every child who joins us, we host a quiet welcome. On Xiaobei's first day, each child and each teacher came forward, introduced themselves, and offered a gentle hug or handshake. One by one, they made space for him.

I watched as Xiaobei reached out his hand, and the moment their hands touched, a smile lit up his face. Maybe he wouldn't remember all their names, but he would remember this—how it felt to be received with kindness. That moment of being included may have meant more than any words of welcome.

Even with all of these gentle touches—the routines, the rituals, the welcome—separation still stirs up emotions. Children may cry. They may resist. They may feel unsure. But in those moments when they seem about to fall apart, someone will always be there. A teacher's arms, steady and warm, waiting to carry them through.

We stay with them. We wait. We breathe through the tears. Because we know those tears are not weakness. They are signs of courage. They are what it looks like when a child begins to walk toward independence.

Separation, though it stings a little, is not the end. It is just another form of love.

And in that small moment of letting go, growth quietly begins.

What Moved You Most? | *Ping Zhang*

Emotions are the most primal and honest bridge between people. We may come from different backgrounds, speak different languages, live different stories, but when it comes to joy, anger, sorrow, or delight, we are surprisingly alike. Feelings like fear, frustration, sadness, or peace become the shared language that helps us enter one another's hearts and connect over the things that words alone often cannot express.

At Tianjin Ruide Kindergarten, we honor each child's emotional truth. Here, children are not asked to hide or suppress how they feel. They are free to express their emotions, and more than that, they are gently guided to understand and accept those emotions through thoughtful, intentional psychological support. We believe that only when a person truly understands what they feel can they begin to see clearly what lies beneath their experiences.

One afternoon, Xiaoru's mother approached me softly and said, "Lately, she's been telling us she has no friends at school and that she's really unhappy. We're quite concerned."

The next day, I invited Xiaoru to our quiet reflection room, hoping to hear what was on her mind. She sat quietly on the little sofa by the window, gripping the edge of her shirt, and said in a soft voice, "All my good friends have graduated. Now that our groups have merged, the other kids don't really like me. Nobody wants to play with me."

I looked gently into her eyes and asked, "How do you feel when you say that?"

"I feel really sad," she whispered. "I miss them so much. I want to talk to them. I don't have friends now. I just feel so lost."

There was something in her voice that moved me deeply. I replied, "Do you think those friends are still your good friends?"

She thought for a moment, then shook her head. "I miss them, but I don't know how to contact them anymore. Maybe … they aren't my friends anymore."

I reached for her hand and said, "What if we recorded a message together, and I helped send it to their families? Maybe they could hear how much you miss them."

She nodded quietly. Then she recorded a short message: "I miss Xiaoyi, Xiaoan, and Xiaole. Are you happy now that you're in elementary school? You haven't contacted me. Does that mean you don't want to be friends anymore?"

Two days later, we received voice replies from all three. They told her, through their parents' phones, that they hadn't forgotten her. They were just busy with school but would visit when they could.

As Xiaoru listened to their messages, her eyes lit up. She took a long breath, and the heaviness that had settled around her seemed to lift. Not long after, Xiaoan and Xiaole came back to visit her.

Still, there was one more worry on her heart. "The kids here now don't like me," she said one morning.

So, we made a plan together. One by one, we went to speak with the other children, face to face. We asked them directly how they felt about Xiaoru.

Each child responded with sincerity. "I like you." "I want to be your friend." I asked Xiaoru to repeat each of their words back to me, so she could say aloud what she had heard and let it sink in.

I could see something shifting in her eyes. In the days that followed, she began running and laughing with the others again. The silence had lifted. Her world was full of voices and joy once more.

This experience stayed with me for a long time.

As adults, we often try to avoid difficult feelings. We fear conflict, awkwardness, or losing control. When pain or confusion arises, we rely on defense mechanisms. We rationalize. We talk over others. Sometimes we fall into silence. But the truth is, every difficult emotion carries a deeper message. If we ignore those emotions, we lose the opportunity to hear what really matters. Over time, misunderstanding builds, and we retreat into our own assumptions, unable to connect with others or even ourselves.

But here, we believe that no matter how small it may seem, nothing about a child's emotions is trivial.

A child is allowed to cry, to shout, to say, "I am not happy." We don't push those feelings aside. We sit beside them and ask, "Why are you sad? What happened? What made you upset?" And in that process, emotions begin to shift. They no longer spiral out of control. They become windows into the child's inner world.

We explore those emotions together, so the children can learn that the world is complex. There will be days of longing, of disappointment, but there will also be days of comfort and reunion. All of these moments are part of life.

We do not ask children to bury their feelings. Instead, we help them move through those feelings with understanding, so they can keep growing with clarity. In the end, this ability to navigate emotions is one of the most profound gifts life can offer.

Chapter 5: Letters From Parents: Seeing Ourselves Through Our Children

Again, include a short blurb here to tell the read what they are about to read.

It really helps to quantify as well. Something like ... Next, I will present three letters from parents of children who blah, blah, blah. Give us a bit more background .

I Thought I Brought my Child to Class, But I Was the One Who Changed

It was one of those soft, quiet evenings when the sky glowed like a watercolor painting. I was walking with my daughter Lele through our neighborhood, the kind of stroll where time slows down just enough to notice the little things. The air was gentle, and the wind carried a calm that made the leaves dance in silence. We looked up together at the clouds tinged with gold, and then down to watch the fallen leaves swaying on the path.

Then, quite suddenly, Lele stopped. She looked up at me with her round eyes and said, "Daddy, I'm really thankful for nature."

I turned to her and smiled. "Daddy is thankful for nature too. Can you tell me why you feel that way?"

She kept her gaze on the sky and answered slowly, like she was choosing each word with care. "Because nature gives me air, so I can breathe. The sun shines on me and makes me feel warm. And the rain helps the grass and trees grow. The air, the sunshine, the rain... they don't belong to me. Nature gives them to me. That's why I feel grateful."

I stood there for a moment, unable to reply right away. She was not yet five years old, and yet what she said carried such clarity and gentleness. It moved me deeply. In that quiet moment, it felt like I had stumbled into something sacred. Like hearing the ocean from far away in the middle of the night, soft but steady, full of life.

This moment, simple and profound, has everything to do with the way Lele has grown up at Tianjin Ruide Kindergarten.

She joined the school when she was just one year and seven months old, and over the past three years, I have watched her grow from a wide-eyed toddler into a thoughtful, deeply feeling little girl. At Ruide, where gratitude and character are woven into the heart of daily life, she has been nurtured not by lectures, but by moments like this.

In today's world, many children grow up as only children. They are deeply loved, but often see the world through a lens centered on themselves. That is why Ruide places character education, especially gratitude, at the core of its approach. Gratitude is the first seed they plant, and the one they hope will take root the deepest.

And this isn't just a slogan. It lives in the rhythm of the children's days. Before lunch or snack, the children recite a gratitude verse, thanking their parents and grandparents, the teachers who prepare their food, the farmers who grow it, and the sun, the wind, the rain, and the soil that make it all possible. They even say, "Thank you, nature, for the air we breathe," and close with a gentle prayer. When someone is unwell, they add their own lines: "Please send your prayers, and may she get better soon."

One day, Lele whispered quietly, "Please pray for me. I caught a cold today." Her voice held a quiet strength, as if she had found her own way to exchange kindness with the world.

I remember another day, during our family dumpling-making party. We were all gathered around the table. Lele came over, holding a bowl of steaming dumplings she had prepared herself. Her little face was full of pride. She said, "Daddy, thank you for everything. These are the dumplings I made just for you. Please enjoy them."

My eyes filled with tears. A mother nearby was watching and wiped her eyes too. She leaned in and said softly, "This is the first time I've ever heard my child say 'thank you' like that. I think she's really growing up."

At Ruide, gratitude is not only about people. It extends to the earth, to labor, to the act of living itself. Children grow their own vegetables and flowers in the rooftop garden, digging through soil, watching butterflies land, and discovering snails in hidden corners. They come to understand that without sunshine, rain, and earth, nothing can grow. And so, they begin to see the world not as something to use, but something to care for.

Lele brought this sense of gratitude home too. Once, I was helping her clean up her toys, and she looked up and said quietly, "Thank you, Daddy." Another time, after her mom had come home exhausted from work, Lele tiptoed over and began to gently massage her shoulders. "Mommy, you rest now. I'll help."

She looked like a tiny grown-up, full of tenderness.

There was another little girl named Ruirui. One day, after learning that her grandmother had caught a cold, she calmly said, "Grandma, since you're sick today, I'll do the dishes." And she did. The kitchen was spotless when she finished. Her grandmother smiled with such warmth that it seemed to light up the whole room.

This is the kind of education that does not rush to fill children with facts. Instead, it lights a small candle in their hearts and lets it grow, slowly but steadily. It reminds them that the world is not here to revolve around them, but is a place to honor, to cherish, and to thank.

This kind of teaching does not shout. It falls like spring rain, quietly nourishing both the children and the hearts of us parents. Our children do not grow up alone. It takes all of us, walking hand in hand. I am thankful for every teacher at Tianjin Ruide Kindergarten, for the gentle love Lele gives me as her father, and for this school that still believes in raising a child not just with knowledge, but with time and care.

Gratitude is not just a feeling. It is a kind of love, a kind of wisdom, a way of living that makes the world a more beautiful place. May we walk this path of thankfulness, alongside our children, step by step.

—Lele's Dad, Yiming Zhou

Parent at Tianjin Ruide Kindergarten

He Did Not Change, I Just Finally Heard Him

It has been just over seven months since Chenchen began his journey at Tianjin Ruide Kindergarten. Looking back now, the changes in him are nothing short of remarkable, and my heart fills with quiet pride every time I reflect on how far he has come.

I still remember those early days. He had just turned two years and one month. His words were still tangled and uncertain, and he relied on his grandmother for nearly everything. She fed him, dressed him, helped him use the bathroom. Their bond was intense. Whenever she stepped away, even for a moment, he would panic and cry out for her with the urgency of a frightened little animal. In the neighborhood, he kept to himself, rarely responding when other children said hello. His world was small, private, and self-contained. At the time, I was deeply concerned. After much thought and many conversations, we decided to send him to Tianjin Ruide.

His first day played out exactly as I had feared. The moment it came time to separate, he cried with a raw, desperate ache. I stood by and watched one of the teachers gently kneel down, gather him in her arms, and carry him into the counseling room. My heart clenched. I wondered if we had made the right decision. Could these teachers truly help him through such deep-seated anxiety?

What I didn't expect was how quickly things began to shift. On the second day, his tears were shorter. By the third, he barely cried at all. Those few drops he did shed felt more like a way of saying goodbye than an expression of fear.

Now, every morning, he wakes up excited. His first words are often, "Let's go to school. I don't want to be late." That once-intense dependence on his grandmother has softened. Now he gives her a gentle hug, says goodbye with a smile, and walks through the school doors with confidence.

He has become more independent in small, everyday ways. At mealtimes, he washes his hands, carries his bowl, and sits down to eat all on his own. During the summer, he started going to the bathroom without asking for help. One weekend, while I was rinsing vegetables in the kitchen, I saw him quietly placing his socks into a basin. He turned on the water, then started washing them himself. When I asked what he was doing, he looked up and grinned. "Washing my socks," he said, as if it were the most natural thing in the world.

At home, he now sweeps the floor, wipes the table, and hands out cleaning cloths with purpose. It isn't just play. He has begun to understand what it means to take responsibility.

He also surprises me with how well he understands rules. He loves the puzzle game on my phone. Before he plays, we agree on a time. When the minute hand reaches a certain point, he will stop. At first, I thought he might argue or pretend not to understand. After all, he's just a toddler. But each time the clock hits that mark, he sets the phone down without being told. On the rare occasion that he forgets, a gentle reminder is all it takes for him to nod and return the phone without a fuss.

Learning at school is woven into games and imagination. He especially loves numbers. The school turned counting into a story called "The Numbers Are Going Home," and he plays with sparkling eyes and endless laughter. He loves spotting bus numbers and pointing them out to his grandmother. She often says that with him around, she never misses the right bus.

He can now count to four hundred, and his interest only seems to grow.

Just the other evening, I saw him sitting quietly with a newspaper spread across his lap. He was murmuring softly, and at first, I thought he was simply pretending to read, the way young children often do. But as I walked closer, I noticed his finger moving carefully along the page. He stopped at the word "apple" and read it aloud. Then came "Central Avenue," spoken with the same quiet confidence.

I decided to ask him a few more words. He looked up at me with a calm smile and read "tiger," then "station," and then "dad" and "mom." Each word came effortlessly. Then, without prompting, he pointed to our names printed on the page and read them out loud, as if it were the most natural thing in the world.

We had never formally taught him to read. It turns out that he had been exploring the school's audio books, choosing stories to listen to on his own. He also recognized words from the places we often passed in the car. He had been learning quietly, stitching sounds and symbols together in his mind.

He has also learned how to express himself and care for others.

When he struggles, he asks, "Can you please help me?" During meals, he shares snacks and knows how to wait his turn. He remembered his mother's birthday and insisted on choosing the cake himself. He tells us when he doesn't like something, and when he sees I'm tired, he gently presses my legs to comfort me. He wanted the whole family to gather for his birthday and even described the kind of cake he imagined. "A big one," he said, spreading his arms wide.

His growth is quiet and full of wonder, showing up in unexpected places. And it hasn't just been his journey. As a family, we have walked alongside him, attending parenting classes and learning together. Each step has helped us become better for him and for each other. The hope I feel now is steady and real. It comes not just from what he learns, but from the love we all pour into helping him grow.

I am deeply grateful to Tianjin Ruide Kindergarten, to Principal Li, and to every teacher who has walked beside him. And I am also thankful to the version of myself who, in a moment of uncertainty, chose to say yes to this path.

—Zhao Junping, Chenchen's father

Thank You, We Are Starting Over as a Family

When Anran first stepped into elementary school, she was not yet six. We chose a boarding school for her, a decision that brought with it real challenges. But just two weeks in, she was already surprising me again and again. Each day she returned home with bright eyes and a heart full of stories, as if every school day had been a new adventure all her own.

Her teachers told me she was enthusiastic in class, eager to participate, and even brave enough to recite Tang poems aloud in front of everyone. I remembered how shy she used to be. Once, when a male relative visited our home, she wouldn't even come near the dining table. She peeked out from behind the doorframe and stayed there, silent. When she liked someone, she wouldn't say it aloud. Instead, she would gently touch the corner of their sleeve and say nothing at all.

Things began to change during a wedding at FMAE. Her counselor, Miss Irene, invited her to be the flower girl. Anran was nervous. She came to me, twisting her fingers and speaking in a small voice. I told her that if she wanted to try, I would be with her every step of the way. We picked out a white dress together, the kind with a skirt that floated like a cloud ready to dance.

That evening, when she came home, her cheeks were glowing like the sky at dusk. She told me, with sparkling eyes, that she had sung a song at the wedding. The groom had pulled her onto the stage. Miss Irene had only taught her the song the day before. She even spent time alone with the bride's family, chatting and smiling with people she had never met. That kind of experience would have been unimaginable for her just months before.

She still refuses to put that dress away in the closet. It is a reminder of the first time she realized she could do something she thought was impossible. When I asked her what made her brave enough to sing on stage, she looked at me and said, "Because it mattered to me."

Now, in elementary school, her world has grown even larger. After her first week, she came home and told me she had made a friend on the school bus. The girl was in fourth grade, and the two of them talked the whole ride like they had known each other for years. She also told me that she had cried twice during the week because she missed her mom. But she quickly added, "I also comforted a classmate who was crying too."

At FMAE, children are never forced to write. Before she started school, the only character Anran could write was our family name. But after just a few days, she came home excited, flipping through her notebooks to show me the new words she had learned. She could write four characters now, and her pride was impossible to miss. She adapted to math just as quickly. For problems with pictures, she didn't need me to read them. She looked at the picture and answered right away. Her teachers said she was focused and positive in class. Her handwriting was still playful, but her attitude was strong and steady.

English has been a new challenge for her. She told me that other kids remembered words after hearing them once, but she had to repeat them several times. Still, she didn't mind. She picked a notebook she liked, drew pictures of the sentences she was learning, and read them aloud while she drew. "English is an important subject," she said. "I want to learn it well." Her determination showed me that FMAE's values had already taken root in her heart. She was not comparing herself to others. She was comparing herself to who she had been yesterday.

That kind of mindset takes time to grow. I remembered when she first learned to roller skate. She improved quickly. One day, the coach pointed at her and said to another child, "Look how well she skates, and she's even younger than you." That child cried on the spot. Anran said nothing then, but on the way home, she quietly told me, "That girl did much better today than last time."

FMAE's influence has shaped more than just her schoolwork. It has become a part of her everyday life. She knows how to manage her time, finishes her homework independently, and packs her own school bag. Sometimes, she even corrects my pronunciation with the seriousness of a tiny teacher. "Daddy," she'll say, "that's not how you say it. Watch how my mouth moves."

Anran joined FMAE when she was just three years and three months old. It's only been a little over two years, but she already seems like someone entirely new. She no longer hides behind doors. She walks up to strangers and says hello. She no longer hesitates. She says, "I can." She may not be six yet, but I can already see her future. It will be bright and full of freedom.

I have always believed that every child is born gifted. What they need is the right place to grow. A friend recommended FMAE to us when Anran was three. I remember feeling unsure at first. The classrooms were not fancy. In fact, they were very simple. But the counselors had something rare. They paid close attention. Their eyes were full of warmth. That is what convinced me to entrust Anran to them. Looking back now, it was one of the best decisions we ever made.

FMAE offers rich experiences beyond the classroom. Anran's favorite is visiting the elderly at the local senior center. One time, we brought gentle soap that would not irritate the skin. Before we left, I reminded her not to leave it in standing water or it would melt. When we arrived, she remembered my words and reminded every elder, one by one, "Please keep it in a dry place."

In her eyes, every living thing deserves respect. Once, we caught a beautiful butterfly. I thought she would be delighted. Instead, she looked at us very seriously and said, "It belongs to nature. It shouldn't be trapped." We listened. Then we let it go.

At home, she is my little helper. When we moved into a new house, she helped us build shelves, paint walls, and organize boxes. She never saw work as punishment. At FMAE, being the classroom helper is a sign of pride. It is part of becoming your best self.

Watching a child grow is a journey full of wonder and love. And FMAE has not only helped Anran become the person she is today. It has also helped us become better parents. Every time I pick her up and see her running toward me, her face lit with joy, I find myself thinking the same thing. Thank you, FMAE. Thank you for not letting her light be dimmed. Thank you for giving our love a place to flourish.

—Lin Qiuyah, Anran's mom

Chapter 6: If You Are on This Path Too

The Mentors' Stories: How They Found Their Way Here

The first time little Yu came to Tianjin Ruide Kindergarten, he was just three years old. His round cheeks and sturdy frame gave him the look of a confident child, yet his body told a different story. His fingers were slightly curled, his steps uncertain, shifting back and forth like a small animal on alert, ready to run at any moment.

His mother stood nearby, her eyes filled with concern as she spoke to me. "He hits people," she said quietly. "He can't sit still. No one at home knows what to do with him."

I crouched down to meet him at eye level and gently called out to him. Yu didn't look at me. His eyes kept drifting, never quite settling. I kept my voice soft and steady. "Yu, I'm Teacher Wang. Are you feeling angry right now?" There was no response. He simply turned his head sharply away.

I slowly reached out and gathered him into my arms. His body went stiff, and he began to struggle with all his strength. "I don't want you to hold me. Let go!" His voice was sharp with fear and resistance, like a wounded animal startled by a sudden touch.

Still, I didn't let go. I didn't rush to soothe him. I held him firmly but gently and said, "You don't like being held this way. It feels uncomfortable, doesn't it? You can tell me that. I'm listening." As I spoke, I softly touched his forehead, letting warmth pass from my hand into that tense little body.

Yu struggled and shouted, and in the midst of it, he began to cry. The sound was tight and brief, like a cry he had been taught to hide. He covered his eyes with both hands and quickly wiped the tears away with a tissue. His movements were fast, practiced, almost mechanical.

I lowered my voice. "When you cry, do you cover your face because you think it looks ugly?" He nodded slightly. "Mom says boys shouldn't cry. Crying looks ugly."

"Does it make you feel better to hold it all inside?" I asked.

"No," he whispered. "It doesn't feel good."

I kept one arm wrapped around him and gently placed my other hand on his small belly. "Is all that not-good feeling sitting right here?"

He nodded again, the sobs coming softer now. "Yes."

"That must feel really heavy. Keeping all that inside must be so hard."

He didn't answer, but something changed. The crying shifted. It was no longer tight with resistance. It opened. It became the kind of crying that only happens when a child begins to feel truly safe.

"You can cry," I told him quietly. "I'm right here. This is a safe place. I'm not going anywhere."

Then the words started to come. Hesitant at first, like a diary being opened for the first time in years.

"Mom hit my bottom … Dad hits me too. My sister took my toy, and I got mad. One day I woke up and Mom was gone. I was all alone. I was scared."

Piece by piece, he let these memories out, threading together moments he had kept hidden deep inside.

"You've been carrying all of that by yourself, haven't you?" I asked.

He nodded. "It's really tiring."

Tears streamed down his cheeks now, freely and openly. His body began to soften. He leaned into me, no longer tight with tension. "I feel like I'm about to fall over," he whispered.

"That's okay," I said softly. "I've got you. You can fall."

In that moment, he let go completely. Like a raindrop finally falling to the earth, he rested in my arms. His eyes met mine for the first time, steady and calm. The storm inside him began to pass. He didn't shout anymore. He didn't struggle. He had found a place to breathe.

None of this came from a special lesson plan or a clever strategy. At Tianjin Ruide Kindergarten, we understand something essential. Young children don't build their worlds through reason. They build them through feeling. Their experience of safety, of connection, of being loved, does not begin in words or logic. It begins in presence, in the unspoken language of touch, tone, and trust. Their sensitivity to emotion runs deeper than we often realize.

Yu's restlessness, his aggression, his resistance, these were not acts of defiance. They were signs of hurt. He wasn't a disobedient child. He was a hurting child without words to say so. When we respond with commands like "Good kids don't hit" or "If you act like this, I won't like you," we teach them something dangerous: that their emotions are wrong. That being real is not allowed. Over time, those messages settle into their bodies. Then the behaviors begin to surface. A child might bite, scream, shut down, cling tightly to adults, wet the bed, refuse to eat, or later on, struggle with anxiety, defiance, or even fall into depression.

At Tianjin Ruide, what we offer is space. A space where emotions are not punished or shamed, but held and heard. Our teachers are trained in early childhood psychology and understand how children between birth and seven move through their inner world. We turn to the simplest things: a steady gaze, a gentle story, a line drawn on paper, the soft shifting of sand, and most of all, the quiet presence of love. With these, we help children let go of what they were once told to keep inside. We gently name each feeling, one by one. We look at where they come from. And, just as importantly, we support the parents, too.

Yu is not unique. Every child who softens in love begins to bloom. Once they feel it is safe to cry, to be angry, to not be perfect and still be loved, something changes. That is when real growth begins.

We have seen so many children bloom like this at Tianjin Ruide. Not because we taught them how, but because they knew, at last, they were safe enough to grow. It isn't our teaching that makes them unfold. It is the atmosphere of understanding that gives them space to do it on their own.

This is the essence of the autopoietic system.

In our framework, each child is not a project to be shaped, but a living system. They are not vessels waiting to be filled. They are complete beings, capable of self-organization, self-renewal, and self-expression. Their language, emotion, movement, and relationships are not parts to be managed separately. They are woven together, like the roots, trunk, branches, and blossoms of a living tree.

When a child's emotions are received, their inner world begins to come into order. When they are no longer labeled good or bad, they begin to feel more freely. When they create through stories and images and play, they are quietly healing, reshaping their understanding of the world and of themselves.

True education does not begin with content. It begins with presence. It begins with honoring the child's inner tempo, their way of being in the world. We are not here to make them into something. We are here to walk with them through all that is messy and unknown, until their steps begin to steady on their own.

Tianjin Ruide is not only a school. It is a place where life is allowed to generate. A place where children are given time to become themselves. We do not rush them. We stay beside them and protect the space where growth can happen.

In a world that moves ever faster, we choose to slow down. We choose to listen. We choose to kneel. Not for efficiency. For the child.

Because real education is not about shaping the child to fit the world. It is about giving them the strength to build a world within, from which they can truly grow.

This is what we do. And this is the path we continue to walk.

This philosophy of education was first proposed by Dr. Jiawei Liu. Tianjin Ruide Kindergarten is one of the places where this vision is lived out each day, in the quiet rhythm of children learning to become fully, beautifully themselves.

Answering With Care

Question 1: Children Competing for Attention

Question. I have thirty-two-month-old twins. They're always competing for attention. The older one especially cries a lot, and once he gets upset, it's really hard to calm him down. What should we do?

Answer. Fang Wang, Tianjin Ruide Kindergarten:

Thank you for your question. I truly understand how exhausting this must feel. Raising twins is already a challenge, and now that they are approaching three years old, their emotions are entering one of the most sensitive stages of early childhood. They are learning to separate from you while still needing to feel completely loved. This inner tension plays out every day, and for parents, trying to soothe two different emotional storms at once can feel like walking a tightrope with your arms full.

Here at Tianjin Ruide Kindergarten, we have walked alongside several twin families. I remember one pair raised separately. The older brother lived with the grandparents, and the younger stayed with the parents. They fought less, but the one who was apart always carried a quiet question deep in his heart. He never said it out loud, but it showed up in his eyes and in his silence. Was I not good enough? Is that why I was sent away? This quiet anxiety about love and belonging can slowly shape a child's inner world.

Another pair lived together with their mother. They were never apart, always entangled in each other's moods. Their home was filled with arguments, tugging toys, shouting matches, and tears. But do you know what we realized? That conflict was not a bad sign. Every shout, every push, every tantrum was a question they did not yet know how to ask. Do you love me just as much? Am I just as important? The fighting was not misbehavior. It was longing.

When twins fight for attention, there are two important things we can do. First, we make sure each child feels clearly and deeply, "You are the one and only in my heart." Love is not a math problem to be split evenly. It is a presence that shows up fully in each moment. You do not need to emphasize fairness, or say who should let the other go first. Just respond sincerely to the child in front of you.

Second, we hold a consistent sense of fairness when it comes to boundaries. A child needs to take responsibility for their behavior not because of birth order, but because they are ready to learn and understand. A three-year-old is already capable of beginning to connect cause and effect. Trust that they can grow into that.

You also mentioned that your older twin is especially hard to calm when his emotions erupt. This is very common in sensitive children. Their feelings run deep, but they often lack the language to describe what they are going through. In these moments, your embrace becomes the most powerful response. Kneel down, hold him tightly, and say softly, "It's okay to cry. It's okay to be angry. I'm here. You are safe. You are loved." Let him know his feelings are allowed. They do not need to be hidden, and they will not cause you to walk away.

Once his emotions begin to settle, you can ask gently, "Were you upset because I held your brother first? Or was it because your toy got taken away?" Help him begin to name what he feels. This makes the world feel understandable again. Later, when he is fully calm, you can offer a quiet invitation. "Next time you feel this way, is there another way you could tell me? Maybe you could say, 'I'm sad right now.' Then we can work it out together."

Sometimes, every meltdown is a message. Not a demand, not defiance, but a soft cry of, "Please see me. Please understand me." He is not losing control. He is simply short on tools. He is asking for help in the only way he knows how.

In these moments, our task is not to demand that he stop, but to walk with him, slowly and patiently, as he begins to learn new ways to say what is true inside his heart.

At Tianjin Ruide, we believe that every child is a living, growing system. They do not need to be controlled. They need to be seen. They do not need to be managed. They need to be accompanied. When we slow down, kneel down, and truly listen, their emotions begin to soften. Eventually, they find their own rhythm. They settle into the shape of their own wholeness.

Thank you again for reaching out. Thank you for your patience, and for the tender effort you bring into your role as a parent. Your children are growing, and so are you. This is something beautiful. I hope my response has offered both warmth and support on your journey.

Question 2: Children Arguing

Question. I have two boys; one is six and the other is three and a half. They argue all the time. As a mom, I often don't know how to handle it. How should I guide and communicate with them?

Answer. Teacher Cao, Tianjin Ruide Kindergarten:

Thank you for your question. When I read your words, "I don't know what to do," I could feel the weight behind them. Raising two boys with different rhythms, different ways of expressing themselves, and endless energy is no small task. Sometimes they go from laughter to fighting in seconds. After a long day, when your own energy is nearly gone, it can feel overwhelming to face yet another round of conflict.

At Tianjin Ruide, we often meet parents going through similar struggles. Sibling rivalry is one of the most common challenges in families with more than one child. A typical scene might look like this: you are in the kitchen cooking while the boys are in the living room. Suddenly someone cries. You rush out to find the younger one sobbing and the older one standing there fuming. Your first instinct might be to ask, "Who hit whom this time?" and before you know it, you have stepped into the role of referee. You scold one for hitting, the other for grabbing. But the more we judge, the more the conflict escalates. The children feel misunderstood, and you feel defeated.

In these moments, try pausing and asking yourself, how do I feel when I hear them fighting? Is it frustration? Guilt? Exhaustion? Often, our wish for peace is tied to our own fatigue. We long for a quiet moment, for harmony. But real growth in children rarely happens in perfect peace. They learn through trial and error. Conflict is how they come to understand boundaries, how to communicate, and how to regulate emotions.

So before trying to fix the situation, take a deep breath. Tell yourself, this is not failure. This is what learning looks like. They are not being bad. They are figuring out how to live together.

What can you do in these moments? First, resist rushing to assign blame. Instead, walk over, kneel down to their level, and say calmly, "I see both of you are upset. Who wants to tell me what happened first?" The younger child may not have the words, and the older one might launch into a dramatic account. That is okay. What matters is that both feel seen and heard.

If emotions are too high, guide them to a quiet space, maybe the edge of the bed or a sunny corner of the room. Let them sit separately for a moment. A change of space often helps children calm down. It also gives you a few breaths to center yourself.

Then you can say, "I know you both feel hurt. Little brother, you are sad because you did not get a turn. Big brother, you are angry because he grabbed it too fast." Try naming their feelings. Even if you only capture part of what they are feeling, they will sense that you are trying to understand. Later, once the storm settles, you might ask, "Next time this happens, what else could we do instead of grabbing?" Let them be part of the solution. Even something as simple as "We could take turns" is a powerful beginning.

At Tianjin Ruide, we believe education is not about control. It is about helping children move through the messiness of life with guidance and love. Every argument between siblings is a chance to learn how to express needs, to test boundaries, and to understand another person. You are not there to eliminate conflict. You are there to help them grow through it.

The next time they fight over a toy, try telling yourself, "They are learning how to be brothers." And you are learning too. You are not the judge. You are not the police. You are the witness, the steady guide, the person who helps them find their way back to each other.

I hope this brings you a little strength and reassurance. Your children are learning to love through their struggles. And you, in all your care and effort, are becoming the mother they will always remember. Not for solving every problem, but for staying close through the hardest moments.

Question 3: Children Hitting or Pushing

Question. My child often hits or pushes other kids in preschool. How should I guide and help them change this behavior?

Answer. Liu Shan Wu / Teacher, Tianjin Ruide Kindergarten:

Thank you for your thoughtful question. At Tianjin Ruide Kindergarten, we often hear this concern from parents. When a child repeatedly shows aggressive behavior in a group setting, it can bring up a mix of emotions for the family. Parents may feel anxious, confused, or even blame themselves. Many begin to wonder if they did something wrong or worry there might be something wrong with their child.

Before you rush to label or correct, I hope you can pause for a moment and offer yourself some kindness. Your child is not broken. You are not failing. Often, what looks like aggression on the outside is really a signal from within, a sign that the child is struggling with something they do not yet know how to say.

The first step is not judgment but observation. How old is your child? How long have they been in the preschool setting? What kind of behaviors are you seeing? Are they pushing, hitting, shouting, or pulling away when other children get close? Do these reactions happen with everyone or only in specific moments? These details matter. They help us begin to see not just the behavior but the feeling underneath it.

At Tianjin Ruide, we have worked with many children who express themselves this way. Some hit out suddenly during play. Some seem hyper-aware and guarded, always watching for danger. Others touch or nudge another child gently but at the wrong time or in the wrong way, which still causes distress. What adults call aggression may actually be a child's way of reaching out, protecting themselves, or asking for space.

Through observation and reflection, we have come to understand several common roots of this behavior:

- Some children feel intense emotions that overwhelm them. They cannot yet say,

  "I am angry," but their fists speak for them.

- Some have experienced being left out or hurt before. They strike first because they do not want to be hurt again.

- Some have a strong need for order. If someone does not play by their rules, they react as if something has gone terribly wrong.

- Some children do not yet have enough language. They use their hands to say what they cannot express with words.

- Some are simply curious. They are trying to connect but do not know the right way yet.

The most important thing we can do is not to punish but to pause and connect. Get close to your child, meet them at their level, and ask gently, "Can you tell me why you did that?" This is not a demand. It is an invitation. You are not scolding. You are offering a chance for the child to be heard.

You might hear, "He took my toy," or "She kept looking at me and I didn't like it." These small responses are openings. They help us understand what the child is really feeling.

Once you have that window into their emotions, you can begin to teach them a new way. You can say, "If you are angry, you can tell him, 'I don't like that.' You can also come to me and ask for help." Model the words with your tone and your presence. If they are afraid someone is too close, show them how to raise their hand and say, "Please stop."

At Tianjin Ruide, we believe all feelings are welcome, but not all actions are okay. Anger is natural. Fear is natural. But hurting others is something we learn to avoid. That is where education comes in. Not with punishment, but with guidance.

Of course, this takes time. Children need many chances to try again. They need the calm voice, the safe space, the adult who will stay and help them name what they are feeling. With enough practice, what used to be a swing or a shove slowly becomes a word. What used to be fear becomes trust.

In our approach to Autopoietic Drama Education, we see every child as a living system in motion. They are not broken. They are becoming. And when we meet their aggression with understanding instead of shame, we give them the chance to reorganize from the inside out.

So please believe this. Your child is not a problem. They are simply a child who has not yet found the right words. And you are not alone. You are the one who can kneel beside them, take their hand, and help them find a new way to speak from the heart.

We hope this response gives you both comfort and clarity. At Tianjin Ruide Kindergarten, we walk with you. Every aggressive moment is not an end, but a beginning. It is a doorway toward deeper connection, and we are honored to walk through it with you.

Question 4: Children Who Are Shy

Question. My child is four years and two months old and has always been shy. Now that he's in preschool, he still seems reluctant to talk to others. He says "Good morning" to his classroom teacher every day, but that's about it. He avoids greeting others and sometimes even says clearly that he doesn't want to. What should we do?

Answer. Yingxue Zheng / Teacher, Tianjin Ruide Kindergarten:

Thank you so much for your question. I can truly feel the care and concern you have for your child. Behind this reluctance to engage with others often lies a complex world of feelings that have yet to be named or expressed. It's not that your child doesn't want to connect. It's more that he's not quite ready yet. His hesitation is not a problem to fix. It's a way of protecting himself while he slowly finds his way into the world.

From what you've described, your child has always been cautious around new people, and that trait hasn't shifted much even after starting school. In our work at Tianjin Ruide Kindergarten, we often refer to this as an "inward style of self-protection." Before a child develops a solid sense of safety and autonomy, it's natural for them to pull inward and be selective about when and how they respond.

So where do we begin? Not with correction, and not with pressure. We begin with listening. We begin by respecting the pace of the child.

Start with what he's already doing well. In a quiet moment, gently say to him, "I noticed you say 'Good morning' to your teacher every day. That's so thoughtful and kind of you." This simple sentence carries three powerful messages: I see you. You're growing. I appreciate you.

Then pause and see what happens. Children are sensitive. When we leave space, they often fill it. He might nod, smile, or even say something like, "But I don't like talking to other people." If he says that, then you've found a window. You've been invited into a deeper part of his world.

Often, children withdraw not because they are impolite, but because they are not yet ready. He might rehearse "Good morning" a hundred times in his mind, but when it's time to speak, his voice freezes and his heart races. Shyness isn't just about unfamiliar people. It's often rooted in the fear of being judged, misunderstood, or rejected. In a four-year-old's world, emotions often outweigh logic.

In addition to gently talking with your child, I'd encourage you to observe a few things:

When did he first start withdrawing? Was it before preschool or after? Did something happen that might have made him feel unsafe or uncertain?

Is your home environment emotionally stable and warm? Children who grow up in homes where feelings are acknowledged and respected usually feel safer expressing themselves in other settings.

Has there been a lot of parental anxiety? Children can feel when we want them to "do well," and sometimes that loving hope quietly becomes pressure. What we intend as encouragement may be heard as "I'm not good enough yet."

Sometimes, children are not resisting. They are waiting. Waiting for a signal that it's safe to step forward. They need to know that they are loved not for what they do, but for who they are. They need to know that you will stay beside them not only when they succeed, but also when they hesitate.

So instead of reminding him to be polite each morning, try turning it into a game. You can role-play together. Pretend to be the teacher, and let him be the child. Or switch roles and have him greet you with a cheerful "Good morning!" When practiced through play, these small social moments feel less intimidating and more fun. He learns not just what to say, but how it feels to connect, all within the safety of home.

You are not trying to raise a child who simply knows how to greet others. You are walking beside a child who is slowly, bravely learning how to step out of his shell.

Please believe this. He is not socially withdrawn. He is gathering courage. And when he is ready, even a soft "Hello" will mark a powerful moment of inner growth.

At Tianjin Ruide Kindergarten, we walk gently with every child, supporting them as they open their hearts and reach out to the world in their own time. And we walk beside you as well, as quiet companions on this meaningful journey of becoming.

Question 5: Children in Relation to Money & Material Things

Question. My child is six years old, and we've noticed that he seems very sensitive when it comes to money and material things. For example, he only gives gifts after receiving one first, and even then, he prefers to give something inexpensive, old, or handmade. We're not sure if this is stinginess or just a lack of gratitude. Is this normal? Should we try to correct it?

Answer. Sha Liu / Teacher, Tianjin Ruide Kindergarten:

Thank you for bringing such a thoughtful and honest question. When a child shows sensitivity around money and possessions, it is often a sign that they are exploring something deeper. At this stage, they are beginning to understand their own boundaries and sense of ownership. They are quietly wondering what belongs to them, why they should give it away, and whether what they offer is truly worth giving. These are not small questions for a six-year-old.

Before I respond more directly, I want to gently invite you to reflect on your own feelings. When you say your child is sensitive about money and things, what comes to mind? Do you worry that he is not generous enough? Do you feel concerned that he is too focused on value? Perhaps, without realizing it, we adults carry similar thoughts too. We may hesitate before buying a gift, wonder if it's too expensive, or feel a little disappointed when someone doesn't give something in return.

We often hope our children will understand generosity and gratitude, yet we sometimes find it hard when they say things like "I don't want to give this" or "That costs too much." But maybe those words come from a place of honesty, not selfishness.

I remember a child who once told me very seriously, "Teacher, I made a drawing card for my grandma because I think it's more special than something I could buy." To him, that handmade card wasn't a cheap gift. It was filled with meaning.

So, I truly understand your question and would encourage you to have a gentle conversation with your child. You might ask:

What made you choose this gift for your friend?

What do you think is special about this gift?

How do you want the other person to feel when they receive it?

You may be surprised by the answers. Many children have their own quiet logic. Some feel that it is only fair to give after receiving. Others might say, "This old toy is my favorite, and I'm giving it because it matters to me." Some will tell you, "I spent time making this, and that makes it better than just buying something."

These responses may sound simple, but they carry something important. Your child is trying to express something real. The language may still be immature, but the effort is sincere.

At Tianjin Ruide, we often see children who only give to those they feel closest to, or who choose to share with care. This is not a rejection of kindness or generosity. It is a process of building emotional safety. When a child gives something small, handmade, or old, it does not mean they lack love. It may simply be their way of showing it right now.

Of course, we can gently guide them too. You might say, "When someone gives you a thoughtful gift, how does that make you feel?" Then ask, "Would you like others to feel that way when they receive something from you?" A child may not fully understand generosity yet, but they will begin to sense that giving is more about connection than transaction.

In our practice of Autopoietic Children's Education, we see every child as a living, evolving system. Each one carries an inner compass that is still forming. Your child is not stingy. He is exploring. He is not ungrateful. He is discovering how to give and receive love in his own language.

That is why education is not about correcting too quickly. It is about standing beside the child, helping them see how they love others and how they wish to be loved in return.

So, take your time. Your steady presence, your honest listening, your gentle words. These are the most generous gifts you can offer. And in receiving them, your child will learn, in his own way and at his own pace, how to give from the heart.

Question 6: Children Who Seem Closed Off

Question. Ever since my daughter started elementary school, she feels like a completely different person. In kindergarten, she was open, cheerful, and would greet strangers with ease. But now, even when familiar people call her name, she ignores them completely, as if she has closed herself off. She refuses to talk about school. Every time I ask, "How was your day?" she answers, "It's a secret." If I ask why, she says, "Because of the thing and the stuff," then says nothing more. It's both confusing and frustrating.

Answer. Fangfang Wu / Teacher, Tianjin Ruide Kindergarten:

Thank you for sharing this. And thank you for choosing to understand your child even when you feel confused or at your wit's end.

Many parents go through this kind of shift when their child enters elementary school. Some children turn inward. Some become protective of their privacy. Some stop talking even to the people they trust most. It can feel sudden or even alarming, but from the child's point of view, it is often a necessary transformation.

The transition from kindergarten to elementary school is more than just academic. It is a shift in emotional geography. Kindergarten is warm, playful, and full of gentle rhythms. Elementary school is structured, goal-driven, and filled with expectations. The child who once greeted the world with joy now faces new systems, comparisons, and demands. She may not feel ready, and yet the journey has already begun.

When your child says, "It's a secret," she may not be trying to hide something. She may be trying to find the words. When she says, "Because of the thing and the stuff," she may not be avoiding you. She may simply not yet know how to explain what she feels inside. It could be fatigue. It could be frustration. It could be the quiet ache of trying to grow into a new role.

At Tianjin Ruide, we have met many children who went through a similar silence. I remember one girl who stopped speaking almost entirely after the first month of elementary school. She would mutter, "I forgot," or "Nothing happened," and look away. So, we stopped asking questions. We began to draw pictures together, walk slowly after lunch, make bread with our hands. One day, as she shaped a ball of dough, she quietly said, "I don't know how to talk about it. I think even if I did, no one would understand."

That one sentence was a doorway. Not because we found the answer, but because we stopped searching for it. From then on, we said less and sat more. We offered presence instead of questions. We said, "I see you," and, "It's okay if you don't want to talk. I'm here."

You can try something similar. Walk together after dinner without talking. Sit beside her when she plays, not asking but simply being there. During a quiet moment, say gently, "You seem tired lately." Not to press for a response. Just to show that you notice.

Sometimes, children close the door not because they want to keep us out, but because they don't know how to invite us in. Let her know you are there, that she doesn't have to be ready yet, that your love does not depend on answers.

If you are looking for guidance, here are a few widely respected books we often recommend to parents at Tianjin Ruide Kindergarten:

- *The Whole-Brain Child* by Daniel J. Siegel and Tina Payne Bryson

- *How to Talk So Kids Will Listen & Listen So Kids Will Talk* by Adele Faber and Elaine Mazlish

- *Raising Human Beings* by Ross W. Greene

- *No-Drama Discipline* by Daniel J. Siegel and Tina Payne

Bryson

- *Parenting from the Inside Out* by Daniel J. Siegel and Mary Hartzell

- *Hold On to Your Kids* by Gordon Neufeld and Gabor Maté

- *Nonviolent Communication* by Marshall B. Rosenberg

These books do not offer formulas. They offer perspectives. They help us see that behavior is communication, and that silence is often a child's way of saying, "I'm still figuring it out."

In the Autopoietic Children's Education system, we believe that each child is a self-generating process, unfolding at their own rhythm. They are not puzzles to solve. They are lives in motion. Our task is not to unlock them, but to wait for them to return, when they are ready, with their own language and their own story.

She may not talk much now. But she will. And when she does, it will be because she trusts that you are the one who never stopped listening.

Question 7: Children Who Seem Hyperactive

Question. My child becomes completely wild when playing. He cannot stop, and no matter how many times I call his name, he doesn't respond. It feels like he's in a world of his own, completely shut off from everything else. Only when I physically hold him does he begin to calm down. But he does not have autism. What should I do about this?

Answer. Dongling Wang / Teacher, Tianjin Ruide Kindergarten:

Thank you for describing your child's state with such care. I can imagine how it feels to watch a little whirlwind race through the house, cheeks flushed, sweat dripping, your heart anxious that he might bump into something while you try again and again to call him back. And yet, it's as if he doesn't hear you. That sense of "not being able to catch him" can be both exhausting and overwhelming.

But please let me offer this first. This kind of wild play may not be a problem at all. It may simply be his way of being. Children at this age are not trying to make things difficult. They are using their bodies and emotions in the most honest way they know to explore their world and release their energy.

How old is your child? That age makes a big difference. Many children between the ages of three and five are bursting with energy and curiosity. Their brains and nervous systems are developing rapidly, especially the prefrontal cortex, which is responsible for self-regulation and impulse control. This part of the brain is still very immature. So, when your child cannot stop or respond right away, it's not because he is ignoring you. It's because his brain is still learning how to shift gears. He is like a train moving at full speed in a world he has created for himself. He isn't being defiant. He truly cannot hear you just yet.

We have met many children like this at Tianjin Ruide. I remember one boy, Rui, who would dive into the sandbox and disappear into another universe. He would plant trees, build castles, and dig tunnels. We could call his name three times, and he wouldn't respond. Sometimes he even frowned at the person trying to interrupt him. His mother was worried. She wondered if he was too obsessive, too difficult to manage.

But then we noticed something. When we walked over to him quietly, crouched beside him, and gently placed a hand on his shoulder while softly saying his name, he would slowly turn his head. His eyes would still be a little dreamy, as if waking from a deep place. In that moment, we knew he wasn't refusing us. He was simply still on his way back.

You mentioned that you have to hold him for him to calm down. That makes perfect sense. A hug is one of the most powerful and direct ways to connect with a young child. For them, language can feel too abstract or too far away. But the sensation of touch, the firmness of a safe embrace, tells them right away, "You are seen. I am here. It's time to return."

So, you're doing something beautiful. You've already discovered a way to connect with your child, and that way is through holding. Many parents, in their frustration, end up shouting or pulling, not realizing that what their child truly needs is not more volume but more resonance. A calm gaze, a low crouch, a whisper close to the ear often works better than ten loud commands.

Of course, if you begin to notice that your child becomes dangerously out of control when overstimulated, or if he shows aggressive behavior or cannot regulate his body at all, it might be wise to observe his behavior in other settings too. In that case, a consultation with a child development professional might help assess whether there are sensory or emotional regulation challenges that need support.

But based on your description, this sounds like a child who is simply using every ounce of his being to experience life. His wildness is full of vitality. His inability to stop is part of his deep desire to engage with the world. Our role is not to suppress that energy but to guide it, giving it shape and rhythm.

You can begin by setting gentle boundaries before play begins. Try saying, "You'll have twenty minutes to play, and then I'll let you know it's time to stop." Five minutes before the end, give him a soft reminder. When the time comes, crouch down and say warmly, "It's time to clean up. I'll help you." These kinds of structured transitions give children the practice they need to learn self-regulation. It also makes the process easier on you.

Children do not arrive in the world knowing how to "listen." They learn it through repeated moments of connection. You're already on that journey. May you continue to feel not only the fatigue but also the joy, the richness, and the life that your child brings to you.

We believe that when a child feels understood, their energy begins to settle into patterns of harmony and direction. And from there, they grow with strength, with clarity, and with light.

Question 8: Children Asking for Things

Question. My seven-year-old son just started first grade. Lately, he's been constantly asking for things that his classmates have. One day it's a pencil case, the next it's a water bottle, then it's a new sticker book. I feel like he's becoming too competitive and materialistic. How can I guide him in the right direction?

Answer. Sha Liu / Teacher, Tianjin Ruide Kindergarten:

Thank you for sharing this, and for opening your heart to talk about something that worries many parents. First, let me say that your child is on the path of growing up, and this journey has only just begun. He is just seven years old, taking his first steps into the small but expanding world of elementary school. His curiosity about others, his urge to imitate, and even his desire to have what his peers have are all natural behaviors at this stage.

I noticed that you used the word "competitive." That word often carries a shadow of judgment, as if this behavior is already a problem. I completely understand your concern. We all hope our children will grow up independent, thoughtful, and able to make their own choices without always comparing themselves to others. But from a child's perspective, this kind of mimicking may not be competition at all. It may simply be how he is trying to make sense of the world.

So perhaps, instead of rushing to correct him or saying, "You shouldn't compare," we can begin by sitting down beside him and gently asking, "Sweetheart, I've noticed that when you see someone with some-thing new, you really want one too. Can you tell me what makes you want it?" That question may seem simple, but it opens a door. Your child might say, "Because it looks cool," or "Because everyone else has one and I don't." Or he might not know how to put it into words at all, and just say, "I just want it."

At that moment, patience matters. You might say, "I see that you really like that pencil case. It is special, isn't it?" Or, "I hear you when you say everyone else has one. Do you feel a little left out when you don't?" This kind of conversation helps him begin to understand his own feelings. It shows that we are listening, not blaming.

This kind of "wanting" is part of social learning. Children use material things to test, in their own way, whether they belong. They are wondering, "Am I part of this group?" or "Will I be liked if I have this too?" It's not wrong. It's a part of growing.

So, what can we do as adults? We can walk alongside them as they explore other ways to feel included. We can help them discover that there are many ways to connect, not just by owning the same object. We can even take them shopping and say, "Let's find something you truly love, not just something someone else has." This gently shifts their attention from copying to choosing.

There was a boy at our school who went through a very similar phase. For five days in a row, he begged his mom to buy shoes just like his classmate's. At first, she was upset. But after calming down, she asked him, "Do you like those shoes because of how they look? Or because you think they'll make you feel cool like your friend?" He paused, then said, "I think he runs really fast in them." That answer revealed something deeper. What he really admired was the idea of speed. So, they found a pair of shoes that he loved and were great for running. They even made a plan to practice running together. He was thrilled, not because they were the same as someone else's, but because they were truly his.

So instead of telling him, "Don't compare," try helping him uncover what he really wants. Is it the design on the pencil case? Is it the feeling of being noticed? Or is it just a way to have something to talk about with friends? When those underlying desires are seen and named, the surface-level "I have to buy it" often fades on its own.

Education is not about teaching children to give up wanting. It is about helping them understand why they want something. Once they understand, the seeds of growth begin to take root.

Please trust that your child does not want to become "the one who has everything." He is simply trying to figure out how to stand tall in this big, complex world. And you are his most gentle and steady guide.

Question 9: Children Who Have Trouble Focusing

Question. My child has trouble focusing and seems obsessed with watching TV.

What should we do as parents?

Answer. Yingying Zheng, Teacher at Tianjin Ruide:

This question may appear simple, but it carries more depth than it seems. When we say a child cannot focus, what exactly do we mean? Is it that they lose attention within minutes of starting homework? That they glance around during meals? Or that they begin reading but soon drift toward the screen?

Before we try to fix anything, it helps to reflect on the specifics. In what settings does your child lose focus most easily? Are there moments when they actually show strong concentration, such as when building with blocks, drawing, or playing a favorite game?

Often, the phrase "lack of focus" is just a label. It rarely tells the whole story. If a child can remain deeply engaged in something they love, their ability to focus already exists. It may just be waiting to be activated in other areas. Instead of rushing to correct, we might begin by observing more closely. What truly interests them? How do they become absorbed? Have we offered them the freedom to explore in ways that invite engagement?

Another important aspect to consider is our own emotional state when the child becomes distracted. Are we already frowning, pressuring, or blaming? Children are remarkably sensitive to these subtle cues. They do not suppress emotions the way adults do. They respond through behavior. The more anxious we become, the more we push for control, the harder it may be for them to remain calm and present.

This is why I often encourage parents to begin with self-awareness. When your child appears to zone out, are you feeling tense? When they turn to the television, do you feel frustrated or helpless? The emotional environment we create has a direct impact on their ability to focus. A household filled with stress rarely fosters the kind of attention we hope to see.

We must also acknowledge something about the world we live in. Screens are incredibly stimulating for a child's brain. The bright colors, rapid cuts, and instant rewards provide a kind of excitement that quiet activities often cannot match. Reading, writing, or crafting require the mind to slow down. Without meaningful alternatives, taking screens away can feel like pulling a child from a festival into an empty room.

In many cases, what appears to be screen obsession is actually a reflection of unmet needs. Some children turn to television because they feel lonely. Others may be longing for real connection or interaction. There are also children who do not feel confident in real-world tasks, and the screen becomes a source of easy satisfaction.

So, when a child cannot concentrate across all areas, the core issue may not be attention itself. It may be rooted in emotion or relationship. That is where we need to begin.

Try speaking to your child gently during a quiet moment. Get down to their eye level. Ask softly, "Have you been feeling upset about anything lately?" or "Do you ever feel like your mind is full and can't hold anything more?" These conversations may not bring immediate answers. But they plant seeds. And over time, those seeds grow.

Creating a calm and accepting home is the first step toward restoring focus. When a child feels understood, their heart begins to settle. When the heart is still, the eyes can follow, and attention begins to return.

So instead of reacting with quick corrections or turning off the TV in frustration, try beginning with understanding. Begin with emotional clarity. Begin with one warm and open conversation each day. When we move one step closer to our children, they often meet us halfway. Growth does not happen in a moment. It happens slowly, through connection and trust.

You are already paying close attention to your child's inner world. That alone is the best place to start. Keep walking with that awareness, and you will find the path that leads to them.

Question 10: Children Facing Challenges

Question. My child always backs down when something feels hard. He says, "I can't," or "It's too difficult," or "I don't want to do it." How should we guide him in a healthy and constructive way?

Answer. Zheng Yingying | Tianjin Ruide Kindergarten:

This is such an honest and common question. When a child meets a challenge and immediately says, "I can't," or "It's too hard," or "I don't want to," it can stir up anxiety in any parent. Why does it seem like they're so afraid of struggle?

But before we label our children as "afraid of hardship," it might help to pause for a moment and gently ask ourselves, "What am I really seeing? And why does this reaction bring up such strong feelings in me?"

For many of us, especially in the way we were raised, "endurance" and "grit" were seen as signs of virtue. Perhaps we were taught not to complain, to keep going no matter how tired or scared we were. Those early lessons often linger in us, so when we see our own children want to give up, something old and unresolved rises up inside us. We feel worried. We feel disappointed. And yes, sometimes, we feel angry too. These feelings are valid. Every parent wants their child to grow up strong, capable, and resilient.

But before we rush in to correct what we see as weakness, we need to understand what the child is really experiencing. What is this child, right now, going through when they say, "I don't want to"?

In the Autopoietic Education System, we view every child as a living, self-organizing system. Each "no," each "I don't want to," is not simply resistance. It is a form of communication. It is the child showing us their pace, their boundaries, and where they are at this moment. Just like an actor on a stage cannot step into a role until they are truly ready, a child who hasn't yet sorted through their internal experience cannot be expected to leap toward a challenge.

So, let's begin with something specific. Say your child refuses to join a physical activity or doesn't want to complete a difficult task. Instead of insisting, you might try kneeling down beside them and gently asking, "What feels hardest right now? Is your body tired? Or does it just feel hard in your heart to keep going?" If they don't have the words to answer, you can help by offering possibilities. "Is it because other kids seem faster?" or "Are you worried you won't make it all the way through?"

When we approach our children with curiosity instead of criticism, they have a chance to truly meet themselves. When we draw near with understanding instead of urgency, they may finally open up about that quiet fear sitting inside. Understanding does not mean lowering expectations. It means we create a bridge to the child's world instead of standing on the other side shouting at them to cross.

Of course, guidance matters too. But true guidance often looks nothing like a lecture. It looks more like a new kind of experience. For example, if you want to take your child hiking and you frame it as "training your willpower" or "good for your body," they may tune out immediately.

But if you say, "Let's become forest detectives today. We're going to find three kinds of leaves and one bug that doesn't fly," you might be surprised how far they are willing to climb.

A child's growth is like a living play unfolding before our eyes. They don't need to become a copy of someone else. They need space to try, to stumble, to test, and to feel for themselves what it means to move forward. And the parent? The parent is not the director shouting cues, but the one in the audience who claps, who waits, who sometimes walks on-stage to hold their hand. We are not here to script their lives, but to walk with them through each hard, beautiful moment.

So, when your child hesitates or pulls back, don't rush to fix it. Stay close. Listen deeply. Be still enough to let them find their own rhythm again. When the inside feels ready, the outside movement will follow. Not because they are afraid to disappoint you, but because they begin to believe, "I actually can." Because real growth is never something taught. It is something awakened.

Question 11: Children Wetting the Bed

Question. My child still wets the bed. How can we help him?

Answer. Zheng Yingying | Tianjin Ruide Kindergarten:

When a child wets the bed, many parents naturally begin by looking at physical reasons. Perhaps the bladder hasn't matured, the child sleeps too deeply, or drinks too much water before bedtime. These are important factors to consider. But often, the deeper cause lies in a space we cannot immediately see. It might be rooted in the child's emotional state, the energy of the home, or an unspoken tension within the family.

Let me share a true story from our school. Xiaoxi, a boy a little over six years old, went through a period when he wet his pants almost every day. We first checked for any health concerns. Everything was normal. That told us his body wasn't the issue. Something deeper was asking to be heard. His behavior was his language. He was telling us something, but not with words.

We did not blame or shame him. We accepted what was happening with patience and began to look more closely at his family environment.

Over time, we discovered that his parents were seen by others as kind and agreeable. They never argued, rarely raised their voices, and always appeared calm. At first glance, the home felt peaceful. But beneath the surface was a quiet tension. There were emotions that had never been expressed. Anger, frustration, sadness. All hidden and unspoken.

Xiaoxi was a sensitive child. He could feel the emotions no one talked about. He didn't try to suppress them like his parents. Instead, he absorbed them. He couldn't yet separate what he felt from what belonged to others. All he knew was that something didn't feel right. He couldn't name it. He couldn't explain it. So, he used his body to release what he could not express.

That is when we began to support him using the Autopoietic Drama-Based Emotional Education approach. We helped him learn to recognize and name his feelings. We helped him begin to understand which emotions were his and which were not. We would gently tell him things like, "Sometimes Daddy feels upset. That feeling belongs to Daddy. You don't have to hold it for him." At the same time, we encouraged his parents to begin expressing more of what they were truly feeling. To let emotions be seen. To allow space for honest expression. Slowly, Xiaoxi began to change. The bedwetting became less frequent. Eventually, it stopped completely.

What touched us even more was how he began to use his new awareness. One day, he noticed something in his father's mood and said, "Are you feeling something right now? What is it? You can say it out loud." That is exactly what we hope our children can do. To understand their own emotions. To sense others. And to respond with clarity instead of fear.

So, when a child wets the bed, please don't rush to correct or control. Don't label the behavior as laziness or misbehavior. Begin by asking, what is this child trying to tell me? Is there something we've been holding back at home? Is the child speaking for us in ways we haven't dared to speak?

From the perspective of autopoiesis, every behavior is an expression of life. The child is not the problem. The child is the mirror. Rather than trying to fix him, begin by listening.

A child's growth is never a path walked alone. It is the movement of the whole family. It is the energy of the household slowly shifting. When we allow old patterns to soften, when we speak more honestly and gently, when emotions are welcomed instead of hidden, then the child no longer needs to speak through the body.

Growth is never just about the child. It is a quiet healing of the family. A shared awakening, tender and deep, that begins with each of us.

Question 12: Children Struggling With School Grades

Question. When a child tries hard but still doesn't get good grades, should parents step in more or ease off?

Answer. Xueming Wang | Tianjin Ruide:

This is not a simple question of "should I control or should I let go." It's an invitation to look deeper and ask what is really happening beneath the surface of a child's struggle with school.

Sometimes, what we see as academic problems are really signals of something else. If a child is living in a tense home, often feels sick, or experiences rejection at school, their focus naturally shifts toward survival. In those cases, their energy is not available for math problems or writing assignments. It is tied up in more urgent emotional needs.

On the other hand, if a child's challenge is rooted in something more practical, like a missing foundation in a subject, irregular routines, or a mismatch between how they learn and how they are taught, then the answer is not to scold or push harder. It is to support them with tools that actually help. Maybe that means a gentle tutor they feel comfortable with, more consistent study habits, or a quieter space for concentration. This is not about controlling a child's behavior. It is about helping them use their energy more effectively.

Still, the most important truth might be this: the fact that your child is trying already means something. The willingness to put in effort, even when results fall short, shows that something inside them wants to grow. That effort itself is the beginning of something strong. It reflects the natural drive of a young life to organize, to improve, and to keep moving forward.

As a parent, you can nurture this drive not by demanding more, but by helping your child find something that responds to their effort. It might not be in reading or math. It might be in painting, building, story-telling, or planting a seed and watching it grow. If they can see their own progress, if they can feel their own power through experience, the desire to learn will rise from within. It will not need to be pushed. It will not need to be forced.

Letting go means releasing our fixed expectations about what a good grade looks like. Holding on means staying present and not letting our disappointment damage their self-trust.

The current education system does not fit every child, and test scores only measure a small part of who they are. So rather than saying, "You must get this grade," you can say, "You can take a different pace or path, but you may not give up on yourself. As long as you keep walking, I will be right here with you."

This is the heart of Autopoietic Drama-Based Emotional Educa-tion. We believe every child carries within them a complete and living sys-tem, one that can grow when it is seen and supported, not when it is man-aged or controlled. Education is not about filling in answers. It is about walking alongside a child as they search for meaning that is their own.

If your child knows they are loved regardless of outcome, and that their effort matters just because it is real and honest, they will begin to trust themselves. When that trust returns, something extraordinary begins. They start growing, not because we told them to, but because they found something inside worth growing for.

Question 13: Children With Repetitive Behaviors (Such as Biting Nails)

Question. My daughter is two years and nine months old. Lately, she has been chewing on her fingers and biting her nails. She also insists on sleeping with the same blanket every night and bites it to fall asleep. I'm not sure how to guide her, and I'm worried it might become a habit. I wonder if this is related to an unmet need during the oral stage or maybe built-up emotional stress. If so, how can I help her?

Answer. Teacher Wang Xueming | Tianjin Ruide:

Whenever young children repeat behaviors like biting nails, sucking fingers, or clinging to a certain blanket, they are often sending out quiet signals about how safe or regulated they feel inside. These little habits may look small, but they are ways of saying, "I'm trying to comfort myself."

Before trying to stop the behavior, it's important to take a step back and understand what might be behind it. As you thoughtfully guessed, it could be linked to needs from the oral stage or emotional tension that has built up over time. At the root of it all, though, is a deeper question. Does your child have a space where she feels safe enough to regulate her own feelings?

In the framework of Autopoietic Child Psychology, we believe every child is a self-organizing and self-regulating being. What might look like a habit or dependency is often a child's way of managing her emotions. Rather than trying to remove the behavior, we can gently guide her toward healthier ways of finding comfort.

There are two areas you might explore:

First, take a look at the energy in your home.

Has the environment felt rushed, tense, or overly controlled? Has your child been frequently interrupted or asked to meet expectations that feel overwhelming? When a home's emotional tone becomes anxious or hurried, children often respond by turning to repetitive behaviors for comfort. It helps to ask yourself honestly, "How have I been feeling lately? Am I calm, or have I been anxious about her habits?" When you begin to slow down and bring steadiness into the space, she will feel that shift too.

Second, avoid stopping the behavior directly. Instead, offer alternatives with warmth and connection.

If you simply tell her to stop chewing or biting, it may feel like you're taking away the one thing that gives her relief. This can create frustration or confusion. A better approach is to join her emotionally. During bedtime, you might say, "Was there anything today that made you feel a little sad?" or "I love snuggling with you. Let's hold this blanket and tell a story together." These moments help her feel seen and understood. They also show her that comfort can come from human connection.

Over time, you can gently introduce something new for her to hold, like a soft scarf or a small stuffed animal that she chooses. Let it become part of a loving routine. There is no need to rush. This transition works best when it happens slowly and with care.

What she needs most is not a correction but a rebuilding of trust and safety. Her habits are not signs of defiance or stubbornness. They are her own way of managing something inside that feels too big to handle on her own. If we can listen to her without judgment, we begin to understand what she cannot yet say in words.

Eventually, when she feels secure and connected, she will naturally let go of those habits. Not because someone told her to, but because she no longer needs them to feel okay in the world.

Her journey is not about being fixed. It is about being understood. And when that happens, she will be able to move forward with a deep sense of peace.

Question 14: Children Who Fidget or Have a Lack of Focus

Question. My child can never seem to sit still or focus during class at preschool. What should I do?

Answer. Teacher Li Mengling | Tianjin Ruide:

When a child struggles to sit still, seems constantly distracted, or finds it hard to focus, what we're really seeing is not a problem to fix, but a window into their developing ability to pay attention. Understanding where a child is in their attention development is the first step in helping them grow.

For children between the ages of two and six, attention develops in stages, and each stage is closely tied to how their nervous system is maturing.

Typically, between ages two and four, children operate mainly with what we call "involuntary attention." This means their focus is easily drawn by outside stimuli and tends to shift quickly, often lasting just three to five minutes at a time.

Around age four or five, children begin to show signs of "voluntary attention," and they may be able to stay focused for about ten minutes.

By age five to six, this voluntary attention gradually strengthens, and some children can sustain focus for up to fifteen minutes, depending on the situation.

These timeframes, of course, are averages. Every child is a unique and living system in motion, adjusting and evolving with their own internal rhythm.

In Autopoietic Child Psychology, we look beyond isolated behaviors. We ask: Is the child surrounded by an environment that allows focus to grow? Does the child have space to regulate themselves without constant interruption? Are there moments—at home or at school—when their concentration is frequently disrupted?

This is where the deeper work begins.

Take, for example, a child who is fully immersed in building with blocks or drawing a picture. A parent might interrupt with the softest of intentions, saying, "Come have a snack" or "Let's take off your jacket" or "I'll get you a different toy." These well-meaning gestures can quietly chip away at a child's ability to stay with the present moment.

The same happens at school. A child might just be entering a focused state when a schedule shift suddenly requires them to stop and move on. Over time, this can teach the body not to trust focus at all.

We must begin to see that a child at play is a child learning. Attention is not something that only exists at a desk. If a child cannot focus during play, they will likely struggle even more during structured lessons.

So, what can you do?

First, protect their focus.

When your child is deeply engaged, try not to interrupt. If you absolutely need to, give a gentle heads-up like, "In five minutes, we'll go wash our hands." This helps the child prepare, and also builds their sense of timing and control.

Second, take a closer look at what "struggling in class" really means.

If a teacher has raised concerns, take time to speak with them. Ask:

In which activities is my child most restless?

Is this happening all the time or only during specific lessons?

Are there any subjects or projects where they seem highly focused?

At home, when does my child seem most calm and engaged?

These questions help distinguish whether the issue is with the teaching method, the content being too easy or too hard, or whether there are other emotional, relational, or environmental factors at play.

We must resist the urge to label a child as "unfocused" too quickly. Often, their behavior is not a problem to be fixed, but a signal that their environment needs adjusting.

Finally, invite your child into the conversation.

You might ask softly, "Do you like art class?" or "Is math class boring or a little hard?" or "Do you ever feel hungry or uncomfortable during class?" Giving your child a voice in their own experience helps them feel seen and respected. That alone can shift their sense of presence.

This is the heart of autopoietic education. We believe every child has the ability to self-organize and grow from within. Our role is not to manage or mold them, but to listen for the rhythm of their becoming.

If we take the time to hear their world, we'll see that most children do not resist focus. What they need is a space where their rhythm is met with understanding, where their silence is not mistaken for disobedience, and where their growth is not rushed but trusted.

Question 15: Children Who Can't Sit Still and Just Wants to Play

Question. My child can't sit still. She doesn't like reading, just wants to play, and spends too much time watching the iPad. What should I do?

Answer. Teacher Li Menglin | Tianjin Ruide Kindergarten:

Before we correct our child, we need to ask why she prefers the iPad, why she plays so much, and why reading doesn't interest her.

Let's start with her love of screens and her constant need to play. First, how much time is she actually spending on the iPad? Many children enjoy screens. So do adults. The issue isn't whether she watches, but how often, and whether it's replacing other important experiences.

You also mentioned that she just wants to play. But isn't that true for every child? Play is their nature. It's how they explore and make sense of the world. Maybe what worries you is that she plays too much and doesn't spend enough time learning new skills or reading books. That's a valid concern, but we need to first understand her world.

Children today are growing up in a world surrounded by technology. Even a toddler can instinctively swipe on a screen. I've seen many families where, when a child cries or fusses, the first response is to hand them a phone or the iPad. At home, if the adults are always on their devices, scrolling or playing games, it's natural for the child to follow that pattern.

But if you really watch closely, you'll notice something important: children actually prefer to play with people. Play is richer, warmer, more satisfying than anything on a screen. No child would rather stare at a device than share laughter and connection with a parent—unless that connection isn't available.

What your child needs is your presence. And not just being in the same room, but a kind of presence that's full of attention, joy, and warmth. When you sit with her, play with her, look into her eyes, and really join her world, she will almost always choose you over the screen.

And when you do spend time with her, make that time count. Put your phone away. Don't take calls. Be fully there. That's what meaningful connection looks like. I once saw a little girl run up to her mother, excited to show the coloring she had done. Her mother looked at it and said calmly, "Oh, you colored it. But that sun is the wrong color. The picture shows yellow. You used green. Suns aren't green."

The child replied, "But I want it to be green."

Her mother said again, "Look carefully. What color should it be?"

The girl insisted, "I just like this one."

The mother kept trying to correct her, and the child's excitement slowly faded. Her joy turned into silence. Her face looked confused and hurt.

What if the mother had said, "Wow, a green sun! That's so creative. I've never seen one like that before." What if she had been curious, instead of correcting? For all we know, maybe the child really saw the sun that way, in her own inner world. Sometimes, we need to set aside our expectations and let ourselves enter our child's imagination, not the other way around.

Now about reading. It's true that some children are born with a love of books. At Tianjin Ruide Kindergarten, we had a boy who was one year and nine months old, and he was already deeply in love with reading. His mom told us that even when he cried, handing him a book would calm him instantly. When we read stories in class, he listens with incredible focus and stays engaged from beginning to end.

Maria Montessori once wrote in The Absorbent Mind that adults can remember and think about things from their surroundings, but children absorb those things. What they see and hear becomes part of who they are. While adults might ignore what's around them, children shape their very self from it. That's why Montessori said the most important thing in education is the environment we create.

So, if you want your child to enjoy reading, then create a reading-friendly home. This means having books available. Create a cozy space for reading. Most importantly, let her see you reading too.

Children don't develop a love of books through pressure or rules. They fall in love with books when they feel curious and safe, when they're invited into a world of stories, not pushed into one.

So before worrying too much, take a moment to ask yourself:

What kind of environment have we built at home?

Are we offering real connection and play?

Are we inviting her into the world of books in a gentle way?

When we choose connection over correction, when we invite instead of demand, we open the door for our children to love learning in their own way and time. Often, that's all they need.

Question 16: Children Respecting Rules and Boundaries

Question. My child is very smart but seems to lack a sense of rules. What should I do?

Answer. Zhang Feifei, Teacher at Tianjin Ruide Kindergarten:

From the way this question is phrased, it feels like you are both proud of your child's intelligence and also concerned about the lack of boundaries. When we talk about a child having "no sense of rules," what exactly do we mean? Is it that the child does not follow the teacher's guidance in class? Does the child struggle with classroom routines, or are there other signs? To answer this properly, we need to look at the specific situations.

It is also important to consider whether boundaries and rules have been clearly set at home. Sometimes, when a child is very smart and picks things up quickly, parents may place a strong focus on academic or intellectual growth and unintentionally overlook the importance of behavioral development. If, as a result, we fail to guide the child in following rules and respecting limits, the child may gradually come to believe, "I can do whatever I want."

This is not about blaming or labeling. Rather, it is an invitation to reflect. When expectations around behavior are not made clear, and when a child is not encouraged to respect shared boundaries, it becomes difficult for them to understand their role in a group setting or why rules exist in the first place.

So before trying to correct the behavior, take time to observe what is happening. Are there consistent routines at home? Has the child been part of conversations about what is allowed and what is not? Do they understand why certain rules are in place?

Establishing boundaries is not about strict control. It is about creating a sense of safety, predictability, and mutual respect. For a bright child, this can be a crucial learning experience. When we introduce rules with patience and clarity, children do not feel restricted. Instead, they feel grounded. They begin to understand that true intelligence includes learning how to relate to others and how to grow within a shared space.

At Tianjin Ruide Kindergarten, we believe that rules are part of a healthy emotional environment. They are not there to limit a child, but to support the development of social awareness and emotional balance. When a child knows what to expect and feels respected within those expectations, they are more likely to develop both responsibility and inner strength.

Question 17: Children Who Are More Cautious and Timid

Question. My child seems overly cautious and timid. How can I help her become more open and braver?

Answer. Li Mengling, Teacher at Tianjin Ruide Kindergarten:

This question reminds me of a little girl named Xiaoyu at Tianjin Ruide. I first met her when she was one year and seven months old. At the time, I was sitting with her parents near the drama corner while she stood silently by the toy kitchen, just watching us without moving for almost twenty minutes. Eventually, she began to play with the kitchen toys and would occasionally come over to interact with us.

After about two months at Tianjin Ruide, Xiaoyu changed a lot. She could greet unfamiliar people and use her voice with confidence, even in new environments. Her mother once told us that while riding the bus, Xiaoyu saw a crowd in front of her and politely said, "Excuse me, please make way." It's hard to believe she was only one year and nine months old.

Another child, not yet three years old, once refused to eat winter jujubes when she first arrived at Tianjin Ruide. She would spit them out immediately. We later found out she had never eaten them before. At the time, I simply invited her to lick the fruit and try its taste. The second time, she managed a small bite. Over time, she learned to enjoy all kinds of fruit and grew to love them.

When we say a child is too cautious or timid, what exactly are we noticing? Some behaviors that seem timid to adults, such as standing quietly and not participating, may actually be the child observing and making sense of their surroundings in their own way.

If adults respond with pressure or phrases like "Don't be so shy" or "Be brave, there's nothing to be afraid of," it can often backfire. The child might begin to believe they are timid by nature, or that something is wrong with them. This can lead to confusion or inner conflict because they are already processing the world with their own understanding, and they long for acceptance.

It helps to first observe when and where your child seems cautious. Are they facing something truly unfamiliar or difficult? Could the situation be too complex or overwhelming? Or does the challenge exceed their current capacity, which makes them hesitate?

The next step is to gently talk with your child. Try to understand why they didn't want to act at that moment. Let them know it's okay not to do something right away. If their hesitation comes from worry or a sense that they are not yet capable, then we can offer the support they need.

Most importantly, we need to look at the whole picture. Take the time to observe your child, to understand them, and also to understand your own reactions. Whenever we feel unsure about how to help our child, the first step is not to change who they are but to support who they are becoming. Our goal is not to reshape them into someone else but to help them grow into the person they already are.

Question 18: How to Talk to my Child's Teacher

Question. Today during PE class, my daughter Shanshan, who is seven, was caught talking to a classmate. The teacher, upset in the moment, pushed her by the shoulder. Shanshan immediately stopped talking, but when she turned around and our eyes met, I saw tears running down her face. At that moment, I didn't do anything. She turned her back to me and kept crying quietly. Later, when I held her, she cried even harder. Her mood stayed very low. She often says she feels useless. Could this be related? What should I do?

Answer. Liu Sha, Teacher at Tianjin Ruide Kindergarten:

May I ask, are you the parent? If so, why were you present during her PE class? Did the school invite parents to observe, or were you there for another reason? More importantly, what did you do when you saw what happened? Was the teacher still nearby when you went to hold your daughter?

These details matter because without knowing what happened before and after the incident, it is difficult to respond fully. But if you, as her parent, witnessed the teacher physically push your daughter and did not intervene or ask what happened, then your child may have experienced more than just the pain of being pushed. She may also have felt abandoned.

At Tianjin Ruide, we do not support any form of corporal punishment. We believe that physical force, even when minor, can damage a child's sense of safety and dignity. This belief is deeply connected to the vision of our founder, Dr. Jiawei Liu, who is a psychologist. Our entire educational philosophy is built on the idea that every child is a living, self-organizing system. When a child is hurt, especially in a setting that is supposed to be safe, their ability to trust, to express, and to grow is disrupted.

What matters most now is how you respond going forward.

First, please take time to talk with your daughter. Let her know that what happened was not okay, not because she was talking in class, but because her body and feelings were not respected. Acknowledge her pain, not just physically, but emotionally. Let her know that she is allowed to feel hurt, confused, even angry. These emotions are real and they deserve to be seen.

Second, talk with the teacher or school. Calmly and respectfully ask for an account of what happened. This is not about confrontation but about understanding. We teach children to say "Stop" when someone touches their body without permission. But for that to work, adults must first model that kind of boundary-setting. If a teacher crosses the line, even unintentionally, it is the parent's role to step in, not with blame but with clarity and protection.

In self-generating education, we believe that children are not passive recipients of rules and discipline. They are participants in a living system of mutual respect. When something goes wrong in that system, the solution is not silence or avoidance. It is repair. Children need to see that the adults around them are willing to stand up for them and speak out when something is not right.

Finally, I want to speak to your daughter's words: "I feel useless." This is heartbreaking. It tells us she is internalizing the shame and perhaps interpreting the teacher's action and your inaction as proof that she does not matter. This is where your response can begin to heal what was hurt. Reassure her that she is important, that her feelings are valid, and that you will always protect her, even if sometimes you do not respond quickly enough.

You might say, "I saw what happened today and I'm sorry I didn't come to you right away. That was my mistake. You didn't do anything wrong by talking. You're allowed to make mistakes, and no one should ever push you like that. I'm here. I see you. And I love you."

It is not too late. At seven years old, Shanshan still looks to you for safety, for truth, and for strength. When we respond with honesty and care, we are not just correcting one moment. We are restoring the entire field of trust in which a child grows.

In the self-generating model of education, growth is never about control. It is about connection, protection, and a deep respect for the child's whole being.

Question 19: How to Interact With a Withdrawn Child

Question. I am a kindergarten teacher currently working with a middle-level class this semester. There is a girl in my class who, as the semester nears its end, has never initiated a conversation with a teacher. When we try to talk with her, she rarely responds with words, and she shows very little physical reaction. When spoken to, she keeps her eyes lowered. Occasionally, I see her smiling and interacting with a few classmates, but as soon as she notices a teacher watching her, her face turns expressionless. How can I communicate and interact with a child like this?

Answer. Wang Dongling, Teacher at Tianjin Ruide Kindergarten:

Based on your description, this child appears to be very withdrawn. It is possible that she is carrying a great deal of tension or fear internally. In this case, the first step is to help her release the emotions that are stuck inside. Only then will it be possible for change to begin.

If her reluctance to speak happens only with teachers, you might want to talk with her parents. Was there a past incident involving a teacher or another adult that left a lasting negative impression? If there was a traumatic experience, it is important to seek guidance from a professional child psychologist as soon as possible.

Before interacting with her, take a moment to observe your own emotional state. With a child like this in your class, are you feeling anxious, frustrated, worried, or helpless? Try to understand the root of those feelings. If you approach her while carrying these emotions, it may affect your interaction. Children are highly sensitive to emotional energy. If you feel anxious, she will likely become tense as well. If you feel frustrated, she may become scared. If you feel helpless, she might distance herself or seem disengaged.

But if you can approach her in a calm, grounded, and emotionally neutral way, you may begin to close the distance between you. Start by simply observing what she enjoys. Notice which activities she's drawn to or what toys she prefers. You can gently join her in those activities or mirror her actions, gradually softening the invisible wall between you.

As she becomes more comfortable and perhaps starts to glance your way, try kneeling down to meet her at eye level and begin talking to her softly. Even if she doesn't respond, that's okay. If she doesn't reject you or walk away, that is already progress. Once you feel confident that she hears what you are saying, even if she chooses not to respond, you can try gently holding her hand or cupping her face, then looking into her eyes.

If she resists, that's alright too. You can begin to guess and reflect on what she may be feeling and what might be behind those feelings. For example, you might say, "Are you feeling nervous or a little scared? Is it because I'm a teacher? What are you worried about?" At this age, children often communicate more through emotion than through words. Understanding how she feels is the key to real connection.

If you guess correctly, she might cry, go silent, or quickly say no. These are all emotional responses. Your role at that moment is to validate her feelings and stay present with her. Let her cry if she needs to. Be there for her. Let her know, "Whatever you feel is welcome here. This is a safe space. I'm here with you because I care about you and I love you."

Throughout this process, your intention to truly connect must come from the heart. Words alone are not enough. When she begins to feel this level of connection, her heart will gradually open to you. After that, communication and interaction will come more naturally.

Of course, this kind of process takes time and requires a great deal of emotional steadiness from the teacher. At Tianjin Ruide Kindergarten, we often use gentle hugs to help a child's emotions flow more freely. We support children through focused presence, careful listening, and heartfelt empathy.

When a child's emotions begin to move, their clarity and vitality return. Your relationship with them naturally becomes closer. In the view of autopoietic education, the child is not a vessel to be corrected or shaped, but a living system in need of resonance. When we attune ourselves to their rhythms with patience and authenticity, the child's own self-regulating capacity will awaken from within.

Question 20: Children Procrastinating

Question. My five-year-old tends to dawdle, especially when it comes to eating and brushing teeth. I have to remind them again and again. What should I do?

Answer. Jiang Dongling, Teacher at Tianjin Ruide Kindergarten:

1. I suggest the adults at home start by reflecting on their own behavior. Do you, as a parent, also procrastinate or take your time with certain things? Children are masters of imitation. Behavioral patterns can be passed down, and they often reflect what they see.

The word "dawdling" is quite general, so it's important to clarify whether it is truly that the child is slow, or if it just feels that way to the adult. Adults and children naturally operate at different speeds. Children with different temperaments also complete tasks at different paces. If the child's abilities are still developing or if this slow pace is part of their natural rhythm, then we should learn to respect that. In general, children's actions are slower than those of adults. Sometimes it is not that the child is too slow, but that the adult is too anxious and overlooks the child's actual capabilities.

2.   If the child only seems to dawdle with certain tasks, we need to understand whether they are encountering difficulties with those tasks, or if they have emotional reactions to them, such as fear or frustration. If there are difficulties, help them solve the problem. If there are emotions involved, then address those emotions first.

3.   Sometimes children carry a heavy emotional burden, which can make them move slowly or appear not to hear what is being said. Their internal energy may be entirely spent managing their emotions. This is often the most confusing situation for parents. I remember a child whose parents were in constant disagreement and emotional coldness filled the home. The child, sensing this tension, became consumed by fear, sadness, and anger but did not know how to express it. What showed up on the outside was a withdrawn, slow-moving child who seemed lost in their own world, barely responding to others.

At Tianjin Ruide Kindergarten, we support children like this through warm physical touch, like hugs, and emotional understanding. We help them release the burden of these feelings before engaging in conversation with the parents to support the child's recovery and bring back their energy.

4.   When boundaries and rules at home are unclear, and parents often compromise, children will tend to test limits. In an environment without stable rules, children feel insecure and will naturally try to see how far they can push. This is when it becomes necessary to create clear boundaries and rules.

I suggest holding a family meeting with your child to discuss and agree on rules for meals and brushing teeth. At five years old, most children are fully capable of having a conversation with adults and expressing their opinions. Rules and limits only make sense and become meaningful to a child when they are built upon respect for their freedom and the space to explore. Only then will they be willing to follow them.

Of course, in my view, the most important factor for change lies in the parents' willingness to keep learning and continuously adjust themselves. This self-work strengthens the bond between parent and child. That bond is the most essential "first glue" of the relationship.

In autopoietic education, we do not see dawdling as a simple behavioral issue. We understand that a child is a self-organizing system constantly adjusting to their inner and outer environment. The real question is not how to make the child move faster, but how we can become better attuned to the rhythm of their unfolding.

Question 21: Children Asking Many Questions

Question. My nine-year-old son asks many questions. Sometimes he cannot answer them himself, and after I respond, he asks another new question. Could you recommend some books or methods to help us parents answer him more clearly?

Answer. Zhang Yiming, Tianjin Ruide Kindergarten:

At age nine, children begin to enter a stage of deeper thinking. It is natural for them to be curious and want to understand the world. This kind of active questioning is a good sign of development.

As parents, it is important to stay calm and patient. If you do not know the answer, it is okay to say so and look it up together. This shows your support and builds a healthy relationship.

Parents should also keep learning. Children can sense when adults stop growing, and it can make them feel disconnected. Facing your child's questions with openness, honesty, and curiosity is the best way to grow alongside them.

Question 22: Children Crying at School

Question. My child has been crying often at kindergarten lately, saying he misses his mom. The teacher couldn't do much to help. Later we found out it was due to a lack of security. How can we effectively strengthen a child's sense of security?

Answer. Zhou Ye, Tianjin Ruide Kindergarten:

Is this your child's first kindergarten? How long has he been attending? When your child cries, how did you conclude that it was caused by a lack of security? Has he shown any signs of insecurity before?

If this is his second or third kindergarten, it's important to find out whether this happened before or if it started only recently. If the issue is new, it's worth reflecting on any recent changes in the child's school or home life. Has anything shifted lately? Is mom experiencing stress from work, feeling exhausted, or dealing with family tension? Children are very sensitive to changes in the emotional environment around them. Even if we don't say anything, they can often sense that something feels different. They might not understand it clearly, but they begin to feel unsettled and express that discomfort by crying or clinging.

If there have been no major changes at home, it's a good idea to check if something unpleasant happened at school. When you're with your child, try to set your own emotions aside so that you can approach them with calm and steadiness. Hold your child gently and say something like, "Sweetheart, I've noticed you've been feeling sad about going to school and missing mommy. It's okay to miss me. It's okay to feel sad. You're allowed to cry when you need to. I will come pick you up at (specific time)." After your child has had a chance to release some emotions, observe how they respond. If you feel your child still seems worried, you can reassure them again by saying, "Mommy knows how to take good care of herself. You can feel safe and trust that I'll be just fine."

This kind of reassurance may need to be repeated many times. What matters most is the parent's emotional presence and stability. It is essential to accept the child's emotions with empathy and stay nearby with patience and warmth.

If your child is just beginning kindergarten, it's entirely normal for them to feel sad and miss their parents. The approach above can be a helpful way to support them through this transition.

If something specific has happened at school, parents need to look deeper into the incident so that they can help the child release the emotional weight of that experience and begin to heal.

Question 23: Children Struggling to Focus on Studying

Question. Lately, I've noticed that my child seems to only go through the motions when it comes to studying. When I'm right there, she performs well enough. But as soon as I walk away to do something else, she loses focus. This has become my biggest headache. What should I do?

Answer. Zhuang Yue, Tianjin Ruide Kindergarten:

Has your child always studied with you sitting beside her? If so, could your constant presence be making her feel watched or pressured, leaving her with little personal space? Does her study routine allow room for her own planning or decision-making?

You might start by having a gentle conversation with her. Ask how she has been feeling lately and what her thoughts are about studying. If she is facing any challenges, be sure to offer your support in a timely and calm manner. At the same time, take a moment to reflect on your own emotional reactions to her study habits. When you talk with her, be mindful not to let your frustration or anxiety color the conversation.

In truth, studying is a personal journey that belongs to the child. One of the most important steps is helping her realize that learning is her own responsibility. Once she understands this, her sense of ownership and motivation will grow, and you'll find yourself needing to worry less.

From the perspective of the autopoietic learning model we practice at Tianjin Ruide, each child is seen as a self-generating system. This means they need space to regulate their own pace, make internal choices, and gradually build an inner rhythm that supports long-term growth. If a child studies only when a parent is near, it may reflect a dependency on external structure. Our role is not to enforce discipline from the outside, but to help them generate it from within.

This can take time, but when children are respected as agents in their own learning, they become more than students who follow rules. They begin to create meaning, build confidence, and learn not just because they are told to, but because it makes sense to them. That is where true learning begins.

Question 24: Repairing the Parent-Child Bond

Question. My eldest son is twelve. Due to family circumstances, he lived with his aunt for two years. At the end of June, I brought him back to live with me. Right now, our parent-child relationship feels distant. He shows little motivation to study and often seems lazy or withdrawn. How can I repair our bond without becoming overly indulgent?

Answer. Wu, Tianmin Ruide Kindergarten:

Before making the decision to have your son live with his aunt, did you talk to him about it? How did he feel at the time? Has the distance between you only appeared recently, or was it already there before he left? If the relationship was already strained beforehand, then the causes likely go deeper. Rebuilding will take more time and a gentler, more thoughtful approach.

Find a moment to sit down with your child, without distractions, and talk through whatever might have made him feel uneasy. It may be the move to his aunt's home, or something earlier. What matters is that you give him space to speak, and that you listen fully. He needs to know that you care enough to hear him out.

During everyday life, keep communicating in ways that show him love. With a twelve-year-old entering adolescence, you will start to see more independence and stronger personal opinions. When you talk, focus on understanding his perspective rather than correcting him. Be open about your own thoughts, but also make room for his.

In the view of autopoietic development, relationships are not fixed or imposed from outside. They are systems that evolve through mutual recognition and connection. Your son is not just adapting to life with you again, he is also reshaping his inner world. What he needs most now is your steady presence, your patience, and your belief in him.

When we stand beside our children and truly see them, the bond begins to grow again. Not from pressure, but from quiet trust. Not from control, but from shared meaning. Relationships take time to mend, but they are alive. And with care, they can become even more whole than before.

Question 25: Children, Privacy, and Boundaries at Home

Question. My daughter is three years old. At home, her father and I often show affection in front of her, such as hugging, touching, and kissing. We are wondering if this might have a negative impact on her. Recently, she has developed a habit of running to the bathroom to watch either of us take a shower. She also asks about the differences between boys and girls. For example, she pointed at me and asked, "Daddy has a little penis, why don't you?" We try to explain honestly, but the grandparents keep saying things like, "A girl should not be around her father, and a boy should not be around his mother." How should we handle this?

Answer. Zhang, Guangtian Ruide Kindergarten:

Your daughter is at a perfectly natural stage of development. At age three, children begin to develop basic awareness of their bodies and start asking questions about physical differences. This is not a sign of anything problematic. On the contrary, it's a sign that her cognitive and emotional systems are becoming more integrated, and that she's ready to begin forming her earliest understandings of identity.

From the perspective of autopoietic development, a child is a self-forming system. She is constantly absorbing, organizing, and making sense of the world around her. At this age, her questions about the body are not sexual in the adult sense. They are about structure, belonging, and meaning. Your role as a parent is not to silence this curiosity, but to meet it with calm, truthful, and age-appropriate responses.

Here are some specific suggestions:

1. Normalize Curiosity:

    Let your daughter know it's okay to ask questions. You can say something simple like, "Yes, boys and girls have different bodies. You are curious, and that's normal." Avoid reacting with shock, shame, or awkwardness. Your emotional tone teaches her just as much as your words.

2. Offer Clear and Factual Information:

Use real terms for body parts, not nicknames or vague expressions. Picture books about the human body can help, especially those designed for toddlers and preschoolers. Read them together so she sees that learning about the body is part of everyday life.

3. Set Gentle Boundaries With Respect:

While it is fine for young children to be curious, it's also important to guide them toward respecting privacy. If she wants to be in the bathroom while someone is showering, you might say, "This is my private time. You have your body, and I have mine." Make it clear that everyone has the right to their own space without making her feel rejected.

4. Teach Body Autonomy and Safety:

Begin basic safety education by explaining which parts of the body are private and that no one is allowed to touch them without permission. Help her understand that she can always come to you if she feels uncomfortable.

5. Respond Thoughtfully to Elder Generational Views:

Traditional sayings like "a girl should avoid her father" often come from a time when open communication about bodies was discouraged. While it is important to respect the elders' care and concern, it is equally essential to follow what modern child psychology and early education research support. You can kindly explain that you are teaching your daughter about her body in a healthy and respectful way.

6. Embed Affection in Respect:

Expressing affection between parents is not harmful when it is modeled with respect and mutual care. Your child learns about relationships first by watching you. What matters most is the emotional tone. Loving gestures help children feel secure. Just be mindful of moments when she seeks reassurance or clarity.

At Tianjin Ruide Kindergarten, we understand that early child-hood education is not just about facts, but about how children experience the world emotionally and relationally. In a self-forming (autopoietic) system, every piece of experience contributes to how the child builds her inner world. What she needs is not less exposure, but more meaning. When you guide her with truth, gentleness, and consistency, you are helping her form a healthy relationship with herself and others.

Let your daughter grow up in a home where love is visible, questions are welcome, and her body is respected. That is how real safety is built, not from avoidance, but from connection.

Postscript

"If a soul be born not to be filled, but to unfold, then what, in truth, is the purpose of our teaching?" Some nights, after everything has quieted down and the children are asleep, I find myself sitting alone, just thinking. And I keep coming back to the same question. Why are we doing all this? What is it we truly hope to give?

Is it so our children can be outstanding? So, they can get ahead in life, win competitions, get into good schools? At first glance, that might seem like enough. But deep inside, I know it isn't. What moves us most isn't grades or prizes. It's the way we are present with our children. It's one life walking beside another, step by step, growing together.

In the work we do, especially within the world of autopoietic drama education, we are not here to shape children into someone else's idea of success. We are learning to wait. We are learning to stay close and present, allowing each child the freedom to grow in their own rhythm. Growth does not appear out of thin air. It begins in the smallest, most ordinary moments. It begins when a child reaches out with curiosity, when they try something new, when they fall and try again, and when they slowly start to recognize who they are becoming. This quiet unfolding is the heart of what we believe in.

Long ago, the Greeks spoke of seven arts. Grammar, logic, music, geometry, things that weren't meant only to be learned, but to help a person polish their soul. These were not tools. They were ways of understanding life, ways of aligning yourself with something larger. I think that is where true education finds its roots.

So, when we say we start with the child, we really mean it. We begin not with what to teach, but with who this person is. What they're feeling. What they're wondering about. What kind of silence they carry. What their eyes are searching for. We're not trying to fit them into a system. We are trying to meet them where they are.

We don't believe in one kind of success. We believe in rhythm. We believe in each child's own pace, their own flavor, their own way of walking through the world. A child doesn't grow like a program. They grow like a tree. With roots buried deep, with branches that stretch toward sunlight. Sometimes they bend in the wind. Sometimes they wait in the cold. Our role is not to cut or prune them into shape. Our role is to protect the roots.

That's what autopoiesis teaches us. That a living system survives by adapting, integrating, and creating from within. So, our work is not to fill children up with facts. It is to keep them connected to that inner source, to that quiet sense of "I am becoming."

And their growth won't look neat. It won't go in straight lines. They will stop. They will circle back. They might fall silent. And then one day, almost by surprise, you'll see it. They've stood up taller. They've found something inside themselves that can hold.

That is why we design our curriculum the way we do. Not just to teach, but to accompany. From a toddler just learning to be with others, to a high schooler beginning to feel a sense of purpose, we are always asking the same thing. What does it mean to walk with a child as they unfold?

At the root of everything, there is something hard to measure. It's not about how much they've learned. It's whether they feel their learning belongs to them. Whether it has roots. Whether it helps them make sense of who they are.

If we could give them anything, I hope it would be this. That they know what they feel, and they are not afraid of it. That they believe the world holds meaning. That they speak and listen not to win, but to connect.

That they see mistakes not as failure, but as part of the path. That they know becoming yourself is enough.

These are not goals we add to them. These are textures that rise up from within, when a child feels safe to grow. And this is where theater matters most. Not as performance, but as a space. A space where they can place what they don't yet have words for. Where they can cry through movement. Where they can laugh in a role. Where they rehearse being themselves. And we, we are just the ones who sit quietly, watching with care, holding space.

In this world, everything is so fast. It's easy to miss the way a child finishes their thought. But if we slow down, if we walk a little closer, if we take the time, we might find something else waiting for us. A world not built by those who win fastest, but by those who are kindest. The ones who notice. The ones who create gently.

We want to be part of that kind of future. To walk with you. Not to turn your child into someone else. But to make sure they get the chance to become fully themselves.

There is an old line from a Chinese poem that stays close to my heart. In Xǐ ér xì zuò, written by Su Shi of the Song Dynasty, he wrote,

"愿儿愚且鲁，无灾亦无忧。" Roughly translated, it means, "I only wish my child to be simple and sincere, and to live free from sorrow." We don't wish for our children to be small. We just hope they are real. Healthy. Joyful. Alive.

Education is not a race. It is not about arriving. It is about staying close. Being patient. Saying, "I see you. You're already enough. We'll take this one step at a time."

Over the years, I've learned that teaching is hard. But seeing a child, really seeing them, is harder. And more beautiful. To see beyond their grades. Beyond their good days. To see their fears. Their pauses. Their hopes they haven't said out loud yet.

Once, in drama class, a boy chose not to play a person at all. He said he wanted to be a rock. He said, "I just want to lie here and say nothing." I didn't push him. I didn't ask him to speak. I sat beside him and asked, "How long would you like to stay like this?" He looked at me and said, "Until I'm ready."

And I remember feeling something deep open in me. Not because he got up. But because he trusted me to wait.

So, what does it mean to truly honor a child? Maybe it means staying close when they feel unsure. Sitting still with them when they feel messy. Whispering, "This is okay. You are okay. We'll figure it out."

We call this autopoietic education. It sounds like a theory. But really, it's just believing that every child is already alive with meaning. They are not containers for us to fill. They are seeds. Some grow fast. Some wait a while. Our job is not to control the shape. Our job is to make space.

That's why we hold onto drama. Not to train performers. But to give them a place to be seen, to be felt, to be heard. Some of them cry there. Some of them laugh. And all of them are practicing being real.

Parents carry love, and with that, the fear of getting it wrong. I saw it. I've felt it. But I also believe the goal is not to run. It is to walk well. If a child grows up walking gently yet firmly, with peace in their spirit and pride in who they are, that is more than we could ever ask for.

We begin gently, close to the ground, where patience makes space for something lasting. We pay attention to whether they smiled today. Whether they lined up their shoes. Whether they tried to understand a friend's feelings. These are not small things. These are the roots.

That's why everything we do has a reason. Emotional learning helps them meet their feelings. Drama helps them speak. Projects help them choose. And we do it all not to win. But to help them grow with peace and with courage.

As teachers, we're growing too. We remind each other to slow down. To breathe. To never treat a child like a task. As we walk with them, we find ourselves learning again how to move through the world with tenderness and truth.

So maybe this letter is not just for you. Maybe it's for me too. To remind myself why we do this. To come back to what matters.

Because education, at its heart, is just one person choosing to walk beside another. It's not loud. It's not perfect. But it's real. And to me, that's everything.

So let us build not from the top, but from the root.

Let us wait with children, and not rush them.

Let us trust the small signs, and not chase big results.

Let us believe in slowness, and honor the unfolding.

Let us speak less to correct, and more to understand.

Let us choose presence over performance.

Let us offer steadiness, not pressure.

Let us shape not their path, but their strength to walk it.

Let us protect the soil, not pull at the stem.

Let us see not a task, but a whole becoming.

Let us remember that a child is not a plan, but a person.

Let us listen, truly listen, even when no words are said.

Let us teach not for the world's approval, but for a soul's freedom.

And let us walk with them, step by step, not to lead, but to stay.

—Jiawei Liu

Father of two children

Acknowledgments

As I was writing this book, I want to give my deepest thanks to Tianjin Ruide International Kindergarten. I am grateful to every teacher, parent, and child there. Their support and the data they shared gave me the foundation to complete this work. Without them, this book could not have been written.

I also want to extend my deepest gratitude to my friend, Dr. Eric Zhou Hanning. We first met during an audition for one of my stage plays, where he came to participate as an actor. Our conversations were a joy, yet what impressed me even more was his humility and the extraordinary depth of his knowledge. As a scholar and an expert in artificial intelligence, his academic journey began during his undergraduate years at Tsinghua University, where he was already engaged in pioneering research in the field. His expertise has since matured into a distinguished doctoral career, and I have learned a great deal from both his insights and his way of being. It was a true honor to invite him to write a foreword for this book. His contribution is more than an introduction; it is a dialogue of ideas that enriches the entire work and reflects the depth of his wisdom.

I am especially thankful to Dr. Mariana Grohowski, who also served as the editor of my doctoral dissertation. She has continued to help me with humility and care. In one of her messages she said, "It was my honor to be able to read and learn from you. Maybe instead of crediting me as an editor an acknowledgment for being an early reader and offering some editorial support is more appropriate." These words show her deep modesty. To me, she has been both a mentor and a friend. Having her support is a true honor in my life.

I must also thank my family with all my heart. While I was working on this book, I was taken to the emergency room twice, once for asthma and once for a sudden heart problem. My wife, while seven months pregnant, stayed with me late into the night and gave me strength and comfort. My elder son, whenever I was tired or weak, ran toward me with love and gave me hope again. I am six feet two inches tall, and he is only 40 inches tall, yet he faces the world with endless curiosity and joy. Too often I have demanded things of him from my adult perspective, and I now see how foolish that was. He has taught me that the most precious gift in life is the simple purity of wonder.

This book was made possible because of the support of Tianjin Ruide International Kindergarten, my editor, my friend Eric, and my family. I also thank Dr. Colleen Bosholm, introduced to me by my brother, for his careful proofreading support. Their love, patience, wisdom, and encouragement made it possible for me to finish. My gratitude to them is beyond words, and this book belongs to them as much as it belongs to me.

References

Achterbergh, J., & Vriens, D. (2010). The social "arche," organizations as social systems: Luhmann. In Organizations (pp. 117–166). Springer Berlin.

https://doi.org/10.1007/978-3-642-14316-8_4

Allen, M., & Friston, K. J. (2018). From cognitivism to autopoiesis. Synthese, 195(6),

2459–2482. https://doi.org/10.1007/s11229-016-1288-5

Bitbol, M., & Luisi, P. L. (2004). Autopoiesis with or without cognition: Defining life at its edge. Journal of the Royal Society Interface, 1(1), 99–107. https://doi.org/10.1098/rsif.2004.0012

Capra, F., & Luisi, P. L. (2014). The systems view of life: A unifying vision. Cambridge University Press.

Emunah, R. (1994). Acting for real: Drama therapy process, technique, and performance. Brunner/Mazel.

Grof, S. (2000). Psychology of the future: Lessons from modern consciousness research.

State University of New York Press.

Jennings, S. (1998a). Introduction to developmental play therapy: Playing and health. Jessica Kingsley Publishers.

Jennings, S. (1998b). Introduction to dramatherapy: Theatre and healing. Archetypes, symbols. and roles. Jessica Kingsley Publishers.

Kauffman, S. A. (2019). A world beyond physics: The emergence and evolution of life. Oxford University Press.

Koskinen, K. U. (2013). Knowledge production in organizations: A processual autopoietic view. Springer.

Luhmann, N. (1984). Soziale Systeme: Grundriß einer allgemeinen Theorie [Social systems: outline of a general theory]. Suhrkamp Verlag [Suhrkamp Publishing].

Maslow, A. H. (1971). The farther reaches of human nature. Viking Press.

Maturana, H. R. (1987). Everything is said by an observer. In W. I. Thompson (Ed.), Gaia: A way of knowing. Lindisfarne Press.

Maturana, H. R., & Varela, F. J. (1972). Autopoiesis and cognition: The realization of the living. Reidel.

Maturana, H. R., & Varela, F. J. (1980a). Autopoiesis and cognition: The realization of the living. D. Reidel Publishing.

Maturana, H. R., & Varela, F. J. (1980b). Autopoiesis and cognition: The realization of the living (2nd ed.). Springer.

Montévil, M. (2015). Biological organization as closure of constraints. Journal of Theoretical Biology, 372, 179–191. https://doi.org/10.1016/j.jtbi.2015.02.029

Montessori, M. (1967). The absorbent mind (C. Claremont, Trans.). Holt, Rinehart, and Winston.

Oxford Reference. (n.d.). Autopoiesis. In OxfordReference.com. Retrieved November 12, 2021, from https://www.oxfordreference.com/display/10.1093/oi/authority.20110803095436328

Siegel, D. J. (2012). The developing mind: How relationships and the brain interact to shape who we are (2nd ed.). Guilford Press.

Teubner, G. (1992). Law as an autopoietic system. European University Institute Press.

Thompson, E. (2007). Mind in life: Biology, phenomenology, and the sciences of mind. Harvard University Press.

Wilber, K. (2000a). Integral psychology: Consciousness, spirit, psychology, therapy. Shambhala.

Wilber, K. (2000b). A theory of everything: An integral vision for business, politics, science, and spirituality. Shambhala.